STUDIES IN
GERMANIC LANGUAGES
AND LITERATURES

Fred O. Nolte

STUDIES IN GERMANIC LANGUAGES AND LITERATURES

In Memory of FRED O. NOLTE

A COLLECTION OF ESSAYS
WRITTEN BY HIS COLLEAGUES
AND HIS FORMER STUDENTS

Edited by Erich Hofacker and Liselotte Dieckmann

WASHINGTON UNIVERSITY PRESS

ST. LOUIS 1963

c

305147

This volume was planned as a Festschrift upon the retirement of Fred O. Nolte, our cherished teacher, our beloved colleague, and a very dear friend to all of us. He knew that the volume was in progress, but it was not granted to him to see its completion. It is now dedicated to his memory.

In his earlier years, Fred Nolte made significant contributions in the fields of modern German literature and literary criticism: The Early Middle Class Drama (1935), Grillparzer, Lessing and Goethe in the Perspective of European Literature (1938), Lessing's Laokoön (1940), Art and Reality (1942). Later he became increasingly concerned about the preservation of the human element in our age of science. During the last decade of his life he worked on a series of volumes bearing the general title The Life of the Spirit. The increasingly high standards he set for himself in regard to the formulation of his ideas prevented him from completing the third volume. A few quotations from the beginning of the second volume Science and Conscience can best illustrate why Fred Nolte was so esteemed and held so dear by his colleagues and students, for he himself was the best example of what he advocated: "Education, art, and civilization do not, like science, offer a presumable formula for life or a theory of life. They are in themselves an immediate embodiment of life. This is why they are religious." "Either we educate the whole man or we do not educate at all. We only train; and we train for evil as well as good." "Only a good man can be wise." "All strong people are gentle."

Fred Nolte was a vigorous man, both physically and mentally. He loved sport, especially baseball, and in his early years he once was a member of an amateur team in Paris. He loved wit and humor and delighted his friends with ever new anecdotes which he had heard or read. On the other hand, he had a disciplined mind and his Belesenheit was the envy of his colleagues. After a heart ailment put limitations to his mental and physical exertion, the gentleness of his spirit and his effort to nurture fine human relations became more and more apparent. Fred's humility and delicate tact would not have permitted us to say in the Festschrift what we have just said about him as an introduction to these studies which are dedicated to his memory.

E. H.
L. D.

Contents

STUDIES IN
GERMANIC LANGUAGES
AND LITERATURES

The Gothic Character X

by ERNST EBBINGHAUS

THE TWENTY-FOURTH character of the Go. alphabet (in the following transcribed as *x*) performs three different functions. First, it is used as a symbol for 600. Second, it makes the first part of the contraction x̄s̄ (x̄ū̄s̄, etc.). In both cases it is used regularly, i.e., no other symbol is ever substituted.[1] However, it does not represent a sound here and is to be considered an ideogram. Third, it is used occasionally in writing Greek borrowings (mostly of Aramaic origin), in which it corresponds with the Chi of the original (Greek) spelling. In addition we find the isolated case of Go. *x* used in the Go. spelling of the PN χρήσκης: *xreskus* (II Tim. 4: 10A [B: *krispus*]).

Whenever *x* is used as a regular letter it must represent a sound, and since it appears to be used to represent the Greek Chi (with the exception of *xreskus*), one might assume that it represents the same sound, i.e., an aspirated *k*. However, the use of Go. *x* is very irregular. In most cases the Go. MSS. use Go. *k* for the Greek Chi, and if we find the *x*-spelling, e.g., *zaxarias* Luke 3: 2, we almost always find at least one case in which the same word is written with *k*, e.g., *zakarias* Luke 1: 5; 1: 12; 1: 13; 1: 21; 1: 40; 1: 59 (in various case forms); *pasxa* John 6: 4; 18: 28; 18: 39 vs. *paska* Matt. 26: 2; Luke 2: 41; Mark 14: 12; 14: 14; I Cor. 5: 7B. Three words appear with the *x*-spelling only, but each of them occurs only once in the texts: *galiugaxristjus* Mark 13: 22; *saixaineiins* Neh. 6: 18; *aiwxaristian* II Cor. 9: 11B. The word *galiugaxristjus* has to be eliminated here; the use of the *x* in *galiugaxristjus* is an entirely different problem, similar to the use of *x* in spellings such

---

[1]For 600 the numeral could have been used.

as *xrist*,[2] *xpistin*,[3] *xristanheid*,[4] that can be found in OHG and MHG MSS.

For the remaining *x*-spellings there seems to be no system. The use of Go. *x* can be attributed neither to particular scribes (in contrast to other scribes using *k* instead) nor to the type of script. In the CodArg. (type II) scribe I uses both *pasxa* and *paska*, while scribe II has *zaxarias* and *zakarias*; and in CodAmbros. B (type I) we find *axaïa* II Cor. 9: 2 and *akaïai* II Cor. 1: 1. On the other hand, one would surely hesitate to attribute such a striking orthographic irregularity to Wulfila and his staff.

In theory there are two possible explanations. One might assume that Wulfila used the letter *k* for the Go. k-sound(s) and for the Greek mute (Kappa), and that he introduced the letter *x* to render the aspirated *k* (Greek Chi). One might further assume that for some unknown reason the later scribes no longer made this distinction, using Go. *k* in all cases, and that the few *x*'s that can still be found in our MSS. are the leftovers of Wulfila's original orthographic system. This seems highly unlikely. If such a clear-cut orthographic system existed, why should it break down?

The other possibility seems much more likely. We may assume that the few instances in which Go. *x* is used are innovations. This was Jellinek's opinion, who regarded the *x* as "gelegentliche Äusserungen gräzisierender Gelehrsamkeit."[5] However, Jellinek did not see that his explanation causes a new problem. How could the letter be used if it existed only as a symbol for the number and as part of the contraction x̄s̄? To assume that it could have been used because of its similarity to the Greek Chi is palaeographically impossible. The letter must have had its proper phonetic value *before* it was used in spelling. For this problem I should like to propose the following explanation.

In the original alphabet the letter *x* had the phonetic value of an aspirated *k*. The Gmc.-Go. *k* in all probability was an aspirate except when preceded by a spirant, in which case it was mute. It is obvious that Wulfila did not have to distinguish here, and he used one letter, the Go. *k*, only. He also used the Go. *k* to render the Greek k-sounds both

---

[2] Bamberg Charm for Stanching Blood; cp. W. Braune, *Althochdeutsches Lesebuch*, 14. Auflage, bearbeitet von Ernst A. Ebbinghaus (Tübingen, 1962), No. XXXI, 6a, line 2.

[3] OHG Physiologus; cp. W. Braune, *Althochdeutsches Lesebuch*, 14, No. XXV, 1.21.

[4] *Ibid.*, 1.70.

[5] Max Hermann Jellinek, *Geschichte der Gotischen Sprache* (Berlin–Leipzig, 1926), p. 33.

the mute (**Kappa**) and the aspirate (Chi). There is, however, one word for which this spelling system is not sufficient, and this word is of considerable significance in Christianity, the Aramaic word *pasq'a*. The original pronunciation of the word was retained in early Christianity for a long time, as the peculiar phonetic development in the Romance languages shows. The word contains an aspirated *k* preceded by a (voiceless) spirant, a combination that was alien to Gothic (as to many other languages). In order to signal an aspirated *k* in that position, Wulfila needed a special character, and he used the Go. *x*, which he derived from the Greek Chi. Once Go. *x* was established as a regular letter with its proper phonetic value, if only of limited use, the way was open for later scribes to show their "gräzisierende Gelehrsamkeit." If this theory is correct, *xreskus* (II Tim. 4: 10A) instead of **kreskus* would be as easily explainable as, e.g., $\chi\bar\iota\tau\varepsilon$ or even $\chi\varepsilon\bar\iota\theta\varepsilon$ instead of $\varkappa\varepsilon\bar\iota\tau\alpha\iota$, which one can find in Jewish catacombs in Rome.[6]

---

[6] Cp. *TAPA,* 58 (1927), p. 228.

The Composition of Eddic Verse

by WINFRED P. LEHMANN

O NE OF THE points of greatest interest in recent study of poetry, especially poetry of the past, is its composition. What were the techniques which a poet brought with him as he set out to produce a poem? To what extent could he innovate, modifying the forms available to him? There has been special interest in the poetry of preliterate societies, wonder whether poets produced their native wood-notes with a genius unhampered by the restraints of writing. This interest has contributed greatly to our understanding of epic verse. After the publications of Parry and Lord,[1] the Homeric question has become largely meaningless. Like many questions it was wrongly put. An understanding of the composition of epic verse permits us to label both sides wrong in part, correct in some of their views. As in other nonliterate societies, the epic ascribed to Homer was produced in accordance with a tradition which supplied the poet with a great number of formulae and required that he use them. Poetic originality did not consist in new statements delicately dipping into predecessors primarily for rhythm, possibly also for phrases, but in vigorous story arranged around the bones furnished by tradition to carry those matters essential to every narrative, such as introduction to narration, indication of movement, and so on. The formulaic construction of Homeric epic had been pointed

Citations are based on H. Kuhn's revision of the Neckel edition *Edda* (Heidelberg, 1962). Although this has the laudable aim of presenting a text which is close to the manuscripts, one is troubled by the resultant irregularities, such as the retention of the established spelling Loki and the abbreviation Vkv. in spite of the altered spellings of Locasenna and of Vǫlundarqviða.

[1] Albert B. Lord, *The Singer of Tales* (Cambridge: Harvard University Press, 1960), gives an excellent account of the findings of Parry and Lord in their study of oral epic which survived to recent times, especially in Yugoslavia.

to by Meillet, and even earlier, in 1878, Sievers had added to his edition of the *Heliand* a list of Germanic formulae; yet only the sustained study of Parry and Lord clarified the artistic use of formulae in epics, shifting attention from philological to literary questions, as Professor Nolte always strongly urged, and as we should like also for Old Norse and other Germanic verse.

Such a shift of attention is also due for Old Norse Eddic poetry and its composition, verse often referred to as epic but quite different from the narrative epic of Homer and Asia through restrictions in length, substance, and form.

With these restrictions, Eddic poetry much more resembles the medieval ballads. The poems are short enough for ready recitation. They present "compressed episodes" dramatically, with an impersonal approach by the author. They were transmitted orally. Yet they lack many of the characteristics of ballads. It is difficult to believe, in spite of some commentators, that like ballads they were ever associated with dance. Nor were they sung. Germanic and Old Norse literature is not, however, without reports of poems sung. Although we cannot be certain of the extent of singing in scenes reported by Tacitus and others, it seems likely that Tacitus knew of song when he described the procession of Nerthus. A millennium later in the Skaldaskáparmál, the two giantesses forced by Frodi to turn the millstones are represented as singing at work. Both occasions are typical for song—songs of procession and songs of labor, well known from investigations in many cultures. The occasions, however, are different from those in which Eddic poems were used. When Thormod is asked to arouse the courage of Olaf's men before the battle of Stiklestad, A. D. 1030, Snorri tells us he recited, not that he sang, the Bjarkamál. We conclude that the Eddic poems were spoken, in contrast with the presentation of ballads.

Moreover, there is in the Edda none of the "excess of iteration, or repetition, of fixed and recurring phrases" which F. B. Gummere considers the essence of balladry.[2] Since Eddic verse is unlike both epic and ballad, in dealing with its composition we cannot compare contemporary activities as Parry and Lord have done for the epic in Yugoslavia and Greece, or as nineteenth-century scholars of the ballad did in the Faroe Islands, in Russia, and as is still being done on the border of Mexico, as by A. Parades, *With His Pistol in His Hand* (Austin, 1958). To determine how the Eddic poems were composed we must

---

[2] See his *Beginnings of Poetry* (New York, 1908), p. 193. He deals with the subject also in *The Popular Ballad* (New York, 1959), as does W. J. Entwistle, *European Balladry* (Oxford, 1939).

look in them for internal evidence and to Germanic literature for the fragments of descriptions which we find on the production and composition of verse.

The extant descriptions deal primarily with its production. From the earliest commentators on the Germans, Caesar, Tacitus, Jordanes, we know that Germanic culture, as do most cultures, included the practice of verse, but the reports tell little besides the fact. Even the *Beowulf*, which like the *Odyssey* reports a bard presenting verse to an audience, permits few sure conclusions. We are merely told that in the rejoicing after the death of Grendel, one of King Hrothgar's thanes made a fine account of Beowulf's undertaking, adding to his poem on Beowulf—the words of which he bound truly—stories of the former heroes Sigmund and Fitela. Except for indications that this poet was trained, that he remembered all of the ancient stories and could speedily put together a new poem, we have little information about him or his techniques.

Such information we have in detail about the composition of skaldic verse in Snorri's *Skaldic Poetics* and *List of Meters*, handbooks with few parallels for any type of verse. Further, in one of the most remarkable passages in the sagas we see the skaldic poet Egil at work on the composition of his head-ransom poem, *Egilssaga* sections 59–61. Besides the details on his procedure—his setting out to labor on a poem, his interruption by a witch in the shape of a swallow while composing it (to our view, his problems in getting down to solid work), and the plain description of his presentation the next morning—this account interests us because it, too, was probably written by Snorri; it therefore gives us Snorri's conception of the process of composition of a skaldic poem, whether or not it reflects the procedure of a skaldic poet in the tenth century.

Yet the poetry we are concerned with here is not skaldic; it is narrative, as compared with the occasional panegyric verse of the skalds. Moreover, it is much less complex in form, lacking the rigorous rime required for skaldic verse, and the variety of meter, as well as the requirements of construction of individual lines. Accordingly, it has been contrasted with skaldic verse as poetry of the farm to poetry of the court. This contrast seems to suggest that Eddic verse is unsophisticated, the poetry of the people, while skaldic verse is studied to the point of artificiality. Such a characterization would lead us to classify Eddic verse with folk poetry, somewhat like ballads.[3] To test their degree of

---

[3] Entwistle, for example, *European Balladry*, p. 202, says, "The older Edda is, therefore, a mediator between the primitive epic and the medieval ballads."

sophistication, their characteristics as folk poetry, we may examine briefly two Eddic poems, the first dealing with gods, the Locasenna, the second with heroes, the Vǫlundarqviða. The Locasenna I examine for general structure, the Vǫlundarqviða for details.

In attempting poetic analyses of Eddic poems, one must set out from handbooks designed with Teutonic thoroughness for philological exercises, not for literary enjoyment. Notes and commentary deal with individual features: an uncertain letter, a strange name, imperfect meter. An important feature of the text is numbering of stanzas, introduced by early philologists and now inviolate. Poems are case histories of individual gods or heroes, illuminating Germanic mythology, informing us on Old Norse life, though their chief purpose was to provide a testing ground for the philological acumen of nineteenth- and twentieth-century textual critics. Sparring with tittles is a pleasant sport, but viewing the Locasenna and the Vǫlundarqviða as works of literature, we have an obligation to attempt to understand some techniques of their composition.

The Locasenna is a satire, not totally dissimilar from satires of Horace such as the dialogue between Ulysses and Tiresias, though Loki carries on his discussion with more speakers than one, and the dialogue is more violent, with the satire directed at the gods themselves, not obliquely at man. Loki enters the hall of Aegir where the gods are carousing and asks the doorkeeper what the chatter is. The doorkeeper replies that they are talking of their prowess in battle, though all are speaking evilly of Loki. Loki pushes past the doorkeeper, saying he will mix their liquor with malice, and is met with silence. On his request that they talk to him, one, Bragi, tells him the gods will never grant him a seat at their parties. Loki turns to Oðin, reminds him of their old days of drinking; Oðin then asks one of his sons to give Loki his seat, upon which Loki gets a drink and greets all the gods but Bragi, who then responds and sets off the further exchanges which continue through the poem—until Loki yields before the threats of Thor.

I am not interested here in discussing the structure of the poem in detail, merely its external form. Apart from the final curse, which Loki mutters as he leaves in stanza 65, the poem consists of 64 stanzas. This number can scarcely seem accidental to anyone who has dealt with Germanic runes and magic with their emphasis on the number eight. The first section consists of twenty-four stanzas, introducing Loki to the doorkeeper, then to the gods and the inhospitable Bragi, with a quarrel developing between Loki and Bragi in spite of the efforts of Iðun, Bragi's wife, Gefion, another goddess, and Oðin. After Loki rebukes his old friend Oðin in stanza 24, the quarrel is on in earnest.

The following sixteen stanzas are clearly a structural unit, with four stanzas devoted to exchanges between Loki and Frigg, Oðin's wife, four to Loki and Freya, four to Loki and Niorð, and four to Loki and Týr.

The next twelve stanzas seem to indicate the victory of Loki, with Freyr bested in one exchange, followed by two allotted to Byggvir versus Loki, in which Byggvir is totally routed; this allotment of six stanzas is repeated, with Loki's opponents now Heimdall, like Freyr depicted as a hapless warrior, and Skaði, derided as the daughter of Thiazi whom Loki helped kill. The four following stanzas consist of exchanges between Loki and the wife of Thor and the wife of Byggvir, suggesting that Thor is approaching but leaving Loki uncowed.

The last eight stanzas contain the Thor-Loki exchange, after which Loki leaves with his curse.

The Locasenna accordingly is composed in four segments, as indicated below, each a multiple of the number eight: the preparatory twenty-four followed by two sets of sixteen each, in which Loki is triumphant, and one of eight, in which he is completely discomfited by Thor.

1. Stanzas 1-24: Entrance of Loki and beginning of quarrel.

2. Stanzas 25-40: Exchange dealing with sexual activity of gods.

    25-28 Frigg and Loki;   29-32 Freya and Loki;
    33-36 Niorð and Loki;   37-40 Týr and Loki.

3. Stanzas 41-56: Exchanges dealing largely with warfare.

    41-42 Freyr and Loki;   43-46 Byggvir and Loki;
    47-48 Heimdall and Loki;   49-52 Skaði and Loki;
    53-54 Sif and Loki;   55-56 Beyla and Loki.

4. Stanzas 57-64: Exchange of Thor and Loki.

    65   Loki's departure and curse.

Such an arrangement is hardly that of an untutored folk poet. To indicate that this arrangement is not wholly external, we may note that in the second section with its emphasis on the sexual unfaithfulness of the gods, there is a progression from the promiscuity of Frigg to the incest of Freya and Niorð, to the adultery of Týr's wife with Loki. In the third section the confident Loki shifts from the sexual activity of his opponents to their martial inactivity and inadequacy, just before he himself is bested by the martial Thor. Loki's attempt in the last section of eight stanzas to reproach Thor for his inability to deal with the giants during his expedition to the east brings Thor at once on the offensive, and makes Loki clearly the loser.

Apart from observing his control of the structure of the poem, it is instructive to see how the poet uses details of poetic composition, as when he gives Thor the offensive. Thor is the first of the gods to use Loki's rejoinder: *þegi þú* "you be silent." Throughout the poem, from his exchange with Iðun, Loki routs his opponents with this clause, so that one might consider it a typical use of incremental repetition like that found in ballads. But the repetition is not automatic as we may expect for ballads. Loki uses it to the gods whom he treats most scornfully: Iðun, Gefion, Oðin, Frigg, twice to Freya, Niorð, twice to Týr, to Byggvir and Heimdall—but not to Skaði, whose favors he seems to remember tenderly. The clause is accordingly applied with discrimination, increasing its force when Thor uses it as his first statement to Loki.

Repetitions have a different use in the Vǫlundarqviða, serving to connect sections of the poem rather than to build up towards a dramatic climax. The poem begins by telling how Vǫlund and his two brothers were suddenly deserted by three Valkyries who had lived with them for eight years. Vǫlund, left also by his two brothers, stays alone in Ulfdal, manufacturing precious jewelry; there he is robbed of a gold ring, by Niðuð's men, which Niðuð gives his daughter Bǫðvild. Vǫlund is then carried off to work for Niðuð. The second section of the poem, stanzas 16–29, tells of Vǫlund's revenge, how he lured Niðuð's sons to his smithy, killed them and made bowls of their skulls which, with other products of his imagination, he sent to Niðuð and his family. When the daughter goes to Vǫlund's smithy to have her treasure repaired, Vǫlund rapes her. In the third section of the poem, stanzas 30–41, Vǫlund tells Niðuð of his revenge as he flies off, a revenge which Niðuð cannot escape for otherwise he would have no heirs; moreover, he has sworn an oath not to harm Vǫlund's wife. The cruelty of the Vǫlundarqviða is generally accepted, but the poem is criticized for its lack of unified story and construction.[4] Before indicating its underlying theme, which makes of it a unity, we may observe how the poet suggests its unified construction through verbal repetition.

The longest such repetition consists of eight lines which first narrate Vǫlund's killing of the sons, 24.1–25.8, and then are modified by Vǫlund in direct address to Niðuð, 34.5–36.4.

---

[4] An earlier version of this paper was given at the meeting of the Modern Language Association in December, 1961. After the presentation, Professor Paul Beekman Taylor very kindly acquainted me with his own work on the Vǫlundarqviða. Professor Taylor examines in greater detail than has been done here the repetitions in the poem, relates them to the Germanic use of formulae, illustrates how the author applied them with effect, and sees in the structure of the Vǫlundarqviða indications that the "tale is a regeneration myth." See now his "The Structure of Völandarkviða," *Neophilologus*, 1963, 228-36.

24.1. Sneið af haufuð húna þeira,
      oc undir fen fiǫturs fœtr um lagði;
      enn þær scálar, er und scǫrum
      vóro,
      sveip hann útan silfri, seldi
      Níðaði.
      Enn ór augom iarcnasteina
      sendi hann kunnigri kono Níðaðar;
      enn ór tǫnnom tveggia þeira
      sló hann brióstkringlor, sendi Bǫð-
      vildi.

34.5. sneið ec af haufuð húna þinna,
      oc undir fen fiǫturs fœtr um lagðac.
      Enn þær scálar, er und scǫrom
      vóro,
      sveip ec utan silfri, senda ec
      Níðaði;
      enn ór augom iarcnasteina
      senda ec kunnigri qván Níðaðar.
      Enn ór tǫnnom tveggia þeira
      sló ec brióstkringlor, senda ec
      Bǫðvildi

With modifications only in pronouns and verbal endings, this repetition closely connects sections two and three of the poem. So do other phrases in section three, e.g., 38.1–2 and 29.5–6

hlæiandi Vǫlundr hófz at lopti

32.2 and 13.4 vísi álfa, and most strikingly 31.1 of section three with section one when, after the disappearance of his children, Niðuð says

Vaki ec á valt vilia lauss

an echo of 11.3–4, where the poem says of Vǫlund deserted by his wife and fettered by Niðuð's men

oc hann vacnaði vilia lauss

Clearly the poet attempted to relate the sorrow of Niðuð with the earlier sorrow of Vǫlund, which Niðuð had in part caused. There are other such similar expressions. When Niðuð's men raid Vǫlund's smithy, they fetter his feet 11.7–8.

en á fótom fiǫtur um spenntan

as does Vǫlund later to the sons of Niðuð, 24.3–4 and 34.7–8.

oc undir fen fiǫturs fœtr um lagði/ lagðac.

Moreover, Vǫlund's Valkyrie wife and Niðuð's daughter are linked by similar expressions: in 3.1 sáto síðan the Valkyries and the three brothers are reported to have lived together, with the same verb that Niðuð uses to question his daughter whether Vǫlund's allegations are true: sáto við Vǫlundr saman í hólmi.

Other carefully introduced repetitions from the poem could be cited. Those given here may illustrate how the poet through them related different segments of a poem which seems disjointed to interpreters who regard the Edda as a repository of Germanic mythology. By this view a first section relates a story of Vǫlund and his two brothers visited by Valkyries, who leave abruptly after nine years; the second section tells of Vǫlund's capture and enslavement by Niðuð; the third tells of his revenge and escape. But when viewed as a whole, as we are directed by the verbal repetitions, the Vǫlundarqviða is a revenge poem, which tells of the evil fates of two men, Vǫlund and Niðuð. Niðuð, the object of the sadistic revenge of Vǫlund, reflects in the loss of his sons Vǫlund's loss of his Valkyrie. If we read the Vǫlundarqviða as such a poem without trying to relate it to other Germanic mythology, we find a story which may have served Freud for terminology; Niðuð's gift of Vǫlund's ring to his daughter seems a Freudian foreshadowing of her treatment by Vǫlund. Repetition of phrase as well as intermeshing story makes clear the unity of the poem.

These two structural characteristics, balance of sections of the Locasenna and repetition of phrase in the Vǫlundarqviða, may demonstrate that the Eddic poems were careful compositions by highly trained poets—not rustic products of peasant conviviality. The unknown poets drew on available themes, as has been the practice in other traditions. Tennyson's Ulysses and Dante's are no more similar than are the Gudrun of Old Norse and Griemhilt of medieval German verse. Like the verse of other traditions, the Eddic poems reflect the experience of their authors, as may be clearest in the Greenlandic story of Atli, which pathetically pictures Gunnar as a Greenlandic chieftain who set out with four companions to visit Atli in contrast with the thousands in the Middle High German version. We may assume that the various Eddic poets modified their story as did the Greenlandic poet. They also drew on available techniques of composition; the formulae of Germanic epics are not aimlessly introduced but are carefully used for artistic effect. While the structural techniques outlined here may seem to ascribe undue artistry to early Germanic writers and audience, we find other highly developed conventions in early Scandinavian society, such as the burial ceremonies described in 922 by Ibn Fadlan (see J. Brøndsted, *The Vikings,* Pelican A459, 1960). An audience accustomed to such involved rites and to the monstrously complex patterns of skaldic verse might also have been expected to require some complexity in poems which were among their favorites. Structural characteristics of the two Eddic poems examined here indicate that their authors were not unskilled in the composition of verse and that they manipulated inherited features of form for their poetic ends.

The Views of Konrad Gesner
on Language

by GEORGE J. METCALF

The *Mithridates* published by the versatile Konrad Gesner (1516-1565) of Zürich in 1555[1] has received merited attention and praise. His ambitious scheme to include as much information as was available about as many languages as possible, including twenty-two versions of the Lord's Prayer, is in itself noteworthy. And its "utter sobriety" is considered its "greatest distinction" by Henry M. Hoenigswald;[2] this is a quality which commends any work of that age to our modern taste. But "sobriety" alone would scarcely justify a more detailed analysis of Gesner's linguistic views such as we propose here; and Hoenigswald's statement that this "is a reference book with the languages listed alphabetically" (*ibid.*), while true, could give a wrong impression. For the author's command of his material, his awareness at any moment of what he has already said and of what he is going to say, is impressive. The alphabetical arrangement should not hinder our recognition of a coherent structure, careful attention to which can provide us with significant insights into Gesner's views on language.

The unity underlying the entire presentation is indicated in a simple

---

[1] *Mithridates. De differentiis linguarum tum veterum tum quae hodie apud diversas nationes in toto orbe terrarum in usu sunt, Conradi Gesneri Tigurini observationes.* Anno MDLV. Tiguri excudebat Froschouerus. I am indebted to the Newberry Library of Chicago for permitting me to have a reproduction of the work made. In quoting from the *Mithridates,* I have made the customary normalizations: resolving obvious abbreviations and employing *ae* and *u* and *v* according to current practice.

[2] "Linguistics in the Sixteenth Century," *The Library Chronicle, University of Pennsylvania,* XX (1954), 2. Gesner's work is discussed by Arno Borst in his monumental *Der Turmbau von Babel,* III, 1 (Stuttgart, 1960), pp. 1086-87, a general treatment indispensable for earlier views on the relationship of languages.

way in the frequent cross references, both general[3] and specific, in looking ahead (*infra*) and looking back (*supra*).[4] Occasionally the same quotation appears several times at appropriate points. Thus Postellus[5] is cited three times to attest that the language of the Georgians forms an intermediate stage (*media*) between Tartar and Armenian: under the discussion of Armenian (p. 10 r), of Georgian (p. 27 v), and of the use of Greek as a sacred language in Georgia (p. 46 r). Repetition rises almost to a *leitmotiv* in references to the many languages whose speakers experienced the Pentacostal miracle of tongues.[6]

The well-knit plan of Gesner's work is particularly clear in his treatment of the *Scythica Lingua* (pp. 67 r–68 v): "Scythica" itself is of vast extent and it is probable (*verisimile*) that there are many and diverse languages in it; but it has been shown above (*supra*) that some claim the Scyths to be *Germani;* Armenian Scythia has been discussed above and Hungarian also: "De Tartarica paulo post dicemus."

Gesner's control of his material does not, however, impose a rigid schematism; there is rather almost an air of informality. Thus he treats the Greek language under one general heading but the Greek dialects under their separate alphabetical entries; the Germanic tongues, however, are discussed within the general and lengthy treatment *De Lingua Germanica* (although even here there is not strict consistency; some of the "remoter" tongues, such as English and Scottish, have their individual treatment).

The impression which Gesner makes on the modern reader might possibly be more adequately termed "open-minded." He is modest in his claims: in writing about all languages he cannot give full satisfaction

---

[3] E.g., "Abasinorum lingua, vide Aethiopum lingua" (p. 5 v).

[4] E.g., "De barbaris linguis plura referemus infra ex Strabone, in Caricae linguae mentione," (p. 4 v); "De Latina lingua nonnihil dictum est supra" (p. 58 r).

[5] Guillaume Postel (1510-1581), Parisian Orientalist and theologian, was accorded highest acknowledgment among his sources by Gesner in his "Epilogus ad Lectorem" (p. 78 r), for his *Linguarum duodecim characteribus differentium alphabetum, introductio* (1538), and his *De Foenicum literis* (1552).

[6] Thus: "Aegypti incolae apostolos sua dialecto loquentes audiunt Hierosolymis in die Pentecostes, & admirantur" (p. 5 v). With only slight variation in phrasing for "Arabes" (p. 10 r); "Asiae incolae" (p. 12 r); "Cappadoces" (p. 14 v); "Cretenses" (p. 16 v); "Elamitae" (p. 17 r); "Libyes circa Cyrenen" (p. 59 r); "Medi & Mesopotamiae incolae" (p. 61 v); "Pamphylii" (p. 62 r); "Parthi" (p. 62 v); "Phryges" (p. 64 r). These of course are the peoples mentioned in Acts 2. 9-11 (except for the "dwellers . . . in Judea, and . . . in Pontus, . . . and strangers of Rome"). Borst, *Turmbau von Babel,* emphasizes the importance of Pentecost as the "corrective" of Babel in many strands of the Christian tradition throughout late antiquity and the Middle Ages (I, 224 and from there on *passim*). Since Gesner at the beginning (p. 1 r) expressly renounces any desire to discuss the "confusio" (he does not even name Babel), his emphasis on the Pentecostal event probably reflects merely his optimistic hope for the further spread of the Gospel in his own time (pp. 1 r-2 v, 45 r-46 v).

with his treatment but rather hopes to stimulate others to work further in the field (in his dedication and in his "Epilogus," p. 78 r). In providing a word-for-word interlinear Latin translation of a Persian prophecy, he is uncertain how well he has succeeded (p. 64 v). His etymological proposals, he is willing to admit, are often "mere conjectures" (p. 29), although he hopes they will not be "inutiles" in discovering the "veras significationes."

In an age of growing and ever more strident nationalism, his voice is still restrained. To be sure, the "noster" is openly applied to the *Lingua Germanica* and to his own Swiss speech.[7] But there is no attempt to admit Germanic speech to the circle of the "Sacred Three": Hebrew, Greek, and Latin. Rather it is subjected to criticism: shortness of the words in Germanic speech, which generally end in consonants rather than vowels, tends to "coarsen" (*exasperare*) the pronunciation and is responsible for that "harshness" (*asperitatem*) which makes it in general inappropriate for poetic expression (pp. 36 r–37 v). Gesner also admits certain blemishes (*vitia*) in the speech of his own area.[8]

To be sure, this very open-mindedness occasionally makes it difficult to determine precisely what Gesner's views are. There is often the very practical problem, inevitably faced in dealing with writers of that age, of determining the precise demarcation between Gesner's quotations and his own remarks. But Gesner will further present opposing statements without attempting to resolve them or even to state his own indecision. Thus he quotes at considerable length from Matthias à Michou,[9] who considers Lithuanian an independent language (with four major subgroups), but concludes briefly: "Others write that the Lithuanians simply speak Slavic" (p. 60 v); on page 55 v the *Lituani* are listed among the peoples speaking Slavic, as they are again in a shorter listing (p. 52 r). Here we would, of course, welcome either a disclaimer of ability to decide or a more positive statement of

---

[7] "Nostrae . . . linguae asperitatem" (p. 37 v) = 'the harshness of Germanic speech'; "linguae nostrae vitia" (p. 38 r) = 'blemishes (errors) of Swiss ("Helvetian") speech'; "vulgus . . . nostrum" (*ibid.*) = 'the common crowd which speaks Swiss ("Helvetian").'

[8] P. 38 r. Gesner points out, however, that such *vitia* occur in all languages. He may have here had in mind the remarks of Fabian Frangk in his *Orthographia:* "Denn sie [die Deutsche sprach] in keiner jegnit oder lande/ so gantz lauter und rein gefurt/ nach gehalden wird/ das nicht weilands etwas straffwirdigs/ oder misbreuchiges darin mitliefft/ und gespürt würde/" (Johannes Müller, *Quellenschriften und Geschichte des deutschsprachlichen Unterrichts* (Gotha, 1882), p. 94). Gesner later cites directly and extensively from this work.

[9] A Polish *canonicus* from Krakow, who in 1517 wrote his *Descriptio Sarmatiarum Asianae et Europianae.* Cf. Alexander Alexandrovich Vasilieu, *The Goths in the Crimea* (Cambridge, Mass., 1936), p. 251 and fn.

ascription. The reliance on varying sources also inevitably introduces an uncertainty into the nomenclature. Thus on one page (27 v) the "lingua . . . Sclavonica" is mentioned in a citation from Bilibald Pirck-heimer,[10] while the "sermo Illyricus," Gesner's more usual designation, appears a few lines later without an indication of source. When this language group is treated more systematically (pp. 52 r ff.), the additional designation "Sarmatica lingua" is added, and the three terms then follow interchangeably according to the particular sources being cited.

Despite his generally sober approach, Gesner does not disdain all the more fabulous reports that had traditionally enlivened linguistic lore. Without comment of his own, he repeats from Diodorus Siculus the story of the islanders with tongues split lengthwise and of the amazing linguistic results (pp. 2 r-3 v). From Herodotus comes the account of the snake-eating Troglodytes with their bat-like voices (p. 3 v). In reporting on Psammetichus' effort to determine the "original language" by isolating two infants from all normal speech (p. 64 r), Gesner is skeptical of the conclusion: for the children's "beccus" had probably no relation to the Phrygian word for bread, but was simply an imitation of the bleating goats who had nursed them. But Clemens Alexander's contention that animals use *dialects* is rejected as "absurdum," since speech in its proper sense must be denied them and hence dialects all the more so (4 r–5 v).

In his efforts to give a survey of all known languages, Gesner inevitably had to encounter the problem of linguistic change, for he was by no means concerned only with current languages but with all languages of which there were significant records, as his very title ("tum veterum tum quae hodie . . . in usu sunt") indicates. He thus treats separately "De Graeca Lingua vetere" (p. 45 v) and "De Lingua Graeca vulgari hodie" (p. 47 v). Another heading is "De Gallica Lingua, vetere primum, deinde recentiore" (18 v).[11]

Such distinctive terminology is required, of course, because language changes. Only one language is happily exempt from the seemingly universal process of change: "Of the languages Hebrew, as it is the first and most ancient of all, so it alone seems to be pure and whole (*pura et syncera*)" (p. 3 v). The caution of the next statement might point to further exceptions: "Almost all others are mixed,"[12] but this hint of other

---

[10] Noted Nürnberg Humanist, 1470-1530.

[11] In this instance, to be sure, Gesner means "the language spoken in *Gallia*," for, as we shall see later, he expressly denies a genetic link between the old and the "more recent."

[12] "reliquae mixtae sunt pleraeque omnes" (p. 3 v).

exceptions is nullified immediately: "For there is no language which does not have certain words derived and corrupted from Hebrew" (*ibid.*). But it is interesting to note that even Hebrew's unique position is later modified somewhat. For Gesner is thinking of Hebrew as the language recorded in the Old Testament itself. The language of the Jews of later times is "obscure" with words of all nations mingled in.[13] Thus it is really only the sacred record of the sacred book which imparts this unique quality to Hebrew.

But Hebrew's distinction is shared at least in part by Greek and Latin, for these three were likewise those languages through which the gospel had been spread: by Hebrew in the Old Testament, by Greek in the New Testament, and by Latin in its missionary tradition (pp. 1 r–2 v, 46 v). The knowledge of these languages throughout Europe, Asia, and Africa (for Arabic was continuing the Hebrew tradition) was enhanced by Europe's revived and spreading competence in all three, a trend that promised to put an end to the old confusion of tongues (*ibid.*). Thus Gesner could cherish optimistic hopes for a reunion of all mankind in a religion (*pura evangelii & Christi doctrina*) being renewed in his own times through a cultivation of the three sacred languages that had nurtured its beginnings and that had found their appropriate consecration on the cross (pp. 45 r–46 v).

But even this sacred status by no means exempts Latin and Greek from change. For Modern Greek (*Lingua Graeca hodie vulgaris*) is no less changed from ancient Greek than Italian and Spanish are from ancient Latin (p. 47 v); Romanian (*Valachia*) is Roman speech, but greatly changed.[14] So great has been the change in the Germanic tongue that even the learned scholar has difficulty in reading the earlier forms (p. 35 r; Gesner is quoting from Aventinus at this point).

Change for Gesner is regularly equated with "corruption." Italian, therefore, is characterized: "Italorum lingua a Latina vetere corrupta est, ut diximus, barbarorum infestatione & imperio" (p. 58 v); it was by the Goths that the Latin language in Italy, Spain, and *Gallia* "corrupta est" (p. 3 r).[15] Of all languages of his day, Gesner finds English

---

[13] "Recentiorum quidem Iudaeorum sermo, qui Thalmud interpretati sunt, ideo obscurus est, quod omnium fere gentium vocabula intermiscuerit" (p. 48 v).

[14] "Sermo adhuc genti Romanus est, quamvis magna ex parte mutatus" (pp. 70 v-70 r).

[15] Even earlier Latin had become corrupted when its empire had increased and its liberty had been lost and various peoples and nations had been admitted into the rights of citizenship; moral and linguistic integrity had declined together: "quo factum est, ut Romana virtus ac loquendi iuxta integritas passim cum moribus degeneraret" (p. 59 v).

"maxime mixta . . . corruptaque" (*ibid.*), but Rhaeto-Romance (to which Gesner gives special attention) uses an Italian speech "omnium corruptissimo" (p. 65 r). There is no language which does not have certain words not only "derived" but "corrupted" from Hebrew (p. 3 v).

This change or mixture or corruption may come about by necessity, as when new and unusual things bring with them their foreign names; or voluntarily, as when the Latins adopted many terms in the arts and sciences from the Greeks; or by foreign rule or foreign invasions (p. 3 r). In general Gesner appears to be thinking of change as the adoption of new vocabulary items (as in the "quaedam . . . vocabula" which all languages have absorbed from Hebrew). But he shows elsewhere that he is aware of other changes as well. Modern Greek has not only an admixture of barbarian words, but also shows a change in sounds and endings.[16] Latin, too, is affected throughout as it is "corrupted" into the modern tongues: "hoc est terminationibus & literis syllabisque mutata & distorta: & insuper vocabulis mixta alienis" (p. 26 v).

The relative age of a language was, for the sacred three at least, a determinable matter. Hebrew, as we have noted, derived its very purity and wholeness from the fact that it was "prima & antiquissima" (p. 3 v). There was valid evidence, furthermore, that Greek was older than Latin: Latin had borrowed many words from Greek but Greek very few from Latin, and the Latins had adapted the Greek characters in developing their writing system (pp. 45 r–46 v). It is interesting to note, however, how relatively little weight Gesner attaches otherwise to this difference in antiquity. Nor is he concerned to any vital extent with the long tradition that sought to account for different languages by relating them to the dispersal of the peoples after the building of the Tower of Babel; both 75 and 72 are mentioned as the possible number of languages,[17] but the latter figure merely serves to introduce the question of the relationship between "dialects" and "languages."

For Gesner is concerned not merely with listing languages (and giving the *paternoster* or other samples), but with ordering and grouping human speech. Thus he asserts: "And there appear to be actually 72 common dialects (languages, rather), as one can discover also in the records of our own people. But the many remaining ones are to be

---

[16] "Graecorum depravatione literis & terminationibus immutatis" (p. 47 v).

[17] Cf. Borst, *Turmbau*, especially III, 1, 1086, whose particular concern is tracing this tradition of the 72 (70) languages.

assigned to common groups which may contain two or three or more dialects."[18]

This grouping, as we shall shortly see, is often synchronic and seeks to establish the relationship between the "dialectus" and the "lingua communis." But in the case of the Romance languages, at least, the genetic principle is clearly asserted and developed. Italian, Spanish, and French are termed the "propagines" of the Latin language,[19] although their corruption by time and common ignorance is again stressed, and they are rated in terms of this corruption: Italian least and French most (p. 26 v: this ranking is confirmed later in the discussion of Spanish, p. 50 v). As we noted earlier, Romanian is also confirmed as descending from Latin, but in this quotation from Aeneas Sylvius the significant term "propago" is missing (Gesner, pp. 70 v–70 r). It is further interesting that Rhaeto-Romance is declared to be "Latine" rather than "Germanice," although it is more immediately assigned to Italian (*sermo Italicus*) (p. 65 r).

Gesner proposes to define "dialectus" in his introductory statements, but he admits from the start the ambiguous nature of the term (an ambiguity which has persisted to the present time). On the one hand a "dialect" is speech displaying the particular note or characteristic of a given locality; on the other hand it is speech which shows the peculiar or common characteristics of a people.[20] Thus, the Greeks are reported as having five "dialects"—Attic, Ionic, Doric, Aeolian, and a "fifth common" (*quintam communem*) (pp. 2 v–2 r). Gesner blurs even this distinction somewhat, proposing to use the term in two senses: in that of a particular language which differs from the common language or from other similar or related languages—the preferred usage of grammarians; or again in that of articulate speech in general. It is thus important to distinguish carefully in each instance which of the meanings Gesner employs.

The broader sense is clearly implied when he himself offers the alternate "lingua" in discussing the 72 major language groupings (cf. footnote 17 above). It is also implied in his reference to "primae &

---

[18] "Et sane videntur revera dialecti (linguae potius) communes duae & septuaginta, ut in nostrorum etiam monumentis proditum reperitur. Reliquae vera multae sub unum genus commune, quod duas aut tres pluresve dialectos contineat, referendae sunt" (p. 2 v).
[19] "Latinae linguae propagines . . . sunt tres hodie vulgares linguae, Italica, Hispanica & Gallica" (p. 26 v).
[20] "Est autem dialectus dictio peculiarem alicuius loci notam seu characterem prae se ferens: vel dictio quae propriam communemve gentis characterem ostendit" (p. 2 v).

generales dialecti" (p. 4 v). Yet even in these instances the sense of relatedness seems inherent in the term "dialectus": for here Gesner is thinking of groupings of related languages.

More prevalent, however, is the specialized sense. Thus the four "regional" Greek dialects are treated both individually[21] and together where they are not only listed but ranked in value: Attic is "elegantior & communi proprior," Doric "crassissima" (p. 46 r). Dialects are also mentioned and evaluated in the discussion of the three major Romance languages: Castilian is preferred among the Spanish dialects (p. 50 v); among the many Italian dialects Tuscan is said to be preferred, while the speech in the Rhaeto-Romance area is "most inept and most depraved" (p. 58 v); Modern French varies considerably as to dialects: the more remote the area, the grosser (crassiores) the dialects (p. 26 v). The distance from the center is also considered in discussing the speech of the Laconians: just as they are further from the center of Greece, so their speech recedes from the "common"—they apparently are to be classified as a sub-group of Doric (p. 58 r).

It is also important to note that the "common" Greek language, however much it may be associated with the "center of Greece," is not equated with Attic and does not have a more specific geographical definition; it is rather the speech of the literate and the cultivated.[22]

Gesner himself must occasionally resort to a critical examination of his sources to determine the precise relationship of a language group; in reporting Matthias à Michou's discussion of Lithuanian, he gives a parenthetical note: "he seems to feel that there is one language but distinguished by four dialects, for he himself uses the term 'linguagium' " (p. 59 r). Gesner also explicitly justifies the use of a common designation for speech communities which show variations.[23]

In dealing with Germanic speech, Gesner again uses "lingua" and "dialectus" in seemingly free variation. He mentions "Brabantica lingua" (p. 39 r) and "lingua Flandrica" (ibid.), as well as the more remote "lingua Islandica" (p. 40 r); the "Bavarorum lingua" (p. 39 r) is matched by the later remark: "Crassissima fere dialectus, Boiorum seu Bavarorum vulgi existimatur" (p. 42 r); a different alternation presents

---

[21] Thus: "Aeolica lingua, dialectus est Graecae communis" (p. 6 v) and similarly for Attic (p. 12 r); Doric (pp. 17 v-17 r) and Ionic (pp. 57 v-57 r) begin without this introductory definition.

[22] "Communem quidem linguam in nulla regione privatim vulgo receptam fuisse iudicarim. . . . sed illam dici communem, quam viri vel literati, vel alioqui sapientes & peregrinationibus cultiores usurpabant" (p. 46 r).

[23] "Nihil tamen impedit quin communi appellatione eadem ac una nominetur, quanquam non usquequaque eadem, sed paululum variata" (p. 22 v).

both "inferioris Germaniae sermonem" and "inferioris Germaniae dialectum" (p. 42 v). The possibility of applying the generic term to the specific is illustrated in Gesner's heading for his Swiss version of the Lord's Prayer: "Oratio dominica in lingua Germanica communi, vel Helvetica" (p. 38 v): "vel" must here be interpreted "more specifically" and not as a denotation of simple equation.

Specific standards of a "common" Germanic language are implied in a negative fashion in Gesner's admission of the *vitia* of his own Swiss speech (see page 17 and footnote 8). Pejorative qualities are also, as was the case with other language families, assigned to the speech of other specific regions: Bavarian is reported as "etiam crassior" than Swabian and "crassissima" in Austria (p. 39 r) and again is judged "Crassissima fere dialectus" (p. 42 r); the Frisians, too, at one time had used a "plane peculiari, dura, & multum a vicinis distante dialecto" (p. 39 r), although they were now, in the eastern area, adapting themselves "ad Brabanticum et Hollandicum sermonem" (*ibid.*).

Gesner on the positive side gives a cautious commendation to the speech of Meissen,[24] and also reports that "many" (*multi*) praise the style of Martin Luther among contemporary authors (p. 42 r).

Gesner is well aware, too, of more complicated linguistic situations: in Sardinia many of the townspeople speak Spanish, which they have learned from their Spanish rulers, while the people of the countryside retain their traditional Sardinian speech (p. 67 v). Scots who inhabit the better, southern part of their land and are "bene morati" and "humaniores" use English, while the "sylvestres & insulani" have a speech which does not differ from that of the Irish (p. 67 r).

Gesner's aim, as we have emphasized earlier, is not merely to list as much and as varied linguistic material as possible, but to provide a classification of this material to show what linguistic groupings emerge among those languages that have elements which are "similar" or "cognate."[25] In determining what was "related" or not, Gesner, like most of his contemporaries, found his greatest opportunity and challenge in the field of proper names. For here the semantic restrictions were almost unlimited: the purpose of such an investigation, in fact, was to discover the "true meanings" of the words in question: "ad inveniendas . . . veras significationes" (p. 29 r). In his discussion of the Germanic area, in fact, he pleaded for someone to list the entire stock of proper

---

[24] "optima [dialectus] circa Misenam, ut audio" (p. 42 r).
[25] In his dedication he maintains: "Videtur autem non tam curiosa quam liberalis hac cognitio, ut quae inter se cognatae sint linguae plus minus, quae omnino distent, intelligamus."

names (both place names and personal names) mentioned both by the ancient writers and the later ones (from Tacitus and Caesar, for example, down to Aventinus and Beatus Rhenanus) so that they could be explained and etymologized (p. 32 r). For it was especially on this basis that he himself attempted to prove that ancient Gaul had spoken the Germanic tongue. But Gesner showed sound linguistic judgment in urging that particular attention be paid to the formative elements, both compounding and derivational, in proper names. The listing which he hoped would be made would thus contain an alphabetical ordering of such elements.[26]

Not only in proper names but in any projected comparison, the concept of "similarity" was crucial. At times Gesner is highly casual, as when he quotes Herodotus in giving the Medan word for "dog" as *spaca* and then asserts that this is similar to (*accedit*) Slavic *pos* or *pas* (p. 61 v). Likewise he equates, without any further explanation, "Sciri, alias Scyri, id est Stirii vel Stirenes" (p. 67 r). He apparently derives from the similarity in the form of the characters the parallelism of ſ and ll[27] in following up Aventinus' proposal to consider the Tacitean Velleda (Veleda) as "Veſeda" and to etymologize the name as "weiß-heit, ipsa sapientia."[28] Phonetic similarity undoubtedly suggested the *ad hoc* equation of *c* and *g* ("c & g consonantes affinitatem habent," p. 30 r) by which he explained Alcis, from Tacitus, as *Halgen* ("id est sanctos, nam & aspiratio saepe a Latinis negligitur" [*ibid.*]).

On the other hand Gesner presents a long list of examples (e.g., "Vuarda vel guarda: Guelphus vel Vuelphus," p. 29 v) to support his claim that *Vu* paralleled *g* and hence the Langobardian "Vuoda" mentioned in Paulus Diaconus should be interpreted as "goda" (*deus*). But Gesner's very expression of this equation shows that it is not to be interpreted as a one-directional linguistic change that has taken place at a given time: "For I often find *Vu* placed instead of *g* and reversely (*contra*)" (p. 29 v). This reversible interchangeability must therefore not be confused with modern "sound-laws." And the references to High German/Low German differences do not necessarily imply a historical priority of one or the other, even where a term such as "mutant" is used (in an apparent reverse of the actual facts) in a quotation from Sebastian Münster: "Septentrionales & maritimi Germani quos inferiores vocamus,

---

[26] "nempe in andus, in manus, in rix vel ricus, in baldus vel boldus, in precht, mar, hart &c" (p. 33 v).

[27] "facile autem fuit ſ. in ll. mutare" (p. 29 r).

[28] To be sure, precisely this and other such speculations are the ones Gesner labels "merae coniecturae" (pp. 29 v-29 r).

ʃ mutant in t. & b. in f. & z. quoque in t." (p. 44 r). In presenting Glareanus' argument that older Celtic was really Germanic, Gesner notes Caesar's reference to differences in the speech of that time and observes that the differences persist: "Celtae [i.e., Germanic speakers of the Upper and Middle Rhine] enim perpetuo habent ʃ, ubi Belgae t. ut Waʃer/watter: Groß/grott: Das/Dat" (p. 21 r). Here again we must beware of interpreting too much into the statement. "Perpetuo" un-doubtedly means "consistently" and does not imply that the specific parallel had persisted since Caesar's time, but merely that the general dialectal grouping had persisted.

How little weight Gesner himself attached to the "Second Sound Shift" becomes evident in his assessment of Notker's *Oratio Domini* and *Symbolum fidei* which he reproduces.[29] Gesner overlooks the character-istically Upper German consonant features of these documents, and on the basis of two vocabulary items and the absence of the "diphthongs" ("ei. & au **pro** i. & u longis," p. 42 r) declares that they approach closely the speech of Low Germany (p. 42 v).[30] In his zeal to interpret the "framea" of Tacitus' *Germania* as related to "Pfriem," Gesner care-lessly confused his proportion. His example is the "Low German" "paffus"[31] as against the High German "pfaffus," but his "law" is: "Solent autem inferiores Germani p. ante f. ab initiis dictionum omittere" (**p. 33 v**). (His example, obviously, should lead him to say "f. post p."). His conclusion fits his revised law: "sic pro pframea dictum fuerit framea" (*ibid.*).

In analyzing his own "Helvetica," however, and in comparing it with "Suevica" and other Germanic tongues, Gesner proceeds in a more consistent and linguistically sophisticated manner: he mentions various phonetic parallels (e.g., long *u* as against *au*), variant infinitive forms of

---

[29] Gesner's source, as he mentions, is Johannes Stumpf (1500-1576) and his *Schweizerchronik* of 1548. Stumpf was quoting from the lost Codex S (Vadianus) and also furnished the misdating of Notker to 870. Except for very minor details (*hinto* for *hiuto;* one *Kelouba* for *Kelaubo*), Gesner follows precisely the text of Stumpf as given in: Paul Piper, *Die Schriften Notkers und seiner Schule,* II (Frei-burg und Tübingen, 1883), xiv-xv.

[30] Jan Agrell's praise of Gesner for touching upon the problems of the Second Sound Shift (*Studier in den äldre språkjämförelsens allmänna och svenska historia,* Uppsala Universitets Arsskrift, 1955, XIII, p. 30) needs to be qualified because of the lack of any basic genetic direction in Gesner's formulations. The specific set cited by Agrell, moreover, is taken expressly from Fabian Frangk's *Orthographia* but with all the normative sharpness removed. For Frangk, concerned in any case only with "oberlendischer sprach," is warning that good German requires a careful distinction among "Mitstimmer" (consonants) frequently confused: w. b. p./ d. t./ (Johannes Müller, *Quellenschriften,* p. 107).

[31] The form is obviously not one that the "inferiores Germani" (p. 33 v) would use, but would be at best Middle Rhenish.

verbs, contractions, and differing vocabulary (pp. 38 v–38 r); a later listing (pp. 38 r–39 v) gives examples to parallel and illustrate these more theoretical statements. In between are given the "blemishes" (*vitia*) which mar his own speech (p. 38 r) but which are usually "emended" in writing. Each "blemish" is illustrated immediately: thus initial *ch* for k ("chrank" for "krank"), the contraction of the article ("ſhanſen" for "des hanſen"). In this section Gesner's powers of ob-servation and of analysis are shown to their best advantage.

Despite the flaws that such a work as Gesner attempted was bound to show (a reliance, for many of the languages treated, on inadequate and often conflicting sources; a lack of any generally accepted rules for critical judgment on proposed etymologies), the product is still one that Gesner's sound good sense makes worthy of our respectful consideration. He did avoid many of the extravagances that his contemporaries were later to fall into. And he did make an effort to present the record in a clear and organized and fair manner.

The Languages of the World
A Classification by G. W. Leibniz

by JOHN T. WATERMAN

I<small>N</small> <small>ADDITION</small> to his better-known accomplishments in such fields as philosophy and mathematics, Freiherr Gottfried Wilhelm von Leibniz was also a keen student of languages. His efforts to further the use of his native German as a vehicle of polite and learned discourse are common knowledge. Not so well-known, however, are his various attempts to employ linguistic theory and evidence as a tool in reconstructing the history of mankind. Toward this end he anticipated certain features of the comparative method by well over a century, although he apparently never hit upon the notion of a reconstructed proto-language. He did, however, champion the notion of a linguistic family tree, even if his efforts to demonstrate a monogenetic derivation of the languages of the world in harmony with a literalistic interpretation of the Book of Genesis caused his proposals to go far beyond verifiable limits.

If his chartings of linguistic filiations seem presumptuous by contemporary standards of scholarship, it must be rememberd that Leibniz was first and foremost a historian on a grand scale—a "cosmologist"—language being only one of his many interests. Furthermore, in all of his scholarly undertakings he strove constantly and consciously to bridge the gap between empiricism and rationalism: the *vérités de fait* had always to be weighed against the *vérités de raison*. In the linguistic realm, this necessarily means that much of what he has to say is deductive and even speculative. Then too, many of his remarks, though apparently based upon observation, are offered without supporting evidence. Determining the reasons and establishing the factual basis which prompted Leibniz to find in favor of a given classification is, indeed, a difficult and sometimes impossible task. There is as yet no complete edition of his works, though the German Academy of Sciences has such a project under way.[1] Moreover, probably most of what he has to say about language is contained in his vast correspondence, much of which is to be found in the material already published by the Academy, some in the several older editions of his writings,[2] but parts of it still only available in the manuscript collections kept in the archives of the Hanover Public Library (formerly the *Königliche öffentliche Bibliothek*).[3] Although I have examined only a part of the manuscript collection and not all of the available published material, a preliminary attempt to establish the theories and the evidence upon which Leibniz based his classification of the languages of the world may be of some interest. The chart appended to this article is a modification of one prepared by Liselotte Richter, who has attempted to schematize Leibniz' many but scattered comments dealing with linguistic genealogy.[4]

Fundamental to his concern with things linguistic was his belief that the historico-comparative study of language is the only reliable method of determining ethnic origins and affinities. Obviously, he equated linguistic with racial pedigree, a generally untenable premise by modern standards but of acceptable validity in his day. In a letter dated January 20, 1692, he writes: "Ex linguarum connexionibus illustrari origines cognationesque populorum indubitata res est, imo eam unicam superesse arbitror viam in abdita antiquitate."[5] Or again: ". . . les langues sont les plus anciens monumens du genre humain, et qui servent le mieux à connoistre l'origine des peuples."[6] Having thus

---

[1] *Sämtliche Schriften und Briefe,* Preußische Akademie der Wissenschaften (Darmstadt, 1923 ff.), 9 vols. to date.

[2] Among which might be mentioned: Ludwig Dutens, *Gothofredi Guillelmi Leibnitii Opera omnia* (Geneva, 1768), 6 vols.; Foucher de Careil, *Oeuvres de Leibniz* (Paris, 1861-75), 7 vols.; Onno Klopp, *Die Werke von Leibniz gemäss seinem handschriftlichem Nachlasse in der Königlichen Bibliothek zu Hannover. Erste Reihe: Historisch-politische und staatswissenschaftliche Schriften* (Hannover, 1864-84), 2 vols.; Helfried Hartmann, *Die Leibniz-Ausgabe der Berliner Akademie* (Berlin, 1939).

[3] Eduard Bodemann has catalogued the Leibniz *Nachlass;* see especially his *Die Leibniz-Handschriften der Königlichen öffentlichen Bibliothek zu Hannover* (Hannover, 1895) and his *Der Briefwechsel des Gottfried Wilhelm Leibniz* (Hannover, 1889). Another valuable bibliography is that of Emile Ravier, *Bibliographie des Oeuvres de Leibniz* (Paris, 1937).

[4] *Leibniz und sein Russlandbild* (Berlin, 1946), Appendix. It is unfortunate that the scholarship of this otherwise excellent monograph has to compete with propagandistic goals.

[5] *Leibniz Briefwechsel,* Leibniz an Tentzel, 20.1.1692. The correspondence, hereafter referred to by the abbreviation *LBW,* is part of th manuscript collection of Leibniziana in the Hanover library; it has been catalogued by Eduard Bodemann (see footnote 3), and is stored in gatherings arranged alphabetically by correspondent.

[6] *LBW,* Leibniz an Bignon, 16.1.1694.

assumed a correlation of identity between language and peoples, Leibniz then set about reconstructing an ethnic-linguistic pedigree, working his way back through larger and more inclusive groupings until he finally arrived at a racially homogeneous *Urvolk*. As Werner Conze, in his monograph *Leibniz als Historiker*, puts it:

> Leibniz schloß . . . dann, indem er ohne Umstände Sprache und Volk als zusammengehörig voraussetzte, auf die ursprüngliche Verwandtschaft und Bewegung der Völker oder Stämme. Von da aus gelangte er nicht nur zu größeren Völkergruppen, sondern schließlich zur Annahme einer Ursprache und damit eines Urvolkes und einer einheitlichen Urrasse, womit durch die philologische Methode der Anschluß an die Tradition der Genesis hergestellt war.[7]

Unfortunately, Leibniz' "philologische Methode" seems to have been limited pretty much to an inspection of vocabularies: etymology, as he understood the term, was his principal linguistic tool. It is not likely that he realized the full significance of systematic phonetic correspondences, nor does he seem to have had any consistently applied criteria for establishing cognates. However, that he (and certain of his colleagues) made a distinction between symbol and sound may perhaps be inferred from a letter written to him by the Dutch scholar Cuper, who warned him against the "dangerous risk" of assuming linguistic relationship on the basis of "similar sounds or letters."[8] In one of the few statements in which he makes clear mention of the principles he followed, Leibniz seeks to reassure his correspondent of his caution and thoroughness, stressing that he insisted not only upon a goodly number of cognates, but that all his conclusions be highly probable: "Ego non facile Ethymologia fido, nisi multis conspirantibus confirmetur, et in conjecturis ipsis verisimilitudinem desidero."[9] He also attached considerable importance to the geographical distribution of the presumed cognates, pointing out the necessity not only of finding as many witnesses as possible, but of trying to establish a spatial continuity. He was reluctant to recognize an etymological relationship between words from widely separated languages if he could find no cognates in the geographically intervening tongues.[10] Most of his suggested etymologies are preserved in a series of studies published in the *Acta Berolinensia* of the Berlin Academy of Sciences (later the Prussian Academy, now the German Academy of

---

[7] (Berlin, 1951), p. 68.
[8] *Op. cit.*, p. 68, fn. 253.
[9] *LBW*, Leibniz an Cuper, 23.1.1703.
[10] *Nouveaux essais sur l'entendement humain*, Book III, chap. 2, par. 1.

Berlin). These were later edited and printed under a separate title; to my knowledge, this valuable collection of essays has not been reprinted.[11]

Turning now to the chart, an inspection will reveal that Leibniz worked out a detailed classification only for the languages of Europe and northeastern Asia, namely, for those which he subsumes under the title "Japhetic." His suggested classification of the "Aramaic" languages of southwestern Asia and North Africa is less complete, whereas his statements concerning other languages are too vague or tentative to be systematized. In answering another correspondent, he specifically mentions his inability to find enough evidence to warrant extending his classification beyond the Japhetic and Aramaic branches:

> Mettant la Sainte Ecriture à part, on ne laisse pas de voir ce me semble que les langues de l'Europe et de l'Asie viennent d'une même source, aussi bien qu'une bonne partie de celles de l'Afrique. Il faut avouer pourtant que les langues de l'Amerique, et les Extrémités de l'Afrique comme aussi la chinoise paroissent très eloignées de toutes les autres.[12]

It will furthermore be noticed that the immediate subdivisions of Japhetic are Scythian and Celtic. His use and interpretation of the term "Scythian" stems ultimately from a combination of religious and geographical considerations. As mentioned earlier, he accepted without reservation the authority of Holy Writ, assuming the *Urheimat* of the human race to have been the valleys of the Tigris and Euphrates rivers. To Leibniz the only plausible exit from this homeland in Asia Minor for those tribes that subsequently settled in northeastern Asia and in Europe was through the mountain passes that lay between the Black and the Caspian Sea. The vast area to the north and stretching indefinitely eastward into inner Asia, he called "Scythia," expanding the term to include much more territory—especially to the north and northwest—than it traditionally encompassed. Assuming as he did that Europe and northeastern Asia were subsequently populated by later migrations from Scythia, he sometimes refers to it figuratively as the *vagina populorum*. And in common with other scholars of his day, Leibniz uses the expression "Celto-Scythian" as a synonym (or near-synonym) for the term "Scythian." Linguistically, this word includes in its definition all the then-known languages and language-families of

---

[11] Johann Georg Eckhardt, *Godofr. Guilelmi Leibnitii Collectanea etymologica, illustrationi linguarum, veteris celticae, germanica, gallicae, aliarumque inservienta* (Hannover, 1717).

[12] *LBW*, Leibniz an Larroque, 26.1.1694.

Europe and Asia: Turkish, Slavic (which he calls "Sarmatian"), Finnish, Hungarian, Germanic, Celtic, Greek, and Latin.

When we consider the limited information to which he was privy, and the lack of any controllable technique for determining specific linguistic relationships, the accuracy of some of his inferences and deductions is quite striking. He decided, for instance, that the Finnish language had spread from northern Scandinavia deep into Siberia. And on the basis of linguistic evidence, he concluded that Hungarian is related to Finnish.[13] Also based upon linguistic considerations is his opinion that the Celtic and Germanic languages had derived from a common source. In a letter to Sperling he writes: "Celtas constat Germanos Gallosque comprehendisse atque ita facile admitto, imo statuo Celtas id est Germanos se Septentrioni infudisse."[14]

Fundamental to all his attempts to establish linguistic pedigrees, it should be emphasized, was his interest in tracing the origins and affiliations of the Germanic languages. The word *Germani* itself Leibniz derived from the "Herminones" mentioned by Tacitus, tracing this tribal appellation back to a Germanic root *erman-* or *irmin-*, meaning "great, powerful." This etymology, though uncertain, is still more acceptable than most and as respectable as any.

In the last years of the seventeenth century, German and Swedish cosmologists were engaged in a running polemic centering on the location of the Germanic homeland. The Swedish scholars, as might be expected, supported a theory that placed the *Urheimat* in Scandinavia. Leibniz opposed this view. He maintained that the Germans had come from Scythia, migrating at an earlier time from Asia Minor through the passes of the Caucasus, and later—from Scythia—spreading out into the Danube valley. From there, he proposed, they had gradually worked their way northward into the area where they were found at the time of Tacitus, although even prior to then some of them had gotten as far north as Scandinavia. This explanation, Leibniz admitted, was offered without proof, but he insisted that it was more probable than the Swedish position (one must bear in mind that he accepted Asia Minor as the birthplace of the human race). To get to Scandinavia by first traversing Russia and the fastnesses of the Arctic regions seemed to him less reasonable than to assume a gradual northward migration from the Danube valley.

---

[13] Louis Davillé, *Leibniz Historien: Essai su l'activité et la méthode historiaue de Leibniz* (Paris, 1909), p. 418.
[14] *LBW*, Leibniz an Sperling, 12.1699 (the day is not given).

In addition to probability, however, he offered three other arguments to support his viewpoint. One was an argument from ancient history, which attests to the presence of Germanic tribes all the way from the Black Sea to the Upper Danube. His other arguments are essentially linguistic in nature. In ancient times, he maintained, the geographical expanse in question showed at least two major language areas: a southern one that extended from the Don to the Danube—the Germanic; and a northern one from the Ob river to Norway—the Finnish. (Leibniz held Finnish to be the Scandinavian substrate; waves of Germanic and Slavic tribes, he believed, had swept over original Finnish territory.) As a third consideration, he pointed out that the historical names for the Swedes and the Goths never stood for all the Germanic tribes, whereas the terms *Germani* and *Teutoni* were generically much more inclusive.

This belief that the Gothic homeland was in the Balkans, though at variance with the position of most modern scholars and probably influenced in large degree by national pride, was nevertheless consistent with his intellectual convictions. Significantly, perhaps, this is one of the few instances I have found in which he gives specific examples of the sort of linguistic evidence upon which he based his contention that the Goths are not of Scandinavian origin.

Leibniz had studied (how thoroughly we know not) the Gothic language of the Codex Argenteus. At any rate, he noticed that the Scandinavian languages, including the Icelandic, are in some respects more like the Old Saxon than like the Gothic. He also comments on certain similarities in the morphology between Gothic and the classical languages. Typical are the observations he includes in a letter to Spanheim:

> Le dialecte du codex argenteus est fort different de tous les autres dialectes Allemands; et même de l'ancien langue suedois; et s'il est Gothique, il ne s'est pas à mon avis à confirmer la pretension de Messieurs les Suedois qui veuillent que les Goths soyent sortis de chez eux. L'ancien suedois, qui est l'islandois moderne, a bien plus de rapport à l'ancien Saxon, aussi bien que le Danois. Au lieu qu'il y a bien des choses dans le Codex Argenteus, qui paroissent tenir du Latin et du Grec; et entre autres il est digne de consideration que l'Allemand de ce Codex n'a presque point de verbes auxiliaires. Ainsi il pourroit bien estre de ces peoples Goths establis dans la Moesie ou dans la Pannonie [roughly present-day Rumania and Hungary].[15]

---

[15] *LBW*, Leibniz an Spanheim, 20.12.1692.

Leibniz predicted a time when "all the languages of the world would be catalogued and then compared with one another."[16] As established in this brief account, his own early efforts in this direction must be regarded as fragmentary and inadequate. On the other hand, a thorough study of his *Nachlass* may reveal a far more empirical basis for his statements than is now assumed.

---

[16] *Nouveaux essais,* Book III, chap. 2, par. 5.

Original Spelling and Terminology

ADAPTED FROM A SCHEMATIZATION BY LISELOTTE RICHTER

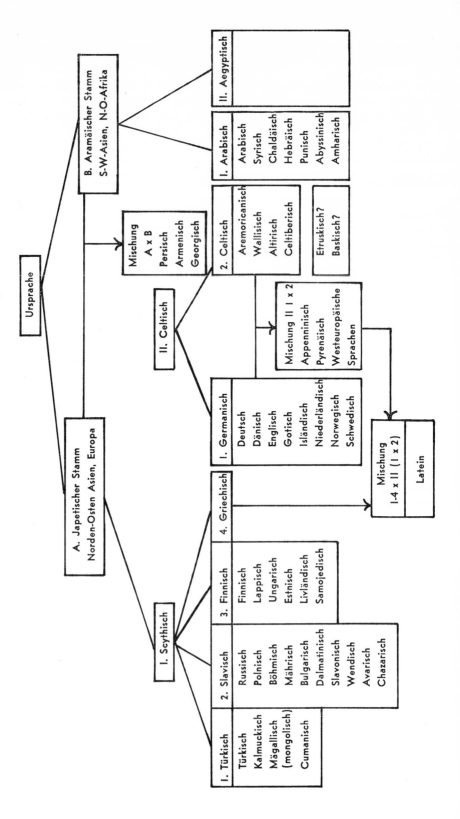

Another Look at Lessing's *Philotas*

by BERNHARD ULMER

"Lessing had no youth," states Nolte (*Grillparzer, Lessing and Goethe,* Lancaster, 1938), and this is a more subtle observation with wider implications than one might at first imagine. It is of particular importance if one wishes to evaluate the dramatist's *Philotas* properly. Upon its anonymous publication in 1759, when Lessing was thirty years old, this drama was first ascribed to Ewald von Kleist, and it is even now too often dismissed as a work of Lessing's "youth," when the author was not yet in control of dramatic technique and subject matter. The language, on the other hand, is usually acknowledged as being of power and beauty, but even here one has too often overlooked its finish, subtle skill, and musicality. In fact, Lessing is not given full credit for being the complete artist in this drama that he was in his later or better known dramas. Despite this, the whole of Lessing's greatness is indeed there if one but looks for it. Also the "small form" of the one-act play, in itself underestimated in importance, is a factor contributing to the neglect of *Philotas*.[1] It is all too easy to forget that at least a good third of Lessing's total dramatic production was in the field of the one-act play. For him it was not a minor form!

Furthermore, the age of the youthful prince has, in large part, been a stumbling block to a just evaluation on the part of the reader or perhaps the listener.[2] The prince's age seemed too scant at first sight for

---

[1] It is significant that the latest book on Lessing by Wolfgang Drews (Rowohlt, 1962, p. 173) lists in its bibliography only two specialized articles on *Philotas,* one by G. Friedrich and another by L. Vincenti, with the widely separated dates 1895 and 1937, respectively.

[2] *Philotas* has in recent years likewise been presented as a *Hörspiel.*

that of a tragic hero. One might note, in passing, that on two other occasions Lessing chose a child as a hero—in *Kleonnis* and in *Das Horoskop,* works which, however, remained fragmentary. Lessing makes a particular point of the fact that years have nothing to do with heroism. It is his contention that even a youngster has the capacity for greatness of action. Just as the latent heroism of a young man must be developed through the circumstances by which he is tried, so it is with the child. What is not latent, however, in the boy will not suddenly be implanted later when he is older. Young leaders mature with the responsibilities imposed upon them. Likewise the child. To be sure, by his years Philotas *is* a mere child, having taken the toga just a few days before the action begins. Therefore, at best, he is in his early teens. But the ancient Romans regarded one of his age as no longer immature, and Philotas in particular is anything but an irresponsible little swaggerer. He has been educated to responsibility and to kingship. He has known little else than preparation for leadership. His toy was a sword. He has had, like Lessing himself, no real youth. Actually then, there is nothing basically false about the actions or speech of Philotas as he is conceived by Lessing, and he deserves to be considered a hero.

It might be noted, furthermore, that the numerous epigrams which Lessing assigns to Philotas are entirely in keeping with the speech the boy has always heard around him at the court. Just so Marwood's daughter Arabella precociously apes her mother's speech.[3]

Returning to the precociousness of the character Philotas, one should not, however, overlook the fact that Lessing is quite aware that this trait verges on the ridiculous. He had, in fact, made fun of himself in *Der Junge Gelehrte.* In characteristic fashion Lessing often also treats Philotas with irony when he allows his hero to talk precociously. Actually Philotas himself is quite conscious of his patent immaturity. His very sensitivity about being a child or being treated as a child is evidence of this. His stoicism about his wound smacks of the bravado of a small boy. Also, like the hero of a baroque tragedy, Philotas feels he must play a role, and with that goes a certain amount of posturing and gesturing. All of this is indeed Lessing's intent in this fine psychological characterization. Lessing understands such a precocious youngster's feelings and mentality from his own personal experience.

---

[3] It seems, incidentally, utter nonsense to refer to our play, *Philotas,* as "the dramatic epigram," as has so often been done. It is far too complex and varied in its themes to suggest an epigram, nor is its exemplary brevity a justification for this "aesthetic" epigram.

Thus, while Philotas is made acutely cognizant of the fact that he is not a man but obligated to play his part as best he can, there is no question here of "leidenschaftliche Kriegslust" as one critic erroneously sees it (R. M. Werner, *Lessing*, 1907, p. 84), although he concedes: "die Sterbensfreudigkeit wird nicht zum Märtyrerfanatismus."

In *Philotas*, perhaps in greater measure than in the later *Minna von Barnhelm,* where Tellheim's and Werner's attitudes are contrasted, Lessing expresses his distaste for war. Nonetheless, if a man finds himself forced into the position of having to defend his country, Lessing expects him to conduct himself patriotically and heroically. He is quite conscious of the ambivalence of war, and he intensifies its tragedy in this drama by having at war two kings who were originally friends. Now, essentially, they are unwilling enemies through circumstances they have not chosen. Thus the whole drama underscores the mutual respect of the adversaries. A hero respects and is respected—anything else would not be in keeping with human dignity. In fact, *Philotas* upholds at every juncture the dignity of man no less than does *Nathan der Weise,* Lessing's more widely acknowledged product of his "Humanitätsideal."

Accompanying the theme of heroism in *Philotas* is that of honor and dishonor. This theme looms very large also in the character of Tellheim, whose exaggerated sensitivity to these concepts is so charmingly ridiculed by Minna as she educates the young officer toward a better understanding of the fallibility and limitations, as well as the strengths, of his humanity. Obviously, Lessing has depicted these limitations much earlier in his child-hero, Philotas.

With such limitations in mind Lessing here, as always, acknowledges man's inability to guide his destiny without divine help and wisdom. It is therefore to be anticipated that the author's deference to divine providence ("Vorsicht") is in great evidence in *Philotas*: the constant preoccupation of the baroque writers with "Glück" and "Kriegsglück," even up to Schiller's *Wallenstein,* is that of the preoccupation with divine foresight which tests and alternately punishes or rewards. King Aridäus consoles Philotas that the youth's capture has been ordained by divine providence, for the fortunes of war have, as it develops, made a captive of Aridäus' own son, thus equalizing the situation of the two enemies.

In the second of Philotas' monologues which show a certain parallelism to those of Odoardo Galotti, the young prince says, at the beginning of the fourth scene (R. Boxberger, *Lessings Werke, Deutsche National-Litteratur,* vol. 59, p. 263): "ich bin zu gütig gegen mich. Darf ich mir alle Fehler vergeben, die mir die Vorsicht zu vergeben scheint." He feels that the dishonor and shame into which he has fallen is not to be pardoned. Here again he evidences his uncompromising youthful nature, which gives him the strength to decide to kill himself. Philotas' suicide will give his own father an advantage over the enemy, who will thus have lost his hostage.

Again and again in the drama Lessing points up the combination of the immature and mature traits in the nature of his youthful hero, sometimes viewing him with irony, as indeed he does with his other soldier hero, Tellheim. Philotas himself, as has been said, worries over his immaturity. At the end of the second monologue (scene 4) Philotas has just rationalized himself into a belief in his ability and worthiness to die the heroic death of a man—all by very logical deductions. Yet in the next instant the duality in this youthful hero is evident. He says (p. 265): "Welche Begeisterung befällt mich. Die Brust wird dem Herzen zu eng! — Geduld, mein Herz!" which recalls to us Odoardo's admonition to himself (act V, scene 2): "Nichts verächtlicher als ein brausender Jünglingskopf mit grauen Haaren!"

Boxberger (*Lessings Werke*, vol. 59, pp. viii-ix) says in part: "Das kleine, aber treffliche Stück . . . kann nicht verstanden, noch recht gewürdigt werden, wenn man sich nicht in die kriegerische Stimmung der damaligen Zeit versetzt." This is only partially true and is a very superficial view of the drama. As the foregoing reveals, the heroic, martial aspects are merely the timely aspects, whereas the timeless aspects of every great work of art are in the inner conflicts and the dilemma confronting the tragic hero. We know Philotas is in a large degree conscious of his deficiency as an adult, and this deficiency results from not yet having attained that harmony of thinking and feeling which the adult supposedly has. Even Odoardo at his age is in danger of losing it, as is evident in the passage referred to above. Aridäus, the father of Philotas' young counterpart, at first also reacts in a highly emotional way when he is faced with Philotas' suicide, and he says in the final scene, not to be outdone by Philotas' heroism (p. 277): "Stirb nur! stirb! Aber nimm das mit, nimm den quälenden Gedanken mit: Als ein wahrer, unerfahrener Knabe hast du geglaubt, daß die Väter alle von einer Art, alle von der weichlichen, weibischen Art deines Vaters sind . . . Was liegt mir an meinem Sohne? Und denkst du, daß er nicht ebensowohl zum Besten seines Vaters sterben kann als du zum Besten des deinigen? — Er sterbe!" But Strato, who had earlier warned Philotas that supposed "Tapferkeit" might only be "angeborene Wildheit," knows that the rational will be victorious in King Aridäus, as indeed it is shortly afterward. Yet as W. Oehlke (*Lessing* 1919, vol. 1, p. 278), very well puts it: "Ein unreifer Held ist keiner."

If Lessing exhorts his fellow men not to surrender to impulse, this does not mean that he does not fully realize the limitations of the intellect alone in the solution of problems. In the fifth scene Philotas says to his father's trusted servant Parmenio (p. 268): "Soldat, kein Vernünfteln!" and later: "Du bist freilich klüger als ich. Aber nicht die Klügsten allein haben die besten Einfälle. Gute Einfälle sind Geschenke des Glückes." And this is Lessing's own conviction. By "Glück" he means that which is divinely inspired.

As to Philotas' "Einfall," the boy says of it (p. 269): "ich getraue mir nicht ihn in Worte zu kleiden." And herewith Lessing is stating that to an even greater degree the *word* is inadequate to clothe the idea. This is certainly a modest admission on the part of an author who is a master with words, one who extracts from them in a terse epigrammatic style the last bit of meaning. But it is because Lessing is so well aware of the ambivalent nature of the word and the thing or idea behind it that, though himself an author, he willingly acknowledges the inadequacy or the deceptiveness and illusoriness of the word. Consequently, just as in the baroque poets' works which precede Lessing, oxymoron, another form of ambivalence, is a figure of speech which occurs frequently in this drama. It occurs, for example, as early as the opening monologue, where Philotas, speaking of his captor's concern for his wound, says (p. 257): "O, der grausamen Barmherzigkeit eines listigen Feindes!" and ends with the words: "Hohnsprechende Höflichkeit!" This principle of verbal antithesis is widened in the structural and ideological elements of the drama as a whole. There is an ironical duality in the situation of *Philotas*' captive young princes. There is a duality in the person of Philotas himself, who is at once child and hero of stature, son and prince, as there is also a duality in the person of Aridäus, who is to his sorrow both father and king. These two characters of royal blood are then paired off, as are their two warriors Strato and Parmenio. With all three of these older characters, singly and in turn, Philotas is paired off in highly effective dramatic and ironical scenes which parallel each other.

Both Philotas and Aridäus Lessing views with detachment and with his characteristically mild irony. One might further say that Lessing is surprisingly modern in his presentation of his characters with their strengths and weaknesses, but always Lessing evidences his all-pervading

love for humanity. We remember that Minna in her love for Tellheim
is not blind to his weaknesses, just as Nathan the Wise is not unaware of
the weaknesses of his beloved Recha. Lessing's attitude toward Philotas
and Aridäus is not different.

If the duality of existence is a basic theme here, there are other themes
and motifs, likewise previously alluded to, which are familiar from other
works of Lessing. Yet nowhere have themes and motifs or imagery been
better used to give unity to Lessing's drama than here in this one-act
play. One such theme already mentioned in passing is "Höflichkeit."
Lessing treats this subject at length in at least two of his famous plays.
It occurs in *Minna von Barnhelm,* particularly in the Riccaut episode,
and in its obverse, namely, the incidents dealing with Just's curtness,
which stems, however, from a basically genuine and decent character.
In *Emilia Galotti* it is especially prominent in the scene where Marinelli
rids himself of Orsina by a courtesy which negates the actual intent of
courtesy. Similarly Philotas, too, may talk in the opening monologue of a
"hohnsprechende Höflichkeit" in his captivity.

The basic theme of heroism and honor is, of course, self-evident
and has been referred to repeatedly. But one should also not overlook
the parallels in the play to Philotas' heroic attitude. There are varying
shades of it mirrored in Strato and Parmenio, and a dramatic height
perhaps is reached (scene 8) in the case of the common soldier who
had captured Philotas and wants the honor of keeping his royal captive's
sword. He is suspected of being concerned with the sword's material
value, but he contemptuously wrenches off the precious hilt, saying
(p. 275): "Vielleicht aber ist es Euch nur um den kostbaren Heft zu
thun." He had won the sword fairly from the little "warrior demon" as
he calls him, and cherishes this honor.

This passion of the little prince is underlined again and again in the
imagery which is so evocative in its precision. Strato calls him (p. 262)
"feuriger Prinz." Parmenio says to him (p. 267): "Ich bin auch Vater,
Vater eines einzigen Sohnes, der nur wenig älter als du, mit gleicher
Hitze." At the beginning of Philotas' second monologue (scene 4) the
prince says (p. 263): "Götter! Näher konnte der Blitz, ohne mich ganz
zu zerschmettern, nicht vor mir niederschlagen. Wunderbare Götter!
Die Flamme kehrt zurück"; and toward the end, the image of fire
(incidentally also a favorite baroque image to contrast the warmth of
life with death's coldness) returns when Philotas says (p. 265): "Welch
Feuer tobt in meinen Adern?" Parmenio, receiving orders from Philotas
(scene 5), takes up the image of flashing and igniting lightning once

again when he exclaims (p. 268): "Ich erstaune, weil ich höre. Es hat geblitzt und ich erwarte den Schlag." And finally in the same scene, Parmenio asks Philotas (p. 270): "Soll ich für Dich durchs Feuer rennen?" And Philotas' reply to his speech begins (p. 270): "O mein bester, feuriger Freund!"

No less effective or striking is an image in Philotas' second monologue where he questions his own adequacy as a hero, saying (p. 264): "Wie alt muß die Fichte sein, die zum Maste dienen soll?" Just as graphic is the statement of Parmenio, for example, in the fifth scene. Hearing of the capture of Aridäus' son, he philosophizes (p. 265): "Ich finde, daß das Glück zu einem kleinen Schlage, den es uns versetzen will, oft erschrecklich weit ausholt. Man sollte glauben, es wolle uns zerschmettern und hat uns am Ende nichts als eine Mücke auf der Stirne totgeschlagen."

There has been discussion earlier of the ambivalence and the antithetical juxtaposition of meanings. In spirit allied to this, of course, is the larger concept of dramatic or tragic irony. This tragic irony which is so extensive in one of the earliest "one-act plays," namely the *Oedipus* of Sophocles, is by no means missing in *Philotas*. In Lessing's play the final scene in its essence is full of tragic irony. Aridäus might well have been warned in the preceding scene where he finds Philotas' remark puzzling. Aridäus there had said (p. 274): "Aber wehe meinem Sohne, meinem redlichen Sohne! Du wirst es ihm schwerlich vergönnen, den Harnisch abzulegen." To which Philotas had replied: "Beruhige den Vater, o König! Ich werde deinem Sohne weit mehr vergönnen! weit mehr!" Had Aridäus understood this ironical remark, he would not have been deceived later by the "child's play with the sword." Lessing subtly uses this irony as the basis for a dramatic and tragic misunderstanding brought about by Philotas' apparent childishness. The boy is thus able to master his dilemma and to choose the heroic death, the right of every free human being in a worthy cause, as he says (scene 8, p. 277): "Sollte die Freiheit zu sterben, die uns die Götter in allen Umständen des Lebens gelassen haben, sollte diese ein Mensch dem andern verkümmern können?"

Where in Lessing is there a greater variety of exalted sentiments on freedom, religion, honor, heroism or humanity than here in this "little" play? Which of Lessing's dramas deserves to be called more carefully and economically constructed than *Philotas*? Which of his larger plays contains finer poetic expression and imagery—or more moving and powerful dramatic tensions? Does this one-act play really deserve to be relegated to his lesser and "youthful" production? Although there might be room for disagreement about the early comedies and even the ideologically mature *Die Juden,* they display a surprisingly profound content and craft considering the time of their appearance. One can safely say that Lessing had no real youth, not even as a dramatic artist.

A Gottschedian Reply to Lessing's Seventeenth *Literaturbrief*

by ROBERT R. HEITNER

THE HISTORY of German literary criticism cannot point to a more incisive and annihilating frontal attack against any individual or any movement than Lessing's quick and total demolition of Gottsched's prestige as a reformer of the German theater in the famous Seventeenth *Literaturbrief*. In comparison with this diamond-hard little essay, Heine's exposé of the Romantic school seems more than ever like a rambling and gossipy collection of anecdotes, and the polemics in which Gottsched himself indulged in the 1740's appear all the cruder and more tiresomely abusive. Not many of Lessing's other writings can measure up to this, the most outstanding of all the *Literaturbriefe;* perhaps only in the supremely caustic speeches of Orsina in *Emilia Galotti* did he achieve the same tone of masterful, irresistible audacity. One by one, like so many steel-tipped arrows, he unleashes his disdainful sentences against the helpless enemy: "Ich bin dieser Niemand; ich leugne es geradezu. Es wäre zu wünschen, daß sich Herr Gottsched niemals mit dem Theater vermengt hätte. Seine vermeinten Verbesserungen betreffen entweder entbehrliche Kleinigkeiten, oder sind wahre Verschlimmerungen."[1] The reader, caught between surprise and amusement, cannot but follow Lessing breathlessly, and ends by agreeing with him wholeheartedly that this Gottsched and his school were little better than misguided fools. We may be thankful that Lessing defied convention and common respect in order to blast this absurd obstruction from the path of the advancing German national theater! How perspicacious of him to see that Gottsched has tried to force foreign French taste on Germany

---

[1] *Lessings Werke,* ed. Julius Petersen and Waldemar v. Olshausen (Berlin, Leipzig, Wien, Stuttgart, n.d.), IV, 56.

when he should have realized that the English theater was more closely akin to the natural genius of the German people! How ingenious and yet how basically right was Lessing's contention that the French drama, for all its "correctness," was far less the heir of Greek drama than the undisciplined English drama, and especially that of the incomparable Shakespeare!

So crushing is Lessing's magnificent tirade, and so eminent is its position in literary history—Danzel called the passage about Shakespeare, for instance, "eins der Ur- und Grundworte der modernen deutschen Literatur"[2]—that any inquiry into its impact on Gottsched and his circle may well seem superfluous. Since Gottsched's actual authority as a literary "dictator" had come to an end long before the appearance of the Seventeenth *Literaturbrief*, one assumes that the reactions of his diminished coterie to Lessing's attack would scarcely be more interesting than the whimpers of any other marrowless creature to which the *coup de grâce* is being administered. As for the aging professor himself, one might imagine, borrowing inspiration from Goethe's vivid anecdote in *Dichtung und Wahrheit* (Part 2, Book 7), that he, sunk in gloom and peevishness, gave his luckless manservant a resounding box on the ear and then returned to his dull daily routine of "scholarship." Perhaps these all-too-easy assumptions explain why the fact has generally been overlooked or forgotten that an answer to the Seventeenth *Literaturbrief* did indeed promptly emanate from the Gottsched circle, and why this answer has never been subjected to the analysis which it merits. Appearing anonymously at Frankfurt and Leipzig in 1759 (although dated 1760), the answer bore a long and explicit title: *Briefe, die Einführung des Englischen Geschmacks in Schauspielen betreffend, wo zugleich auf den Siebzehenten der Briefe, die neue Litteratur betreffend, geantwortet wird.* It is ironical that this, one of the last and least-known efforts of the Gottschedians, should also have been one of their best. In that sense, it was truly a swan song.

The existence of the *Briefe* is not, however, a secret. They are mentioned and their contents are more or less briefly indicated by Danzel,[3] Creizenach,[4] Schmidt,[5] Schlenther,[6] Waniek,[7] and Reichel.[8] Of

---

[2] Th. W. Danzel and G. E. Guhrauer, *Gotthold Ephraim Lessing. Sein Leben und seine Werke* (2nd ed; W. v. Maltzahn & R. Boxberger, Berlin, 1880), I, 440.

[3] *Ibid.*, p. 448-50 (1st ed.; Leipzig, n.d. [1850-54]), I, 454-56.

[4] Wilhelm Creizenach, *Versuch einer Geschichte des Volksschauspiels vom Doktor Faust* (Halle, 1878), pp. 77–78; also *Zur Entstehungsgeschichte des neuren deutschen Lustspiels* (Halle, 1879), pp. 21-22, 24-25.

[5] Erich Schmidt, "Zur Vorgeschichte des Goethe'schen Faust. I. Lessing's Faust," in *Goethe-Jahrbuch*, ed. Ludwig Geiger, II (Frankfurt am Main, 1881), pp. 76-77;

the standard editions of Lessing's works, Hempel (1868-77) gives the title in a footnote, along with a statement that the author was Karl Christian Canzler;[9] Lachmann-Muncker (1886-1924) lists the title along with a surmise that Christian Gottlieb Ludwig and Frau Gottsched were the principal authors;[10] Petersen-Olshausen (1925-35) does no more than this, and Rilla (1954-58) omits mention altogether.[11] The *Briefe* exist in just one edition and have nowhere been reprinted in their entirety or even extensively quoted. Only the concluding pages with their satirical footnotes to Lessing's Faust scene have attracted significant attention. These pages were reprinted by Schlenther,[12] Tille,[13] and Petsch,[14] who took them from Tille and not from the original text. Danzel also quoted a passage from the Faust section, plus a short passage about Gottsched's knowledge of French, and the historically interesting account of how the Harlequin role was first abolished in 1728 by Johann Neuber without Gottsched's intervention;[15] this is also quoted by Reichel.[16] Prior to 1850 Danzel wrote that ". . . dieses Büchlein verdient der Vergessenheit entris-

---

these remarks are repeated and enlarged in his *Lessing. Geschichte seines Lebens und seiner Schriften* (Berlin, 1884), I, 367-68, 413; see also 3rd ed. (Berlin, 1909), I, 377-78.

[6] Paul Schlenther, *Frau Gottsched und die bürgerliche Komödie* (Berlin, 1886), p. 48.

[7] Gustav Waniek, *Gottsched und die deutsche Literatur seiner Zeit* (Leipzig, 1897), pp. 335-36, 633-34.

[8] Eugen Reichel, *Gottsched* (Berlin, 1908-1912), II, 254, note 4.

[9] *Lessings Werke,* ed. R. Pilger, C. C. Redlich, *et al.* (Berlin, n.d.); IX, 79, note 1.

[10] *G. E. Lessings sämtliche Schriften,* ed. Karl Lachmann (3rd ed.; Franz Muncker, Stuttgart, Leipzig, Berlin, 1886-1924), XXII, part 2, 389.

[11] Petersen-Olshausen, Sec. 2, I, 113; G. E. Lessing, *Gesammelte Werke in 10 Bänden,* ed. Paul Rilla (Berlin, 1954-1958).

[12] *Op. cit.,* pp. 258-67.

[13] Alexander Tille, *Die Faustsplitter in der Literatur des sechzehnten bis achtzehnten Jahrhunderts nach den ältesten Quellen* (Berlin, 1900-1904), No. 278, p. 645 ff.

[14] Robert Petsch, *Lessings Faustdichtung mit erläuternden Beigaben.* Germanische Bibliothek, IV (Heidelberg, 1911), pp. 51-56.

[15] Danzel, *op. cit.,* I, 455, 456 (footnote), 496 (footnote); 2nd ed., I, 449-50, 450 (footnote), 491 (footnote).

[16] *Op. cit.,* II, 254, note 4. This version of the Harlequin's routing from the stage is not taken into account by Friedrich Johann von Reden-Esbeck, *Caroline Neuber und ihre Zeitgenossen* (Leipzig, 1881), who speaks only of Frau Neuber's abolition of the Harlequin and of Gottsched's supposed connection with that in 1737 (pp. 85, 210). The same is true of Eduard Devrient, *Geschichte der deutschen Schauspielkunst* (new ed.; W. Stuhlfeld Zürich, 1929), pp. 101-102; of R. E. Prutz, *Vorlesungen über die Geschichte des deutschen Theaters* (Berlin, 1847), pp. 239-41; of W. H. Bruford, *Theater, Drama, and Audience in Goethe's Germany* (London, 1950), p. 61; of Hannah Sasse, *Friederike Caroline Neuber* (diss. Freiburg in Breisgau, 1937), pp. 11-13. Wilhelm Cosack, *Materialien zu Gotthold Ephraim Lessings Hamburgische Dramaturgie* (2nd ed.; Paderborn, 1891), p. 129, mentions the account in the *Briefe* but remains unimpressed by it. Obviously the *Briefe,* if only for this one historical detail, should be better known.

sen zu werden,"[17] but the opposite has occurred. The only edition has itself become a rarity[18] and its contents remain generally unknown. Yet the reader can derive from the *Briefe* a fuller understanding of Gottsched's theatrical reform, of its necessity, and of its accomplishments. This anonymous defense not only constitutes an answer to Lessing's apparently unanswerable charges but also makes one wonder whether the Seventeenth *Literaturbrief* was not a less important milestone in the history of the German theater than the Gottschedian effort which it condemns.

The *Briefe* are three in number. The first is the least interesting to the literary historian, although it is very amusingly written and should certainly not be included in the description "long-winded" with which Erich Schmidt and Paul Schlenther dismissed the whole work.[19] Nor does it really detract from the letter's quality and originality if one must agree with Schmidt when he, in a somewhat belittling way, says that the style is an imitation of *The Spectator*.[20] Both stylistically and tactically the first letter is a clever introduction to the main body of the *Briefe*. Ostensibly written by a book dealer whose name is an anagram, "Sead," the first letter is addressed to "Herr Niemand" (Lessing: "Ich bin dieser Niemand"), and it describes in a seemingly good-humored, relaxed fashion what effect the Seventeenth *Literaturbrief* has had on Sead's niece and nephew, i.e., the younger generation. The niece is an empty-headed girl who is fond of Harlequin and horrors on stage. She thinks the theater in Leipzig—Gottsched's reformed theater—is dreadful because when you go there you feel like crying instead of laughing. To her, the Seventeenth *Literaturbrief* is an excellent tract, for she understands it to be a confirmation of her own theatrical tastes. The nephew is enthusiastic about it also, as he has taken it into his head to repudiate Gottsched categorically and therefore approves of everything, uncritically, that comes out against him. The implication, of course, is that only uncultured people and young ruffians welcome the Seventeenth *Literaturbrief*. An old physician, however, a friend of Sead's, defends Gottsched from the brutal attacks of the young people and of "Herr Niemand." Sead himself maintains a politely questioning air throughout his narration of the situation. But this is just the first, and rather gentle, sally.

---

[17] *Op. cit.*, I, 455; 2nd ed., I, 449.

[18] The copy used for this study is to be found in the *Theatersammlung* of the *Österreichische Nationalbibliothek* in Vienna.

[19] Schmidt, "Zur Vorgeschichte des Goethe'schen Faust," p. 76; Schlenther, *op. cit.*, p. 48.

[20] Schmidt, "Zur Vorgeschichte des Goethe'schen Faust," p. 76.

The second letter is sharper and more aggressive, although the playful ironical tone is still preserved. It is written by one signing himself "Andrews Sead," cousin to the first writer. Claiming to have been very favorably impressed by the Seventeenth *Literaturbrief*, Andrews starts off with a passage of absurdly exaggerated praise for Herr Niemand and for Shakespeare as well. He then concentrates on the statement in the *Literaturbrief* that Gottsched should have realized that German taste is closer to that of England than that of France. This statement prompts the writer, who displays a remarkable familiarity with seventeenth-century drama and was probably one of Gottsched's collaborators in the compilation of the *Nöthiger Vorrath,* to embark upon a comical listing of old German plays "with English taste" which might be revived now with profit. He mentions an *Oedipus* and *Die Zerstörung Jerusalems;* the latter of these two plays by Hans Sachs is "durchaus sehr tragisch mit Harlekins Lustbarkeiten" (*Briefe,* p. 16). Next comes *Das jüngste Gericht*: "Es hat zwar das den Fehler, daß weder Blut noch Mord dabey zu sehen ist; aber desto mehr Geister und Teufel mit der ganzen brennenden Hölle. Und das ist auch etwas!" (*Briefe,* pp. 16-17.) Then there are an *Adam und Eva* and a *Mammons Sold.* The latter work, written by Wolfhart Spangenberg and published in 1614, was first listed in the second part of Gottsched's *Nöthiger Vorrath* (1765)[21] without comment. But here it is described as follows: "Diese Tragödie ist in so weit sehr englisch, oder recht zu reden, altdeutsch; denn der Teufel, und wie der Autor fälschlich glaubt, sein Bruder, der Tod, sind immer auf dem Platze, und es kommen 6 Personen um; aber ewig schade ists, daß sie nicht bluten, und daß die aristotelischen 3 Einheiten so sklavisch beobachtet sind. Inzwischen glaube ich doch, daß man durch einige bescheidene Veränderungen dieses Stück zu unsrer neuen Bühne zurechte machen könnte" (*Briefe,* p. 17). The mimicry of Lessing's own words in this last sentence is clever; moreover, the writer has made a valid point, pricking holes into Lessing's bland generalities about the natural dramatic taste of the Germans. If Lessing had been as familiar with the primitive pre-Opitz dramas as were the Gottschedians who unearthed them, he might have been more careful about his blithe assumption that this so-called native taste was a proper one. A play from the latter part of the seventeenth century, *Der wunderthätige und gen Himmel fahrende Elias* (1680), is adduced to demonstrate that the native taste in drama, when untouched by the influence of Opitz and Gryphius,

---

[21] *Des nöthigen Vorraths zur Geschichte der deutschen Dramatischen Dichtkunst Zweyter Theil, oder Nachlese* (Leipzig, 1765), p. 245.

did not improve with time. When the serio-comic listing is done, the writer implores Herr Niemand to finish his own magnificent *Faust,* or at least to publish it entirely. Thus Lessing's pretense that someone else had composed the Faust scene is quickly penetrated, and the letter writer can sarcastically remark that if an author wants to be praised rightly, he must praise himself—as the author of the Seventeenth *Literaturbrief* has done.

The first two letters are merely skirmishes in comparison with the third and last, in which irony and humor are forgotten, so that a serious, lengthy refutation of the Seventeenth *Literaturbrief* may be undertaken. The writer calls himself "Jemand," thereby emphasizing his positive stand. He is identified as the old physician of the first letter—for which reason Waniek concluded that he was in reality Christian Gottlieb Ludwig (1709-73), a professor of medicine at Leipzig and a member of Gottsched's circle since the 1720's.[22] Ludwig was only fifty years old when the letter was composed; but if he *was* indeed the author of it, he spoke in the tones of a much older person. This was fitting, since the whole situation was looked upon by the Gottsched circle as a struggle between two generations, the one experienced and full of worthy accomplishment, the other presumptuous and upstart. They viewed Lessing's call for freedom and Shakespeare as a return to barbarism and a step backward contrary to the progress of civilization and culture in Germany. The alarm and disappointment with which they received this "reactionary" movement can scarcely by imagined today. With the chorus of spirits in *Faust* they could lament,

> Weh! weh!
> Du hast sie zerstört,
> die schöne Welt . . .

It was perhaps poetic justice when a few years later Lessing himself, as is shown in the last section of the *Hamburgische Dramaturgie,* had to contend with an upsurging younger generation and was forced to play the bitter old man before his time.

The writer of the third letter does not mask his feelings under badinage and satire. He complains openly and volubly about the insolence of Lessing's opening words. Then he points out that Gottsched could not have wrought the worsening effects on the German theater of which he stands accused, because it had already reached its nadir in the 1720's and could not possibly descend further. As to any improvements being

---

[22] Waniek, *op. cit.,* p. 335, note 1.

"trifles," as the Seventeenth *Literaturbrief* said, was it a trifle to have introduced reason and grandeur where previously there had been only nonsense and bombast, where the prevailing spirit had been that of plebeian smut? Was it a negligible trifle to have introduced verisimilitude to a stage which before had known only silly and incredible adventures? (*Briefe,* p. 57.) Dr. Jemand is indignant that Herr Niemand repeats Bodmer's heavy witticism about Gottsched's *Cato,* that it is a tragedy made with paste and scissors out of two tragedies by other authors.[23] In the first place, says Jemand, borrowing material from other authors is a time-honored practice, and no one blames Vergil for having plundered Homer, or Terence for having made a new comedy out of two by Menander, or Corneille for using Spanish sources. Then he adds that Gottsched—and this fact is often overlooked—had never made a secret of the origin of his *Cato* but in the preface to the first edition (1732) had openly admitted his use of the tragedies by Deschamps and Addison, "und sich hierdurch außer allem Verdacht eines plagii gesetzet . . ." (*Briefe,* p. 66). Gottsched had not acted out of a desire to increase his own fame as a poet; his wish was to bolster the slim repertory of the new stage: "Er wollte gern den Deutschen ein gutes und regelmäßiges Trauerspiel in die Hände geben: und er wollte sich nicht der Gefahr aussetzen, ihnen vielleicht zuerst in dieser neuen Bahn ein mittelmäßiges zu liefern" (*Briefe,* p. 66). To our modern eyes, as to Lessing's, *Der sterbende Cato* may well be even worse than "mittelmäßig"; but as the model and standard-bearer of a new style it was extraordinarily successful in Germany, and Gottsched had a right to take pride in the accomplishments of his adopted brainchild.

Herr Niemand had admitted that in the German theater of the early eighteenth century, "Man kannte keine Regeln; man bekümmerte sich um keine Muster" (Petersen-Olshausen, IV, 56). Here Dr. Jemand interposes, "Herr G——d kam und lehrte die Regeln. . . . Herr G——d kam und bekümmerte sich um Muster . . ." (*Briefe,* p. 68). To support Gottsched's procedure in providing models Dr. Jemand draws some historical parallels: Translations of Corneille and Racine—such as were advised and carried out by Gottsched in Germany—were also the means of routing bad Spanish taste in Italy; similar translations were the means of restoring good taste to the Dutch theater (*Briefe,* pp. 70-71). He can cite Johann Elias Schlegel (who had been mentioned with great re-

---

[23] See Bodmer's 'Sinnliche Erzählung von der mechanischen Verfertigung des deutschen Original-Stückes, des Gottschedischen Catos," in *Sammlung Critischer, Poetischer und anderer geistvoller Schriften* (Zürich, 1741-44).

spect in the Sixteenth *Literaturbrief*) as an example of a dramatist inspired by Gottsched's rules and models: "Ich weis, daß der selige Schlegel öffentlich betheuert, daß er niemals auf die Gedanken gerathen wäre, für die Bühne zu arbeiten, wenn er nicht durch G——ds Regeln und Beyspiel dazu wäre ermuntert worden. So machte er seine Dido bereits auf der Schulpforte, nachdem er dessen kritische Dichtkunst gelesen hatte" (*Briefe*, p. 72).[24]

There was in the Seventeenth *Literaturbrief* a remark implying that Gottsched's suppression of extemporized dialogue in plays had removed one of the characteristic features of German theater. But Dr. Jemand, quoting Riccoboni on the subject,[25] points out that extemporizing was neither a native German trait nor part of the English tradition. Instead, the Germans took over this practice, which is injurious to the literary quality of drama, from the Italian *commedia dell'arte*. How, Jemand asks, would Herr Niemand like to see extemporizing introduced, for instance, into *Miss Sara Sampson*? (*Briefe*, pp. 75-76.) The reference to *Miss Sara* is a clear indication that the Gottschedians had guessed the identity of Herr Niemand, although Germany as a whole did not for twenty more years penetrate the anonymity affected by the editors of the *Literaturbriefe*.[26]

It strikes Dr. Jemand as most unfair and incorrect that Gottsched is accused of having forced a Frenchified theater on Germany. From his classical viewpoint the French theater was not French but merely the latest incarnation of a world-wide, changeless, timeless universal theater based on reason: "Wenn ich in Pohlen einen Palast von Italienischer Bauart finde, und ich nehme den Riß davon, und lasse in Sachsen nach demselben, auch einen Palast aufführen: wird man den für ein Polnisches Gebäude erklären? . . . und eben auf diese Art hat G——d die deutsche Bühne auf französischem Fuß aufgerichtet" (*Briefe*, pp. 78-79). Then Jemand clinches his argument with a keen thrust: If it be admitted that this universal theater is a rational one, is it not an insult to the Germans to say it is not suited to them? (*Briefe*, p. 79.)

---

[24] Schlegel's inspiration through the *Critische Dichtkunst* is at least partially corroborated in Eugen Wolff, *Johann Elias Schlegel* (Berlin, 1889), pp. 6 and 12. Wolff's statements are based on those of Schlegel's brother, Johann Adolf. See also the preface to *Orest und Pylades* in *Joh. Elias Schlegels Werke*, ed. Johann Heinrich Schlegel (Kopenhagen and Leipzig, 1761), Erster Theil. The first drama, however, was not *Dido*, but *Hekuba* (later called *Die Trojanerinnen*).

[25] Luigi Riccoboni, *Réflexions Historiques et Critiques sur les differens Théâtres de l'Europe* (Amsterdam, 1740), p. 162.

[26] See Lessing, *Gesammelte Werke*, ed. P. Rilla, IV, 569; also Schmidt, *Lessing*, 3rd ed., I, 412. Herder was apprised of the secret by Nicolai in 1768: see *G. E. Lessings Gespräche*, ed. Flodoard von Biedermann (Berlin, 1924), pp. 79-80.

From this point Dr. Jemand goes on to explore Herr Niemand's assertion that German and English taste are closely related. Lessing has often been congratulated for his penetration in detecting this relationship, but the Gottschedians saw nothing remarkable about the comparison. So-called English taste is nothing more than untutored taste, and the untutored taste of every country is the same, Germany included. Dispensing with romantic notions about a multiplicity of tastes, Jemand distinguishes only between a "right"—the classical, and a "wrong"—everything else. The wrong is as universal as the right: "Wenn das folget, daß wir deswegen einen englischen Geschmack von Natur haben, weil wir in unsern alten Stücken voller Unsinn so viel mit ihnen gemein haben: so schlagen die Holländer, die Italiener, die Spanier, ja die Franzosen selbst in diesen Geschmack ein. Denn bey allen diesen Völkern finden wir, daß sie vor der unternommenen Verbesserung ihrer Bühne bey der lächerlichsten Unwahrscheinlichkeit in den Trauerspielen, das Ungeheure, das Blutgierige, das Wunderbare affectiret, und die Lustspiele mit Verwickelungen überladen und mit Schwänken und Zoten angefüllet haben" (*Briefe*, pp. 81-82). One can see that the Gottschedians regarded their reforms in a semi-religious light. Just as Christianity regarded the multiplicity of religions under the single heading of "wrong" and through missionary zeal attempted to consolidate all peoples in one faith of a universal and eternally "right" nature, so did these *Aufklärer* try to consolidate all literature under the banner of *reason*. They were missionaries, too, of a secular kind, and Dr. Jemand describes their success: "Nur nach und nach gab man der Stimme der Vernunft, der Wohlanständigkeit und den guten Sitten Gehör. Man lernte einsehen, daß ungeheuer und groß, tragisch und abscheulich, schmutzig und scherzhaft, bessernd und verschlimmernd zweyerley sey . . ." (*Briefe*, p. 83).

Lessing, on the other hand, argued for multiplicity and a healthy doubt about what was right and wrong, not only in the theater, but also in religion, as can be seen in *Nathan der Weise*. There the Christians, especially the Patriarch and Daja, are prototypes of these Gottschedians, who see only one truth to which everyone must be converted. Lessing was willing to concede to each people both the trappings of its own religion and the peculiar aspects of its own theatrical taste; but from each religion he demanded the production of virtue, and from each theater a strong effect on men's hearts. Thus the Christians come off short in *Nathan der Weise* because they demand compliance with their ideas, but produce few good works; and the Gottschedians come off short in the Seventeenth *Literaturbrief* because they demand compliance with their rules but their plays have little effect on human hearts.

For Dr. Jemand the moving quality of English dramas was of no consequence, not because the Gottschedians were uninterested in drama's effect on the emotions, but because they insisted first on rationality of form and content. Thus the orthodox Christian believes that *no* good works can be performed until grace has been received. Jemand looks on England as a perversely backward country (much as Charlemagne looked upon Saxony) where the new enlightening doctrines are stubbornly resisted: "Bloß die Engländer haben dasjenige, was sie in Ansehung des Wilden, des Unmenschlichen, des Unanständigen, mit alten unausgebildeten Theatern gemein hatten, zum Theil nicht bessern können, zum Theil nicht bessern gewollt; sondern sich vielmehr ein Verdienst daraus gemacht, dieses Unwesen aufs höchste zu treiben" (*Briefe*, p. 83). This judgment may be smiled at as absurdly unesthetic, but one should not be too quick to write off Dr. Jemand as an insensitive person. He may have felt the attraction of English plays; he had learned, however, as an enlightened rationalist, to control his instinctive sympathies and to accept instead what reason had instructed him was correct. He does not condemn Shakespeare out of hand or attempt to deny his genius. It is just that genius, like any other powerful natural force—water, fire, electricity, etc.—has to be trained and controlled through rational restrictions (rules) if it is to redound to the good of mankind: "Niemand läugnet, daß Shakespear ein außerordentlicher und großer Kopf war; und daß er, hätte er anders gute Muster und Regeln gekannt, es mit dem größten tragischen Dichter würde haben aufnehmen können. So aber war er ein unstudirter Mensch, der bey einer umschwärmenden Bande ein Komödiant und ein Erfinder von Stücken geworden" (*Briefe*, p. 85).

Jemand was well acquainted with the type—every wandering troupe in Germany was supplied with such an actor-author—but, fortunately for Germany, none had ever been a genius! It was nothing but a confounded misfortune for England that Shakespeare lived when he did. Coming before the advent of the new rational revolution, he wrote powerful but bad dramas which made the correct but weaker works of later dramatists impotent to influence the English people. The old gods had too strong a prophet against whom the missionaries could not prevail. If this misfortune had struck France and Germany as well, the same lack of progress would be observed, but luckily in both these countries the most outstanding prerational dramatists were men of little talent: "Wäre Jodelet, wäre Hanns Sachs ein Shakespear gewesen, was würde Corneille, was würde Herr Gottsched zur Einführung des guten Geschmacks haben thun können?" (*Briefe*, p. 85.) Nevertheless, it occurs to Jemand that the English people themselves are generally mild-mannered and not bloodthirsty, so that Shakespeare is an exception among them. Then comes an astonishing explanation for this apparent anomaly: "Shakespear war ein Räuber, eh er Komödiant ward. Bey dieser seiner Handthierung hat er nun Gelegenheit genug gehabt, sich an blutige, schreckliche und grausame Vorfälle zu gewöhnen; und seine mit einer natürlichen Ungestümigkeit verbundnen großen Gaben, machten in der Folge Blut und Abscheu auf dem Englischen Theater nothwendig. *Wäre Shakespear gehenkt worden*, eh er sich der Bühne weihete: so hätten vieleicht die Engländer kein von allen europäischen Nationen so verschiedenes Theater" (*Briefe*, pp. 85-86). One can see that Jemand devoutly wishes that Shakespeare had met this fate and saved the English—and now the Germans—so much trouble. This startling portrait of Shakespeare as a highwayman was a bit too much for Erich Schmidt, who burst out with the following denunciation: "Der sieche Gottschedianismus . . . trat . . . 1759 mit 'Briefen,' gegen den unbekannten 'Herrn Niemand' hervor, einer thörichten Schrift, welche Lessingen die Sehnsucht nach Schwulst, Greueln, Pöbelstücken, verschlechterten Haupt- und Staatsactionen unterschiebt und den wilden englischen Geschmack aus dem—Räuberhandwerk des jungen Shakespeare erklärt! . . . Gegen dieses Gefasel."[27] But Schmidt need not have been quite so scornful of the robber theory, which at least shows that the Gottschedians had been keeping abreast of the current Shakespeare scholarship. The tradition about Shakespeare's youthful poaching escapades, which began with Nicholas Rowe and the Rev. Richard Davies in 1709, was accepted throughout the eighteenth century, and the question is still seriously discussed today.[28] From poacher to highwayman was not a great step if one considers that Dr. Jemand probably read a garbled version of the incident (*Wilddieb* to *Dieb* to *Räuber*). To be sure, it would have been much better if the whole matter had been omitted, for it only weakens, with its personal judgment of Shakespeare's character, Jemand's main thesis that the untutored drama of *any* nation is bound to be full of blood and thunder.

When it is Lessing's turn to betray some naïveté, namely, in saying

---

[27] Schmidt, *Lessing* (Berlin, 1884), I, 413.
[28] See Frank O'Connor, *Shakespeare's Progress* (Cleveland and New York, 1960), p. 19.

that a Frenchified theater does not provide enough for the spectator to see, Dr. Jemand pounces on him, perhaps too ponderously. He accuses Herr Niemand of having childish tastes: "Sonder Zweifel will das sagen, es giebt uns zu wenig Mordthaten, es giebt uns kein Blut, keine Teufel, keine Gespenster, keine Hexenmeister, keinen Harlekin, kein Gelache, keine Schlachten, keine Blitze, keine Ungereimtheiten zu sehen" (*Briefe*, p. 87). If this is what Lessing wants the Germans to see (and it can hardly be denied that there is an abundance of such things in Shakespeare's dramas), then he is trying to make plebeians of them again, coming to the theater only to feast their eyes (*Briefe*, p. 88). To the Gottschedians, anyone who liked Shakespeare must like the *whole* Shakespeare. Instead of charitably supposing that Herr Niemand might be overlooking the more gruesome aspects of Shakespearean works, these doughty polemicists immediately assumed that he reveled in them. With heavy sarcasm Dr. Jemand imagines that Niemand advocates a return to the pig's bladders of blood which were a commonplace of the pre-Gottschedian theater, and he asks, "Gehöret das auch zur schönen Natur?" (*Briefe*, p. 90.) He illustrates the need for restraint on stage with a classical example from the history of painting: "Warum verbarg der Künstler der Opferung der Iphigenia das Gesicht Agamemnons? konnte er keine zärtliche, mitleidige, traurige und bey alledem große Mine malen. . .? Er würde es gekonnt haben, und vieleicht gut; aber niemals besser als er wußte, daß sich jeder das Gesicht dieses unglücklichen Vaters, sobald er nun die Verfassung in der er war wußte, selbst malen könnte. Man lobte ihn darum; und man tadelt doch die dramatischen Dichter, die eben so in ihren tragischen Gemälden verfahren!" (*Briefe*, p. 90). Lessing uses the same example, which was presumably a learned commonplace, six years later in the second chapter of his *Laokoon*, where he too declines to see in the veiling of Agamemnon's face a confession of the artist's inability. Lessing, however, interprets the artist's decision to veil as compliance with the law that plastic art must depict only the beautiful, while a face contorted with grief is ugly (Petersen-Olshausen, IV, 301). Jemand's idea that art should stimulate rather than satisfy the imagination does, nevertheless, find its corroboration in the third chapter of *Laokoon*, when Lessing writes, "Dasjenige aber nur allein ist fruchtbar, was der Einbildungskraft freies Spiel läßt" (Petersen-Olshausen, IV, 304). Furthermore, in the *Hamburgische Dramaturgie*, Stück IX, Lessing calls for a measure of restraint on stage: "Gut, wenn . . . die erhitzte Einbildungskraft Blut zu sehen glaubt; aber das Auge muß es nicht wirklich sehen" (Petersen-Olshausen, V, 59).

What is the nature of the great and terrible called for in the Seventeenth *Literaturbrief?* Dr. Jemand cannot conceive that these qualities
exist only in English dramas where everything is painted in the shrillest
colors. It seems to him that a Cato, a Brutus, and a Horace can also
instil terror, at least in the heart of a cultured and rational person.
Jemand's words are dignified and thoughtful: "Wer malt den Teufel
schrecklicher, der ihn schwarz, mit Hörnern, Krallen und einem Pfer-
defuß malt, oder der von ihm spricht: Er ist ein Mörder vom Anfang.
Das wahre Große und Schreckliche liegt im Innern der Handlung und
der Gedanken, und nicht in der Vorstellung und im Ausdruck. Der ist
nur das Kleid" (*Briefe,* p. 99). The ideal which is intimated here is very
high indeed. The Gottschedians had been working for a theater of the
most intellectual sort. Any appeal to the masses was disdained. The
masses must be trained to *come up* to an appreciation of this super-
refined theater, as had already been done in France. In contrast to this,
Lessing put the emphasis on emotions—once emotions are aroused,
people can be improved through them. Therefore he was willing, within
bounds, to return to the natural taste of the people, in a word, to compromise. Dr. Jemand scornfully agrees with Herr Niemand that the
Germans would have found much greater enjoyment in a translation
of *Hamlet* than in the Gottschedian translations of Corneille and Racine:
"Das Volk, wenn das Volk der Pöbel heißt, würde an dem englischen
Tragödienschreiber nichts auszusetzen gefunden haben; es würde dessen
übersetzte Stücke eben so gerne gesehen haben, als es seinen lieben
Doktor Faust, seine Circe, seinen Masaniello: denn es würde geglaubt
haben, sie wären auf einem Beete gewachsen" (*Briefe,* p. 107). Here
again the similarity of English and old German taste is not denied, but
both are branded as wrong.

   With considerable justice Dr. Jemand asserts that it would have
been a grave mistake to furnish the Germans with translations of
Shakespeare in the 1730's: "Wir würden vieleicht bald Dichter gesehen
haben, die Shakespearischer, als Shakespear selbst ausgeschweift, geflogen
und gekrochen wären . . . Und wenn man vollends das Recht bekömmt,
widernatürlich, unregelmäßig und ungezogen zu seyn; wie leicht kann
man sich da nicht entzünden lassen, um in den Genie-Stand erhaben zu
werden?" (*Briefe,* p. 107.) That is to say, a kind of premature Sturm
und Drang period would have arisen! The *Haupt- und Staatsaktionen,*
instead of being suppressed, would have gained a powerful new impetus.
But the dramatists who under Gottsched's aegis began copying Racine
and Corneille at least produced something entirely different from what

had been seen on German stages before, and the rules they observed gave their works at least a semblance of literary style. Dr. Jemand says, again with some justice, that if Johann Elias Schlegel and Cronegk had lived longer they would have been able to produce some real master-pieces within the confines of the rules. Some years later he could have made the observation that Lessing himself did not wander too far from classical regularity in his three great plays—certainly there is little influence of Shakespeare on *Minna, Emilia,* and *Nathan.* Genius is only enkindled by genius, the Seventeenth *Literaturbrief* had proclaimed en-thusiastically, and therefore Shakespeare should have been made known to the Germans. Dr. Jemand punctures this statement by asking which genius it was, then, who enkindled Shakespeare himself? (*Briefe,* p. 108.) He also counters the glowing statement that Shakespeare seems to have accomplished everything through the direct inspiration of nature and without the painful efforts of art: "Alle schönen Wissenschaften scheinen alles bloß der Natur zu danken zu haben, und doch gründen sie sich auf Regeln. Lese ich Gellerts Fabeln, so kommt mir alles, so leicht, so natürlich vor: daß es mir scheint, als hätte er alles bloß der Natur zu danken; und doch sagt er mir in der Vorrede zum andern Theile ganz was anders" (*Briefe,* p. 109). As for Shakespeare, he should have exercised more *art,* for then his works would appear more *natural.* Jemand fears that many would-be authors, who are either too lazy or too incompetent to master the rules, will have a heyday now that Shake-speare has been recommended to them as a representative of easy ir-regularity: "Diese Aufmunterung ist einnehmend; und es müßte sehr schlecht seyn, wenn wir nicht in Jahr und Tag wenigstens eine Mandel Shakespearische Scheniee hätten, wenn nur dieser englische Schenie zwischen hie und der Michaelis-Messe deutsch lernt" (*Briefe,* p. 111). Here his bitterness has turned Dr. Jemand into a fairly accurate prophet; for the future dramatists of the Sturm und Drang were indeed inspired by their liberation from the rules. One is much less likely now, however, to characterize the young "geniuses" as incompetent.

The latter part of Lessing's argument in the Seventeenth *Literatur-brief,* containing the brilliant maneuver whereby Shakespeare is said to be closer to the ancient Greeks than are the French, is largely ignored by Dr. Jemand. He simply remarks that if it is a question of coming close to the Ancients, why not go *directly to* the Ancients, as Gottsched has always advocated? (*Briefe,* p. 112.) In sum, Herr Niemand is just wasting his time trying to foist an unlearned poet like Shakespeare on an advanced and cultured modern society, and it is useless to transform obvious faults into specious virtues. The man was simply ignorant and, although it is a pity, the fact remains as it is. "Shakespear kannte die Alten und ihre Regeln nicht, sonst würde er ihnen gefolgt, und groß wie sie geworden seyn. Herr Niemand kennt sie, und will, daß wir sie vergessen; und den, der sie uns gelehrt hat, für seinen guten Dienst mit ihm schimpfen sollen" (*Briefe*, p. 115). There the case rests, solidly and logically based on its own premises—premises, however, which Lessing (and posterity with him) rejected.

Dr. Jemand does not permit his letter to end without an attack on the Faust scene which Lessing, probably in haste, was unwise enough to append to his *Literaturbrief*. Into this breach the Gottschedians rushed with glee, no doubt scarcely able to believe that their opponent had exposed his flank in such a gratuitous manner. The Faust scene contains perhaps the poorest dramatic writing that Lessing ever published, and it owes its undue prominence only to the fact that it is the first literary treatment of the old popular theme. It basks in the reflected glory of Goethe's *Faust* like a great man's commonplace or stupid ancestor. Lessing has had few more faithful admirers than Erich Schmidt, but even Schmidt felt obliged to answer Lessing's eager question, "Was sagen Sie zu dieser Szene? Sie wünschen ein deutsches Stück, das lauter solche Szenen hätte? Ich auch!" (Petersen-Olshausen IV, 60) with the blunt retort, "Wir nicht, antworten wir dies Mal mit den Gottschedianern und versagen dem Fragment, das jeder Wirkung auf Gemüth und Phantasie bar, lediglich den Verstand beschäftigt, unsern Beifall."[29] It is difficult to understand why Lessing let this scene be printed as an illustration of his thesis in the Seventeenth *Literaturbrief* when it could only serve to weaken or refute his argument about the salutary effects of the English influence. The Gottschedians chastized him thoroughly for his lack of judgment by reprinting the scene in full at the end of their third letter, accompanied by a set of harshly critical footnotes (*Briefe*, pp. 118-128). Dr. Jemand's answer to Lessing's question, "Was sagen Sie zu dieser Szene?" is "Daß Faust und die Teufel einander zum Trutz witzig sind, und unter diesem ewigen Witz das wahrhafte Große ersticken; daß solche ganz epigrammatisch und ganz unnatürlich ist . . ." (*Briefe*, p. 127). These footnotes are not only merciless, but trenchant; the thrusts are made with a rapier, not a club. Schmidt admits, ". . . dem Unerbittlichen ist während seiner ganzen Schriftstellerlaufbahn, weder vorher noch späterhin, so übel mitgespielt worden."[30] To use a figure of speech

---

[29] Schmidt, "Zur Vorgeschichte des Goethe'schen Faust," p. 74.
[30] *Ibid.*, p. 77.

popular in that day, there was still a last powerful sting left in the trampled Gottschedian worm.

The several nineteenth-century commentators on the *Briefe* agreed that the footnotes were the work of Frau Gottsched,[31] for who else in Gottsched's circle would have had wit enough to write them? Surely the time has now come, however, to cease characterizing the people in Gottsched's circle as "schale Köpfe," "tölpelhafte Gegner," and whatever other choice epithets were in fashion among eighteenth- and nineteenth-century critics, and to restore to them their dignity as sincere representatives of an older school of thought. Conjectures about the authorship of the *Briefe* are somewhat useless. If there is good evidence that Professor Ludwig wrote the whole third letter, there is, on the other hand, no good evidence to prove that he did not write all three letters and the satire on the Faust scene as well. Or it may be that Ludwig and Frau Gottsched, Canzler and Gellius[32] and Gottsched himself *all* contributed to the work. The important thing is that the *Briefe* are a brave last attempt of the Gottschedians to summarize their achievements and to define their goal. As such, the work merits a thoughtful reading by anyone interested in the historical development of the German theater.

---

[31] Included are Danzel, *op. cit.*, I, 456 (2nd ed., I, 450); Schmidt, "Zur Vorgeschichte des Goethe'schen Faust," p. 76; Schlenther, *op. cit.*, p. 48; Waniek, *op. cit.*, p. 633.

[32] Johann Gottfried Gellius (1732-81), a private scholar in Leipzig, was given as the author of the *Briefe* by Christian Heinrich Schmid, *Chronologie des deutschen Theaters* (1775), ed. Paul Legband. Schriften der Gesellschaft für Theatergeschichte, I (Berlin, 1902), p. 134.

José Ortega y Gassets
Verhältnis zu Goethe

by EGON SCHWARZ

A̲n José Ortega y Gasset hat die deutsche Kultur einen ihrer
besten Kenner und Verfechter verloren. Dies ist zur Genüge bekannt.
Und dennoch ist seine Stellung zum Deutschtum keineswegs geklärt.
"Einer der Hauptzüge meines Werkes war es," rühmt sich Ortega, "den
spanischen Intellekt um den Strom des deutschen Geistesschatzes zu
bereichern."[1] Bei einem anderen Anlaß aber spricht er ein Bekenntnis
aus, das sich schwer mit dieser offenbar hohen Wertschätzung verein-
baren läßt: "Man mag es mir glauben, daß wohl niemand eine größere
und ursprünglichere Abneigung gegen die deutsche Kultur empfunden
hat und empfinden wird als ich" (I, 209). "Das System, in welchem sich
die Widersprüche einer Existenz vereinen" (IV, 408)—so definiert
Ortega nämlich das Wesen der Biographie—ist eben für ihn noch nicht
gefunden, jedenfalls nicht auf seine Haltung der deutschen Kultur
gegenüber angewandt worden.

Symptomatisch für diesen Zustand ist Ortegas Goethe-Bild, sowohl
in Bezug auf die Zwiespältigkeit der Vision als auf die mangelnde
Klärung von außen her. Es gehört zu den Rätseln der internationalen
Kulturbeziehungen, daß die deutsche Reaktion auf die frische Kraft, die
Ortegas Goethe-Anrufen innewohnt und von vielen Deutschen auch
empfunden wurde, so schwach und unbedeutend gewesen ist. Das
Schweigen der zum Sprechen Berufenen fällt ebenso auf wie die überaus
undeutlichen Vorstellungen von dem, was Ortega tatsächlich sagen

---

[1] José Ortega y Gasset, *Obras Completas* (Madrid, 1946-1947), IV, 404. Alle
ferneren Hinweise auf Ortegas Werke beziehen sich, sofern nicht anders vermerkt,
auf diese Ausgabe und werden von nun an innerhalb des Textes belegt. Die
Übersetzung ist von mir.

wollte. Daß noch zu einem so vorgerückten Zeitpunkt wie 1946 und an so hervorragender Stelle wie in Fritz Strichs *Goethe und die Weltliteratur* mit diesen Mißverständnissen in keiner Weise aufgeräumt wurde,[2] hat die vorliegende Arbeit mitveranlaßt.

Die Gründe, warum Ortegas lebenslängliche Beschäftigung mit Goethe für die deutsche Kulturwelt so bedeutsam ist, sind mannigfaltig. Seine gründliche Bekanntschaft mit Goethes Werk und Leben, seine Kenntnis der Goethe-Forschung, seine umfassende Belesenheit auf dem Gebiet der gesamten deutschen Bildung sind freilich nur Vorbedingung hierfür. Aber eine solche unleugbare Sachkenntnis mußte gerade diejenigen am tiefsten beeindrucken, denen die gewöhnliche spanische Unbekümmertheit um fremdes Kulturgut kein Geheimnis war. Im Hinblick auf Grillparzers Aufnahme in Spanien hat schon Marcelino Menéndez y Pelayo seine Landsleute wegen ihrer "Vernachlässigung oder Unkenntnis jeder ausländischen Literatur, mit Ausnahme vielleicht der gestrigen französischen," getadelt.[3] Dafür, daß dies von Goethe in fast dem gleichen Maße gilt, fehlt es uns nicht an Zeugnissen.[4] Was Wunder also, wenn die Deutschen die Ohren spitzten, als nun plötzlich in eben diesem Lande eine zwar scharfe, aber informierte Stimme sich erhob und souverän mit den eigentlichsten und unantastbarsten Geschenken des deutschen Geisteslebens an die abendländische Gesamtheit zu schalten begann.

Längst waren aber die Akzente dieser Sprache den Eingeweihten— und um die geht es ja immer bei Ortega—geläufig.[5] Nicht ein Germanist etwa ergriff hier das Wort, sondern einer, dessen Recht auf den Titel eines Philosophen allgemein anerkannt war. Scherzhaft in der Form, aber durchaus ernst in seinen Absichten erklärt sich Ortega einmal über seine eigentümliche Art, Essays zu schreiben. Es werde dem Leser zuweilen sein, sagt er, als befaßten sich seine Schriften verhältnismäßig

---

[2] Bern, 1946. *S.* 394–96.

[3] "Crítica de *Lope de Vega en Alemania*" (Barcelona, 1936), Besprechung von Arturo Farinellis Buch, zuerst erschienen in *La España Moderna. Revista de España,* LXXII (Dic. de 1894).

[4] García Morente, "Goethe und die hispanische Welt," *Jb. d. Goethe-Gesellschaft,* 18. Bd., S. 81: "Deswegen breitete sich der Einfluß Goethes in Spanien nicht so stark und so weit aus wie in anderen Ländern." Vgl. dagegen Udo Rukser, *Goethe in der hispanischen Welt* (Stuttgart, 1958).

[5] Ortega wurde in Deutschland durch jene Schriften bekannt, in denen er zuerst die Probleme Spaniens und dann diejenigen ganz Europas erörterte: *España Invertebrada,* 1921; *El tema de nuestro tiempo,* 1923; *La rebelión de las masas,* 1930. Auf deutsch jetzt in José Ortega y Gasset, *Gesammelte Werke in vier Bänden* (Stuttgart: Deutsche Verlags-Anstalt, 1954-1956): Aufbau und Zerfall Spaniens, II, 7–78; Die Aufgabe unserer Zeit, I, 79–141; Der Aufstand der Massen, III, 7–155.

wenig mit ihrem vorgegebenen Thema. "Eigentlich handelt es sich um kritische Studien," fährt er fort, "aber es will mir scheinen, als sei es gar nicht die wichtigste Aufgabe der Kritik, die literarischen Werke nach ihrer Güte oder Mangelhaftigkeit abzuwägen und einzureihen. Mit jedem Tag liegt mir weniger daran, die Dinge abzuurteilen, ihren Richter zu spielen, sondern ich ziehe es vor, ihr Liebhaber zu sein. Ich erblicke in der Kritik die leidenschaftliche Bestrebung, das auserkorene Werk zu potenzieren." (I, 325.) Dies, auf Ortegas Goethe-Aufsätze angewandt, bedeutete, daß sich der deutsche Leser vor die Aufgabe gestellt sah, zugleich zu einem neuartigen Goethebild und einer ganzen, anspruchsvollen Philosophie, Ortegas Rationalvitalismus Stellung zu nehmen.

Die letzte und tiefste Ursache, warum diese ketzerischen Ansichten mit Respekt aufgenommen wurden, war Ortegas Europäismus und die außergewöhnliche Rolle, die er dem Deutschtum darin einräumte. "Europa. Alle Schmerzen Spaniens beginnen und enden für mich mit diesem Wort" (I, 128), bekannte der junge Ortega zu einer Zeit, da Aufnahme und Verbreitung deutscher Kultur ein wesentlicher Punkt seines Programms zur Wiederbelebung Spaniens ist und er z.B. das Studium der deutschen Sprache an allen Zweigen des höheren Unterrichts in seinem Vaterlande fordert (I, 210). Aus der gleichen Epoche seines Lebens stammt auch die schlagendste Formulierung eines ähnlichen Gedankens: "Die romanischen Völker können gar nichts Besseres und Ernsteres tun, als das Deutschtum sich wieder einzuverleiben . . . Schließlich werden wir auch in der deutschen Kultur finden, was es in der romanischen etwa an Unsterblichem geben mag" (I, 209). In dieser Gesinnung spricht sich eine jener fruchtbaren Synthesen aus, welche die einzelnen Nationen auf ihrem Wege zur Europäisierung eingegangen sind.[6] José Ortega y Gasset zumal, mit seinem spanischen Erbe, seiner deutschen Bildung und seiner europäischen Orientierung, ist ein Sinnbild der Annäherung, Verschmelzung und Steigerung der deutschen und

---

[6] Wie passend der Begriff Synthese hier ist, wird erst recht deutlich, wenn man dagegen hält, was ein Ernst Robert Curtius über das moderne Spanien zu sagen hat, und zwar bezeichnenderweise in einem Aufsatz, der, wenn er auch vorgibt, sich mit dem gesamten spanischen Panorama unserer Zeit zu befassen, doch größtenteils der Erscheinung Ortegas gewidmet ist. "Wir brauchen die Berührung mit romanischem Wesen," heißt es da unter Betonung einer von vielen Deutschen mehr oder minder erkannten Notwendigkeit. Spaniens spezifische Aufgabe sei es in diesem Zusammenhang, uns die lateinische Form von einer ganz anderen Seite zu zeigen, unseren Begriff vom Romanentum gegenüber der französischen und italienischen Art zu erweitern und zu ergänzen. "Spanische Perspektiven," *Die neue Rundschau*, 1924, S. 1229.

spanischen Kulturwelten.[7] In diesem Lichte besehen, mußte es eben besonderes Interesse erwecken, wenn Ortega in einer Reihe von Aufsätzen und Ansprachen es übernahm, die Frage nach Goethes Bedeutung für unser Jahrhundert zu untersuchen[8]—Goethe, in dessen Gestalt sich für viele sowohl das Deutsche wie auch das Europäische einmalig und großartig verkörpert.

Und dennoch ist die deutsche Goethe-Forschung, wie es mir scheinen will, den in diesen Essays an sie gestellten Anforderungen nicht gerecht geworden. Ortega, der wie Goethe die Frage der Wirkung sehr wichtig nahm, hat einmal einem jungen argentinischen Schriftsteller gegenüber sehr prägnant ausgedrückt, was er sich für seine Schriften wünscht: "keine großartigen Lobesworte für den Verfasser, dafür aber etwas weit Schmackhafteres, Schmeichelhafteres: Verständnis" (III, 255). Und gerade an diesem so nachdrücklich geforderten Verständnis ist in Deutschland, was seine Goethe-Kritik betrifft, ein Mangel gewesen, der um so auffallender sein muß, als seine Goethe-Arbeiten ja keineswegs unbemerkt geblieben sind. Erstaunen, Ablehnung, gelegentlich wohl auch Zustimmung, das alles gab es, bloß kein Eingehen, kein Ernstnehmen, keine Diskussion. Das drückt sich zunächst in dem zahlenmäßigen Mißverhältnis zwischen den vielen Erwähnungen und den wenigen Erörterungen aus; viel bedeutsamer sodann aber darin, wie in diesen überaus seltenen Fällen die Aufgabe gelöst wird. Wir wählen als Beispiel Fritz Strichs Buch *Goethe und die Weltliteratur*, wie schon anfangs gesagt wurde, weil es wegen seines zeitlichen Abstandes von Ortegas ersten Goethe-Kritiken und des Ranges seines Autors Hoffnungen auf eine endgültige Erledigung des Themas "Ortega und Goethe" erweckt. Was jedoch Ortega dort widerfährt, ist, nach kürzester Angabe seines Standpunktes, eine moralisierende, vom Vorwurf nicht freie Zurechtweisung, aber keine sachliche Entgegnung. Ein einziger Mißton sei in der allgemeinen Lobeshymne erklungen—so eröffnet Strich seine Untersuchung von Ortegas Beitrag zum Goethe-Jahr 1932 und verurteilt ihn bereits durch diese Wortwahl. Und mit ähnlichen Scheingründen, an denen nur eins überzeugend wirkt, nämlich Strichs Abneigung, endet er

---

[7] Ortega y Gasset studierte 1906-1910 (mit Unterbrechungen) an deutschen Universitäten.

[8] "Goethe, el libertador." Ursprünglich als Vortrag an der Universität Madrid, dann *Neue Züricher Zeitung* (März 1932); "Pidiendo un Goethe desde dentro," *Revista de Occidente* und *Die neue Rundschau* (April 1932); "Concerning a Bicentennial Goethe," in *Goethe and the Modern Age*, hrsg. von Arnold Bergstraesser (Chicago, 1950), S. 349-362. Hinweise auf diesen Aufsatz erscheinen von nun an im Text selbst unter der Abkürzung *CBG*, gefolgt von der Seitenzahl.

auch wieder: in Zeiten der Krise müsse man sich mit erneuerter Energie
an die Tradition klammern; sich der Klassiker unter solchen Umständen
entledigen, hieße "mitten im Sturm den Kompaß über Bord" werfen;
"nicht daß er nach Weimar ging, war schuld daran, wenn sich die
Goethesendung nicht erfüllte, sondern daß die Welt nicht diesem Weg
nach Weimar folgte."[9] Mit solchen Wendungen mag man sich aus einer
Affäre ziehen, aber es ist und bleibt ein Rückzug. Denn gerade der
Kenner ist sich im klaren, daß diese als völlig unbezweifelbare Wahr-
heiten hingestellten Behauptungen seinerzeit schon Ortegas Grund-
problematik ausmachten. Es zeigt sich also, daß ein derartiger Versuch
der Annäherung an die eigentümliche ortegianische Position eine kreis-
förmige Bewegung ist, die schließlich an den Ausgangspunkt zurückführt.

Was aber ist dieser Ausgangspunkt, was diese Position? Es wird
vielleicht nützlich sein, in diesem Zusammenhang, und da Ortegas
Stimme nun für immer Schweigen bewahren wird, noch einmal seine
Fragestellung ins Gedächtnis zu rufen: Das menschliche Leben ist ein
Kampf mit mehr oder minder feindlichen Gegebenheiten; nämlich mit
der durch Zeit und Ort bestimmten Umwelt, aber auch mit Innerlichem
wie Charakter, Seele, Bewußtsein. Gegen diese Mächte gilt es, das
Projekt, die Idee des eigenen Daseins durchzusetzen. Was seine Bestimmung ist, mag dem Einzelnen vielleicht nicht deutlich vor Augen stehen,
und er wird sie auch nie völlig erreichen; aber eine innere Stimme wird
ihm zurufen, ob er auf dem rechten Wege ist. Jeder Schritt in der
vorgeschriebenen Richtung wird mit dem Hochgefühl des Glückes
belohnt, jedes feige Zurückweichen rächt sich durch Mißmut, Unlust,
Verdrossenheit. Dieser Kampf wird in jedem Augenblick des Lebens
ausgefochten, also in der Gegenwart, er wird aber von der Zukunft her
bestimmt, für die Zukunft geführt; die Vergangenheit mit ihrem Schatz
an Erfahrungen ist das Arsenal, aus dem sich der Kämpfende jeweils mit
strategischer Theorie und Waffen versieht. ("Die Zukunft ist der
Gesichtskreis der Probleme, die Vergangenheit das feste Land der
Methoden." IV, 396.)

Diese Auffassung des Lebens trifft auf den Einzelnen so gut zu wie
auf eine ganze Gesellschaft. Ob aber das eine oder das andere, in Zeiten
der Krise zieht sich der Träger des Lebens auf das einzig Unfragliche
zurück, auf seine nackte Existenz. ("In der Stunde der Gefahr trachtet
das Leben, sich zu entblößen, sich auf den reinen Muskel, den reinen

---

[9] Strich, S. 395 f.

Nerv zurückzuziehen." IV, 397.) In einem solchen Zustande der Gefährdung, wenn die Zukunft mit Vernichtung droht, wird auch die Vergangenheit, das Erlebte, Ererbte, Erworbene, problematisch, oft sinnlos und unbrauchbar. Ortega hat diese Lebensdeutung durch das Gleichnis vom Schwimmer anschaulich zu machen gesucht: vom feindlichen Element umgeben, muß er sich durch ständige, zweckmäßige Bewegung, nicht etwa durch planloses Umsichschlagen, was einer zwar emsigen, aber fruchtlosen Geschäftigkeit gleichkäme, über Wasser halten. Gerät er in bewegte Strömung oder treibt er gar einem Strudel, einer Stromschnelle zu, so kann ihn nur die äußerste Anspannung aller intellektuellen und körperlichen Kräfte retten. Erfahrungen aus früherer Zeit können ihm nur dann nützlich sein, wenn sie über ähnlich bedrohliche Situationen Aufschluß geben. ("Ich schenke nur den Gedanken von Schiffbrüchigen Glauben." IV, 398.)

An diesem Punkte setzt Ortegas Goethe-Betrachtung ein. Wir durchleben—so sagt er—eine schwere Krise unserer Kultur. Unsere ganze Vergangenheit ist fragwürdig geworden. Wollen wir überstehen, so müssen wir aus dem Schatz unserer Überlieferung das ewig Wahre, das in allen Gefahren Gültige auswählen, alles andere preisgeben. Vor einem Tribunal von Schiffbrüchigen, gleichsam, muß sich unsere Tradition auf ihre Brauchbarkeit hin verantworten. Wie würde Goethe vor einem solchen Gerichtshof bestehen?[10]

Goethes Leben entspricht nicht der Forderung nach einem kraftvollen Durchsetzen seiner wahren Bestimmung. Sein Leben verzettelt sich auf der Suche oder deutlicher: auf der Flucht vor sich selbst. ("Goethe ist der ewige Deserteur seines innersten Schicksals." IV, 410.) Ist Goethe nicht sein Leben lang vor jeder Entscheidung geflohen, bis er endlich vor dem, was das wirkliche Leben ausmacht, nämlich vor unwiderruflicher Festlegung, vor dem Einsatz der Person, eine Mischung von Furcht und Abscheu entwickelte? In seiner Jugend flüchtet er vor seinen Liebschaften, später vor seinem Dichterberuf nach Weimar, von dort nach Italien, und schließlich vor der Wirklichkeit auf den Olymp, nach dem Orient, in den Symbolismus. Ist es nicht höchst merkwürdig, daß ein Mann, dessen Hauptwerke vor seinem dreißigsten Lebensjahr zumindest begonnen wurden, sich noch an der Grenze der Vierzig fragen muß, ob er ein Dichter, Maler oder Wissenschaftler sei?

---

[10] Vgl. Bernhard Blume, "Sein und Scheitern: zur Geschichte einer Metapher," *Germanisch-Romanische Monatsschrift* (Juli 1959), S. 281 f.

Wie ist es erklärlich, daß jemand, dem nach Aussage der Biographen alles im Leben so trefflich gelang, nachweisbar die meisten seiner Erdentage in übler Stimmung verbracht hat? ("Die anhaltende schlechte Laune ist ein überaus deutliches Symptom dafür, daß ein Mensch gegen seine Bestimmung lebt." IV, 409.) Hierher gehört auch sein steifer Gang, seine allzu aufrechte Haltung, ein physiognomisches Zeichen für die innere Unzufriedenheit mit sich selbst.

Goethe bietet also den Anblick eines Mannes von wundervollen Gaben, Begeisterungsfähigkeit, ausgezeichnetem Charakter, jedoch ständig untreu seinem Schicksal. Daher die ewige Mißstimmung, die Steifheit, der Abstand von der eigenen Umgebung, die Bitterkeit seiner Haltung. Im besonderen aber war es Weimar, dieser Liliputhof mit seinem lächerlichen Scheinleben, was Goethe sich selbst entfremdete, wohin er sich begeben hatte, um einige Semester "Iphigenismus" zu studieren, wo er aber zu seinem Unglück dauernd verblieb. Beinahe Tag für Tag können wir die versteinernde Wirkung Weimars auf Goethe verfolgen, sehen, wie der Mensch sich in eine Statue verwandelt. ("Weimar ist das größte Mißverständnis der deutschen Literaturgeschichte." IV, 410.)

Was Goethes eigentliche Lebensaufgabe gewesen wäre, ist klar genug. Er war berufen, die deutsche Literatur dank seinen seltenen Gaben von Sturm (Phantasie und Gefühl) und Maß (Harmonie, gesundem Menschenverstand), die sonst in der Welt nur getrennt auftreten, die er aber in sich vereinigte, von Grund auf neu zu gestalten, zur ersten der Welt zu machen. Dazu hätte er aber ein Leben ohne Weimar führen müssen, ein Wanderleben, ausgesetzt dem Aufruhr der Kräfte im damaligen Deutschland, preisgegeben jeder Unbill, wirtschaftlich und gesellschaftlich ungesichert—mit einem Wort, ein Leben in jedem Punkt das genaue Gegenteil von seinem wirklich gelebten.

Und dennoch gibt es in Goethe eine Seite, die für diese Verfehlungen entschädigt, einen Goethe, in dem das neue Bewußtsein einer anderen, wahreren Auffassung des menschlichen Lebens dämmert. Diese Seite aufzusuchen, klarzustellen, ist die Pflicht der modernen Goetheforschung. Jener Goethe des Wahlspruchs *Hic Rhodus, hic salta*, hier ist das Leben, hier muß getanzt werden, der zum Leben entschlossene Goethe, ist der Dichter, der uns heute noch etwas zu sagen hat. Jetzt muß gezeigt werden, wie der Goethe, der seinem Ich untreu war, dennoch der Mann gewesen ist, jeden einzelnen von uns die Treue zu dem unsrigen zu lehren. Denn es gibt nur einen Weg, den Klassiker zu retten, nämlich indem man ihn rücksichtslos zu unserer eigenen Rettung ausbeutet. Das erreicht man aber, indem man absieht von seiner Klassik, ihn uns nahe bringt, ihn modernisiert, ihm neue Kraft aus unseren eigenen Adern einflößt, deren Inhalt aus *unseren* Leidenschaften und *unseren* Problemen besteht.

In ähnlich vereinfachenden Umrissen soll nun an diesem Goethebild Kritik geübt werden, wobei das betreffende Material der Übersichtlichkeit halber unter vier verschiedene wenn auch unter sich verwandte Gesichtspunkte angeordnet worden ist. Dabei schien es ratsam, sich diskussionslos in *medias res* zu begeben, d. h. Ortegas Standpunkt einzunehmen und von daher die etwa nötigen Korrekturen einzuzeichnen.

1. *Typus der Kritik.* Zunächst taucht die Frage auf, was denn eigentlich Ortega unter dem Wort "Goethe" vorschwebt, das ja in den westlichen Sprachen kein bloßer Eigenname ist, sondern einen Kulturkomplex bedeutet. Die Antwort ergibt, daß seine Kritik weder das Leben noch das Werk Goethes unmittelbar trifft. Man liest bei ihm zwar zuweilen herausfordernde Bemerkungen über Goethes schöpferische Gebilde: z. B., daß er in die Figur des Faust ein Äußerstes an Paradoxie gelegt habe. Faust sei nämlich der Mann, der das schlechthin Unwiederholbare, sein Leben, zu wiederholen suche (*CBG*, 349); im Falle von *Hermann und Dorothea* habe "der orthopädische Apparat des Hexameters" sein fremdes Gerüst zwischen ursprüngliche Eingebung und ausgeführtes Werk geschoben (IV, 416); die Lösung im *Wilhelm Meister*, nämlich daß der Held Wundarzt wird, sei willkürlich, frivol, des Autors unwürdig (IV, 408). Worauf aber Ortega immer wieder hinauswill, begreift man vielleicht am besten an einer zusammenfassenden Formulierung: "In einem gewaltigen Teil von Goethes Werk—in seinem Werther, seinem Faust, seinem Meister—werden uns Geschöpfe vorgeführt, die durch die Welt irren auf der Suche nach ihrer wahren Bestimmung—oder auf der Flucht vor ihr" (IV, 407). Es wird also nur allzubald klar, daß der Sinn solcher Aussprüche nicht die ästhetische Würdigung der Werke ist, sondern etwas ganz anderes. Wieder ist es Ortega selbst, der uns den Schlüssel zu seinem Verständnis an die Hand gibt. Man fühlt sich nämlich an sein Wort erinnert, in dem er kurz mit der Kunst im allgemeinen abrechnet. "Die Kunst," heißt es da, "jede Kunst, ist eine sehr ehrwürdige Angelegenheit, und doch ist sie oberflächlich und leichtsinnig, wenn man sie mit dem schrecklichen Ernst des Lebens vergleicht" (IV, 403). Darauf zielt also Ortega auch hier wieder ab: den Ernst des Lebens—allerdings nicht Goethes, sondern

unseres eigenen modernen Lebens. "Die Absicht dieser Schrift ist weder eine biographische, noch geht sie auf Deutung und Würdigung der Goetheschen Dichtung. Sondern ich frage: Was ist der geistige Sinn der Goetheschen Existenz überhaupt?" Diese Worte stammen freilich nicht von Ortega, sondern sie stehen in dem Vorwort zu Georg Simmels *Goethe*,[11] den Ortega denn auch als das einzig lesbare Buch über diesen Gegenstand bezeichnet hat (IV, 398). Kein Wunder, denn die Verwandtschaft ist offenkundig. Diese Worte sind mit gleichem Recht der vollkommen entsprechende Ausdruck von Ortegas eigenem kritischen Standpunkt in seinen Schriften über Goethe. "Was ist der geistige Sinn?" fragt Simmel; "das . . . Werk zu potenzieren," ist Ortegas Vorhaben. Im Grunde haben es beide auf dasselbe abgesehen: die Erfassung ihres Zeitbewußtseins als Spiegelung in einer großen, das Menschliche umspannenden Gestalt. Ortega ist es vor allem um das europäische Lebensgefühl von 1932 zu tun, und erst in zweiter Linie kommt Goethe als Einzelphänomen in Betracht. Darum auch die sonderbare Verquikkung von zwei anscheinend so disparaten Themen: einer umstrittenen Tagesphilosophie mit der Zergliederung einer Dichterexistenz aus der deutschen Klassik. Er sagt es ja selbst: "Dies 1932 nimmt uns viel zu stark in Anspruch, als daß wir in der Lage wären, jenes 1832 heute irgendwo unterzubringen" (IV, 395).

2. *Die fraglichen Punkte.* Selbst bei der größten Bereitwilligkeit, sich auf den Standpunkt Ortegas zu stellen und die Dinge mit seinen Augen anzusehen, bleiben logische und psychologische Bedenken zurück, die den Ausblick teilweise verdunkeln. Jedermann wird wohl die Lehre von der Nützlichkeit willig aufnehmen. Gerne läßt man sich davon überzeugen, daß die Überlieferung statt Bürde Werkzeug und Reichtum unseres Lebens sein soll. Aber auf dem Wege zur praktischen Anwendung zeigt es sich, daß die Idee von der Vitalisierung des Vergangenen auf methodische Schwierigkeiten stößt. Wie macht man sich die Vergangenheit zunutze? Lernt man besser aus den Fehlern oder nach dem Vorbild vergangener Generationen, mehr durch Nachahmung oder Widerstand? Ortega fordert uns zu einer erneuerten, gesteigerten Beschäftigung mit Goethe, der Klassik, der ganzen Kultur auf. Mit diesem Programm kann man übereinstimmen. Daß sich jede Generation das ihr eigentümliche Verhältnis zu ihrem Erbe erst erkämpfen muß, ist heute Gemeinwissen. Wie man aber im Ernste und mit Vorbedacht an eine solche Aufgabe herantritt, hat uns auch Ortega nicht gezeigt. Aus

---

[11] Leipzig, 1913.

Goethes Werk und Lebensgeschichte jene Partien hervorzuheben, die mit den Grunderfahrungen der modernen Menschheit in Einklang zu stehen scheinen, kann höchstens ein allererster Anfang sein. So wie die Dinge stehen, wird man Emil Staigers Einwand schwer von sich weisen können, wenn er sagt: "Gerade dann aber, ja nur dann, wenn uns die Frage: Was hat uns Goethe heute zu sagen? angesichts seiner Wirklichkeit auf den Lippen erstirbt oder sich in die angemessenere verwandelt: Wie bestehen wir heute vor ihm?—dann ist es geglückt, ihn neu zu gewinnen und so der Zeit den Dienst zu leisten, den niemand leistet, der sich von ihr die Gesetze des Denkens vorschreiben lässt."[12]

Eine weitere Fragwürdigkeit—und zwar zentraler Art—liegt in Ortegas Theorie der Bestimmung oder des inneren Berufes. Wenn schon der Einzelne seinen Lebenszweck womöglich nie erkennt, was der Philosoph selbst zugibt (IV, 401), um wieviel schwerer muß es einem andern, einem Nachlebenden fallen, ihn hinterher noch festzustellen. Und dennoch ruft Ortega pathetisch aus, vielleicht in dem unbewußten Bedürfnis, die Unsicherheit durch den Brustton der Überzeugung zu verdrängen: "Die Bestimmung Goethes! . . . Wenn etwas in der Welt klar ist, so ist es dies" (IV, 411). Es sei "offensichtlich," daß es Goethes Mission auf Erden gewesen wäre, die Dichtung seines Vaterlandes und durch sie auch diejenige der ganzen Welt völlig umzustürzen und neu zu gestalten ("revolucionar"). Da dies aber nach Ortega aus den nun schon bekannten Gründen nicht geschehen ist, scheint es dem unvoreingenommenen Leser gar nicht mehr so durchaus offenkundig zu sein, daß dies unbedingt Goethes Aufgabe gewesen sein soll. Mit diesem Zweifel stellt man sich zwar außerhalb der erlesenen Reihe jener Eingeweihten, an die sich Ortega etwas anmaßend, wie es scheint, wendet. "Die volle Klarheit über das, was hier dem Kenner ("buen entendedor") angedeutet wird," heißt es bei ihm, "kann nur die Erörterung der Bestimmungstheorie erbringen" (IV, 411 Anm.). Diese aber, mit besonderer Anwendung auf den Fall Goethe, ist uns Ortega, meines Erachtens, schuldig geblieben.

Wir erfahren, daß es in Goethes Macht gelegen hätte, der Weltliteratur eine Bewegung aus *Sturm* und *Mass* zu verleihen, kraft seiner Begabung mit diesen beiden Eigenschaften, deren erste sonst ausschließlich in Deutschland, die andere nur in den romanischen Ländern anzutreffen sei. Was an derartigen Behauptungen so unbefriedigend wirkt, ist nicht, daß sie wohl immer unbewiesen bleiben werden—denn das sind schließlich viele überzeugende Einsichten—sondern, was weit

---

[12] *Goethe* (Zürich, 1952), S. 11–12.

schlimmer ist, daß ihnen eben auch die rechte Überzeugungskraft fehlt. Und dieser Mangel wieder liegt daran, daß die Goethe angeblich aufgetragene Sendung zu allgemein ausgedrückt ist. Sonst wäre es wohl nicht möglich, daß Ortega dem deutschen Dichter vorwerfen kann, er sei dem Ruf seines Schicksals nicht gefolgt, während Fritz Strich behauptet, er habe es ganz und gar erfüllt. "War denn nicht gerade Goethe der morgendliche Rufer, der die Welt aufrüttelte . . .? War das nicht Sturm? Aber er wußte um die Gefahr des Sturmes und um den Segen des Maßes, und so hat er den Sturm in sich gebändigt und das Maß gewonnen."[13] Es ist angesichts dieser gegensätzlichen Behauptungen schwer denkbar, daß die beiden Kritiker von derselben Sache sprechen, ob sie schon die gleichen Ausdrücke gebrauchen.

Nicht minder anfechtbar ist der logische Schluß, auf den Ortega in seinen Folgerungen kein geringes Gewicht legt: Anhaltende Verdrossenheit ist Zeichen eines verfehlten Lebens—Goethe war stets schlechter Laune—also war Goethes Leben verfehlt.[14] Daß der alternde Dichter oft mißgestimmt war, daß er selber von seinen freudlosen Tagen gesprochen hat, ist natürlich bemerkt und ausgelegt worden. Für den einen Forscher sind die Verstimmungen des älter werdenden Goethe Symptome nicht für seine Untreue gegen sich selbst, sondern für den Mangel an Widerhall, die fehlende Wirkung nach außen, das Bewußtsein, den Deutschen kein Wegweiser zu sein;[15] ein anderer sieht in dem mißgelaunten und zurückgezogenen Greisentum Goethes etwas viel Allgemeineres und Grundlegenderes, nämlich die tragische Tendenz des Genies zur Selbstzerstörung:[16] ein dritter packt das Problem von einer ganz anderen Seite an: er wendet sich gegen diejenigen, die Goethe immer jung haben wollen, und geht dann ganz realistisch daran, die Vorteile und Einbußen, die sich für Goethe an den Namen Weimar knüpfen, gegeneinander abzuwägen.[17] Dies, um nur einige wenige, nicht minder einleuchtende Erklärungen neben Ortegas Hypothese anzuführen. Woher will Ortega wissen, daß all diese Symptome die Flucht

---

[13] Strich, S. 395 f.

[14] Vgl. Gerhart Mayer, "Ortega y Gassets Verhältnis zur deutschen Dichtung," *Die Sammlung* (Oktober 1960), S. 667, Udo Rukser, a.a.O. (Anm. 4), S. 193, und Robert Pageard, *Goethe en España* (Madrid 1958), S. 72 ff.

[15] Bernhard Blume, *Thomas Mann und Goethe* (Bern, 1949), S. 14.

[16] Hermann Hesse, "Goethe und Bettina," *Die neue Rundschau*, 1924, S. 1061–67. Es ist sonderbar zu beobachten, wie ein Goethe so nahestehender Dichter sich von der Kälte, die der alte Geheimrat ausstrahlt, abgestoßen fühlt. Er fragt sich, ob "diese schrecklichen Greise" überhaupt noch Menschen sind, und ihre unheimliche Existenz bestätigt ihm nur "die Tendenz des Genies zur Selbstaufhebung . . . als Folge der Selbsterkenntnis." S. 1066 und 1067.

[17] Barker Fairley, *A Study of Goethe* (Oxford, 1947). Vgl. besonders Kapitel XIV: "Profit and Loss," S. 149–67.

vor der inneren Berufung anzeigen? Er wird doch nicht glauben machen wollen, daß es keine anderen Quellen für den Verdruß gibt, keine anderen Ursachen für die Vereinsamung?! Überhaupt müßte die Rolle und Funktion jener "inneren Stimme" noch genauer erklärt werden, die einen Menschen darüber belehrt, ob er auf dem Wege der Erfüllung oder der Verfehlung seines Lebenszweckes wandelt, ja darüber hinaus seine Aufführung mit Glück- und Unglücksgefühlen belohnt bzw. bestraft. So wie sie jetzt erscheint, sieht diese Stimme dem von Ortega verabschiedeten christlichen Gewissen verdächtig ähnlich. Es ist, als habe sich dasselbe, mit einem immoralistischen Mäntelchen bekleidet, durch eine unbewachte Hintertür wieder auf die Bühne des Lebens geschlichen. Mit dem christlichen Gewissen wird diese Stimme dann aber auch die Eigenschaft teilen, daß sie nur demjenigen vernehmbar ist, dem sie angehört, und sonst niemandem.

Ortega hat zu wenige und zu unscharfe Züge aus Goethes Leben herausgegriffen, als daß man ein überzeugendes Gesamtbild daraus formen könnte. Goethes steifer Gang (will Ortega allen Ernstes die physiognomische Zauberei erneuern?),[18] seine Haltung in Liebesdingen, sein Ausharren in Weimar, seine "Versteinerung" im Alter sind Erscheinungen, die schon so manchen Interpreten angelockt haben. Ortegas Deutung ist nur eine unter vielen und nicht einmal die zwingendste. Im großen und ganzen wird es wohl dankbarer sein, zu erforschen, was ein Dichter geleistet und allenfalls, was er dabei verfehlt hat. Mit der Frage, was er hätte erreichen können oder gar sollen, begibt man sich auf höchst unsicheren Boden.

3. *Das Gültige in Goethe.* Goethe ist für Ortega jener Mensch unserer abendländischen Kultur, "in dem zum ersten Mal das Bewußtsein aufdämmert, daß das menschliche Leben der Kampf des Einzelnen mit seinem innersten, ureigensten Schicksal ist, d. h. daß dasjenige, was die menschliche Existenz im Grunde ausmacht, das Problem ihrer selbst ist" (IV, 403).[19] Daraus geht hervor, daß Ortega Goethe einen Ehrenplatz in der Entstehungsgeschichte des modernen Lebensgefühls anweist, aber auch, daß er ihn nur dort gutheißt, wo er sich dieser Weltanschauung nähert; dies war zu erwarten, da sich der Dichter ja auch nur

---

[18] "Es wird wohl nicht unerlaubt sein, Sie zu einem 'physiognomischen Fragment' über Goethe anzuregen" (IV, 409).

[19] Dieser Gedanke taucht bei Ortega y Gasset immer wieder auf. Z. B.: "Die Entdeckung der dem Leben innewohnenden Werte war bei Goethe und Nietzsche, trotz des zoologischen Vokabulars, eine geniale Einsicht, die ein zukünftiges Ereignis von größter Bedeutung vorwegnahm" (III, 192). "Ich glaube nicht, daß jemand vor Goethe in Europa so viel über das Thema des menschlichen Lebens nachgedacht hat wie er" (*CBG*, 353). Vgl. auch III, 189.

mit jenen Partien seines Schaffens die Ungnade Ortegas zugezogen hatte, die dieser Weltanschauung entgegenstanden. Es ist also durchaus Positives vorhanden, nur ist es schwer zugänglich, denn "Goethes Auffassung des menschlichen Lebens, wie denn auch sein ganzes Werk, leidet unter einer Zweiseitigkeit, wozu noch kommt, daß die beiden Seiten in Widerspruch zueinander stehen" (*CBG*, 353). Die zwei widerstreitenden Seiten voneinander zu trennen, wäre nun unsere Aufgabe. Ortega löst sie nicht, aber er macht einen Anfang. Das, was er Goethes "Botanismus" nennt, die Naturphilosophie, der gemäß das Leben unter dem Bilde einer harmonisch sich entwickelnden Pflanze erscheint, ist ein Erbteil der klassisch-humanistischen Bildung Europas und nicht nur der am wenigsten originelle, sondern auch der unbedeutendste, unfruchtbarste Teil von Goethes Gedankengut. Das Leben ist eben keine organische Entwicklung, sondern Kampf. "Goethe—oder sein besseres Selbst, jenes Selbst, mit dem er über die Ideen seiner Zeit hinausragte— wußte das alles sehr wohl" (*CBG*, 353), und der Niederschlag dieses geheimen, besseren Wissens findet sich allenthalben in seinen Schriften. Indem er zu den vier Lebenskomponenten des Macrobius: Daimon, Ananke, Eros und Tyche noch Elpis, die Hoffnung, jenes unbotanischste aller Lebenselemente, hinzufügt, verrät er sein intimes, freilich von allen möglichen Vorstellungen seines Jahrhunderts verdunkeltes Verständnis für die eigentliche Beschaffenheit unserer Existenz. Ortega selbst unterzieht sich nicht der Arbeit, dieses Ideengeflecht aus Goethes Werk herauszulösen, aber er stellt die Forderung an die Goetheforschung. In Goethes "Idearium" oder Gedankenrepertoire gäbe es drei große Bezirke: seine Erkenntnis der Persönlichkeit, seine Haltung gegenüber der Kultur, und die Art, wie er sich zu den Demütigungen verhielt, die uns das Leben zufügt. Dies alles gelte es, zu sichten und zu ordnen. "Die Betrachtung dieser Ideen ist, was ich Beschäftigung mit einem Autor nenne—sei er Dichter oder Denker, und Goethe war beides zugleich" (*CBG*, 353). Mögen immerhin oberflächliche Schriftsteller behaupten, daß man auf solche Art gar nicht mehr über Goethe spreche: Ortega jedenfalls sehe nicht, "wie man heutzutage Nutzen aus seinen Werken ziehen kann, ohne sich auf andere als die gewohnte Weise das Problem seiner Existenz zu stellen" (IV, 399).

Auch Ortega ist also, wie viele vor ihm—Gegner sowie Bewunderer —in den Bann von Goethes Universalität geraten. Auch ihn hat eine der zahllosen Schichten von Goethes Vielseitigkeit ergriffen und seinen Tribut gefordert. Diese ihm wertvoll erscheinende Schicht hat Ortega durch zahlreiche Zitate einzufangen gesucht. Ein oft wiederkehrendes und daher aufschlußreiches ist das alte Faustwort "Nur der verdient sich Freiheit wie das Leben,/ Der täglich sie erobern muß—" und die so verwandten Verse "Was du ererbt von deinen Vätern hast,/ Erwirb es, um es zu besitzen—,"[20] nur dass sie hier mit einer neuen Überzeugung ausgesprochen und daher mit neuer Bedeutung befrachtet sind.

Erst so wird es voll verständlich, wie Ortega einen ganzen Aufsatz dem scheinbaren Widerspruch widmen konnte, daß Goethe in seinem Kampf, sich selbst zu einer neuen Sicht des Daseins zu befreien, unterlag und doch, oder vielmehr gerade dadurch, unser aller Befreier geworden ist.[21]

4. *Inneres Verhältnis zu Goethe.* Ist Ortega ein Goethe-Gegner? Diese Frage mußte natürlich bei Ortegas zwiespältiger Stellung zu Goethe auftauchen. Aber auch hierauf ist die Antwort ausgeblieben. Daß Ortegas unpolemische, von reinem Wahrheits- und Wirksamkeitstrieb beseelte Auseinandersetzungen mit Goethe nicht zu jenen subalternen Ablehnungen gehören, von denen Karl Jaspers spricht, wird wohl jedermann bereitwillig einräumen. Was bleibt, ist, wieder nach Jaspers, "die Aufgabe, Goethes Grenzen zu sehen. Die Erfüllung dieser Aufgabe ist unerläßlich für die Aneignung Goethes in unserer Welt."[22] Gerade dies ist aber stets Ortegas Zweck und Verdienst gewesen. Er wollte die heutige Welt aufrütteln, sie zu einer angemesseneren Goethe-Betrachtung, zur allein möglichen Goethe-Aneignung aufrufen, und ihr dabei noch einmal—zum wievielten Male?—ihre historische Situation vor Augen halten. Es ist höchst unwahrscheinlich, daß man unter solchen Umständen von einer Feindschaft gegen Goethe sprechen kann.

Aber man ist nicht auf bloße Spekulation angewiesen. Ortegas Faszination durch Goethe läßt sich konkret belegen. Zu ganz verschiedenen Perioden seines Lebens trifft man ihn über intensiver Beschäftigung mit Goethe an. Schon 1914 spricht er von einem Goethe-Essay, den er dann freilich nicht geschrieben hat (I, 325). Im Jahre 1932 versichert uns sein Mitarbeiter García Morente, daß José Ortega y Gasset "an einem Buche über Goethes Leben" arbeite, "das uns durch seine ganz neuen Perspektiven sicher angenehm überraschen" werde.[23] Diese Biographie ist zwar auch ausgeblieben, die Überraschung aber—ob jedem auch angenehm, braucht nicht untersucht zu werden—traf richtig ein, als Ortega im gleichen Jahre seine beiden Aufsätze veröffentlichte:

---

[20] Nur einige Stellen, wo eines dieser Worte aus dem *Faust* von Ortega zitiert wird: I, 135; IV, 405; *CBG*, 358.
[21] "Goethe, el libertador," IV, 421–27.
[22] *Unsere Zukunft und Goethe* (Zürich, 1947), S. 16–18.
[23] García Morente, S. 92.

"Pidiendo un Goethe desde dentro—Um einen Goethe von innen bittend" und "Goethe, el libertador—Goethe, der Befreier." Und noch im Jahre 1949 trat er mit zwei Vorträgen hervor, "Concerning a Bicentennial Goethe" anläßlich einer amerikanischen und "Über einen zweihundertjährigen Goethe" anläßlich einer deutschen Zweijahrhundertfeier.[24]

Man hat darauf hingewiesen, daß im Hintergrunde von Börnes Anschuldigungen gegen Goethe eine große Bewunderung stand und daß gerade diese Anschuldigungen einen unbegrenzten Glauben an die Autorität des Dichters beweisen; und in Anbetracht seiner immerwährenden Beschäftigung mit dem deutschen Klassiker mag man sich versucht fühlen, auch für Ortega einen ähnlichen Modus zu postulieren. Damit würde man aber alles auf ein emotionelles Verhältnis reduzieren und dem ausgedehnten Bezirk von Ortegas völlig rationaler, oft durchaus positiver Stellungnahme zu Goethe keine Rechnung tragen. Ortegas Werke sind voll von Berufungen auf Goethe und Zitaten aus seinen Schriften. An der Art, wie Goethes Gestalt heraufbeschworen, ein Wort von ihm in fremder Umgebung wiedergegeben, ein Vers in den heterogensten Arbeiten immer wieder zitiert wird, merkt man, daß Ortega jeweils auf Goethe zurückgreift, weil er einem Teil seines Geistes tiefe Wahrheit, der Gestalt als ganzer aber unantastbare Autorität zuschreibt, und die Wirkung von beiden auf seine Leser voraussetzt. Goethe wird von ihm in den meisten Fällen als letzte Instanz zur Schlichtung von Streitfragen oder zur Klärung eines dunklen Sachverhalts angerufen. Aber auch die direkt von Goethe handelnden Essays sind, wie gezeigt wurde, durchsetzt mit Positivem. Und ein Blick auf die Art, wie das Negative vorgebracht wird, der intime subjektive Briefstil des Hauptessays, die fragende Haltung in allen vieren, ist aufschlußreich. "Wie Sie sehen, statt Ihnen etwas für Goethes Jahrhundertfeier einzuschicken, muß ich vielmehr Sie darum bitten" (IV, 398); "Glauben Sie nicht, daß es sich verlohnte, ein Leben Goethes von diesem einzigen wirklich *inneren* Gesichtspunkt zu konstruieren?" (IV, 402); "Die Operation, der man Goethe unterwerfen müßte, ist zu ernst und zu grundlegend, als daß sie ein Nicht-Deutscher vornehmen könnte" (IV, 398); "Diese Seiten sind Fragen, die ich an Sie richte, Probleme, um deren Erhellung ich Sie bitte" (IV, 407). Man halte diese zögernden Vorschläge, halben Anklagen, widerwilligen Zugeständnisse, dieses Frage- und Abwehrspiel nicht für bloße Rhetorik: die äußere Form ist auch hier wieder bezeichnend für die innere Haltung des Verfassers.

---

[24] IV, 395–427; *CBG*, 349–62. Vgl. auch Anm. 8 in "Über einen zweihundertjährigen Goethe," *Hamburger Akademische Rundschau*, 8–10, 1949.

Wenn man nun alle diese mannigfaltigen Einzelzüge zusammen-
hält, so ergibt sich das Profil eines Schriftstellers, der bei der erstaun-
lichen Vielseitigkeit, der Wendigkeit und dem Reichtum seiner Gedanken immer wieder zu Goethe zurückkehrt, wie zu einem Zentrum von
Kraft, um zu bejahen und zu verwerfen, vor allem aber um zu zehren. Es
scheint mir daher am richtigsten zu sagen, Ortega habe Zeit seines
Lebens wohl *um* Goethe gerungen, keineswegs aber *gegen* ihn.

Es bleibt noch übrig, einige offengebliebene Fragen zu beantworten
und scheinbare Widersprüche zu beseitigen, eine Aufgabe, die eigen-
tümlicherweise, sei sie lösbar oder unlösbar, hinter jeder Beschäftigung
mit Ortega steht. Wie können wir die "Zweiseitigkeit" erklären, die
nicht so sehr an Goethe liegt, wie Ortega meinte (siehe oben), sondern
an Ortega selbst, wie wir glauben? Wie dürfen wir ferner, da sich aus
unseren eigenen Erläuterungen die Subjektivität und Fragwürdigkeit
von Ortegas Goethebild ergibt, der deutschen Goetheforschung vorwerfen, sich nicht ernsthaft auf Ortega eingelassen zu haben? Dazu
kommt noch ein dritter verwirrender Faktor: Ortegas provokative
Goethekritik ist typisch, ja stellvertretend für die Fragestellung des
zwanzigsten Jahrhunderts geworden und kann, rein historisch gesehen,
als Wendepunkt in der Goethebetrachtung unserer Zeit gelten.

Wir beginnen am besten bei diesem letzten Problem. Es ist zwar
unleugbar, daß sich kaum jemand direkt und ausdrücklich mit Ortegas
erstem und interessantestem Aufsatz auseinandergesetzt hat. Trotzdem
ist Ortegas Stellung seit 1932 zum Ausgangspunkt fast jeder Gesamt-
beschäftigung mit Goethe geworden. Ob es sich um Gegner oder
Anhänger, oder überhaupt um Kenner der ortegianischen Gedanken-
gänge handelte, alle derartigen Schriften sehen wie Antworten auf
Ortega aus, sonderbarerweise ohne daß sein Name auftaucht. Man
braucht sich daraufhin nur etwa die Einleitung zu Staigers Goethebuch
(s. Anm. 12) und Jaspers' *Unsere Zukunft und Goethe* anzusehen (s.
Anm. 22), keineswegs als einzige, sondern nur als besonders charakteristische Beispiele. Dies führt aber zum zweiten Punkt: Die Frage nach
der Logik ist ja bei Problemen des Lebensgefühls nie ins Gewicht
gefallen und so ist es kein Widerspruch, daß eine so anfechtbare Sicht
Goethes wie die Ortegas zur Grundlage für weitere Bemühungen werden
konnte. Irgendwie spricht sich in ihr der Konsensus der Zeit aus, der
Wunsch nach glaubwürdigen Führerfiguren, aber auch die Furcht vor
Täuschung; und selbst wer andere Wege gehen wollte, sah sich unter
geheimem Zwang veranlaßt, seinen Vorstoß von dieser Position her zu

unternehmen. Dies ist es, wozu die Goetheforschung Stellung nehmen muß.

Was aber die Brüchigkeit des ortegianischen Goethebildes selbst betrifft, so ist sie nur bezeichnend für seine Haltung gegenüber der ganzen deutschen Kultur.[25] Die Phänomene des Deutschtums haben für Ortega eine Doppelbedeutung. Einerseits sind sie Wesenheiten der Erscheinungswelt und müssen als solche in Betracht gezogen und im Lichte der Erfahrung immer wieder neu ausgelegt werden. Aber sie haben noch eine andere Funktion: sie sind autonome Symbolwerte in Ortegas philosophischem System und dienen dem Versuch, die Krisenlage der modernen Kultur erklären zu helfen. Dies scheint mir eine der Hauptquellen für die Zweideutigkeit zu sein, die man als erregendes Schillern in dem Bild wahrnimmt, das Ortega von der deutschen Kultur entwirft.

---

[25] Vgl. meinen Aufsatz, "Ortega y Gasset and German Culture," *Monatshefte* (März 1957).

The Character and Function of Buttler
in Schiller's *Wallenstein*

by WALTER SILZ

Buttler, commander of Wallenstein's dragoons, is one of the most versatile and, in the same measure, most contradictory of Schiller's minor characters. He appears as a model soldier and a traitor to his chief, the embittered foe and savior of his emperor, a brutal villain and an exalted judge, a taciturn man of action and an eloquent orator; a messenger, a chorus, an executioner—in short, a most useful man in a play but an inconsistent poetical character, illustrating an antinomy in Schiller's dramatic art. This will become clear as we follow Buttler's course through the extensive plot.

He is first mentioned in the *Lager*[1] as a shining example of the heights an ordinary man can reach in Wallenstein's army. Originally an unlettered stable-boy from Ireland, he was, thirty years ago, a mere private; now he commands an important arm of the service. Immediately after his, Wallenstein's own case is cited as an instance of ascent from modest beginnings. Thus, at the very first mention, Buttler is emphatically singled out as exemplary, and paralleled with Wallenstein himself.

Buttler's exemplary character is corroborated many times thereafter. His advance is declared a "Sporn" and "Beispiel" for others (*P* 49 ff.), his conduct a "leuchtendes Muster" and "geachtet Beispiel" (*P* 1978 f., *T* 1456 f.). Octavio points to him as an illustration of the "Kühnheit" that makes the ideal soldier (*P* 260 ff.). He is the army's representative

---

[1] Lines 440 ff. Hereafter references will be given in parentheses in the text, *L* designating *Wallensteins Lager; P, Die Piccolomini; T, Wallensteins Tod.* Roman numerals are used for acts, Arabic for scenes and line numbers.

man, risen by sheer merit from the ranks, a soldiers' soldier. At sixty he
is a toughened veteran of forty years of campaigning, a serious, almost
sober professional, dedicated to his calling. He exemplifies the soldier's
ordained isolation from bourgeois life (cf. *L* 917 ff.). Without wife or
child or human attachments, he has made the camp his home, and the
commander-in-chief his sole heir. A self-made, self-reliant man with a
hard core, ambitious, energetic, and resolute; a man of probity and principle, not easily swayed from his allegiances; proud and "touchy," the
more so because he is conscious of his humble origin and lacks the assur-
ance of one born to high station. With a natural prejudice against
aristocracy of birth, he is content to see old names displaced and new
ones emerging from obscurity (*P* 2018 f.). Such is the picture of Buttler
we obtain from the *Lager* and the *Piccolomini.*

He is present at the start of the action of the play proper and at
most important junctures thereafter, until his strong and sinister figure
comes to dominate the two final acts of the great trilogy. Toward the
end, he is "in charge" in every sense: the chief doer, the hand and mouth
of retributive justice, of history, and of fate.

We see him as the curtain rises, and hear his voice before ten lines
of the text are spoken. On behalf of the author, as it were, he calls our
attention to the crucial nature of the situation: "Auch Frau und Tochter
ruft der Fürst hieher?/Er ruft hier viel zusammen" (*P* 34 f.). Only
later does Octavio enlarge on this hint (*P* 313 ff.). Very early, too,
Buttler strikes a gloomy note and functions as the bringer of bad news.
His short words "Auf Gallas wartet nicht" (*P* 22) fall with an ominous
weight; they mark the beginning of the defection and of Wallenstein's
downward course. There is something somber about Buttler; he is a
typical representative of the "düstre Zeit" of which the *Prolog* speaks. He
has the dark hue of Shakespeare's figures of violence and crime.

In reply to Illo's concerned question, he tells tersely of Gallas'
attempt to detach him from Wallenstein, and his stalwart refusal. His
punctiliousness is shown by his hesitating to accept congratulations on
his recent promotion because it has not yet been confirmed by the
government. He speaks and acts as a loyal follower of Wallenstein and
is genuinely shocked at the suggestion that Wallenstein may give up or
lose the command.

In the next scene, too (*P* I, 2), Buttler figures as a stanch partisan
of Wallenstein. After all the others have had their say, Schiller, who
has held Buttler in reserve (save for one short, sharp utterance against
the court [161 ff.]), brings him forward as the chief spokesman for the

army: in a long and eloquent summary (210–57) he pleads the case for Wallenstein's unique and indispensable leadership. A little later, he is one of a select small group of commanders invited to hear Questenberg's official message (*P* II, 7). He is the first of them to speak up (1149). He seconds Wallenstein on further questions (1195, 1209), and voices the army's hostility to the emissary of the court (1287 ff.). Buttler's expressions of attachment to Wallenstein, all through the early part of the play, are too warm and positive to be explained by such a purely negative factor as resentment at the court for having denied him a favor.

Buttler is absent from Act III, which is dominated by the Max-Thekla action, and from Act V, which is taken up with the Max-Octavio *Aussprache*. In the masterly banquet scenes, however (*P* IV, 4-7), he figures prominently, declaring himself and working vigorously for Wallenstein's cause. He volunteers his help to Illo and Terzky in their plot and avows his unconditional loyalty to his chief (1962 ff.). He speaks not only for the ambitious Wallenstein but for Schiller, the philosophical historian, as he surveys this whole age of radical change and endless opportunity for the strong man:

> Es ist ein großer Augenblick der Zeit,
> Dem Tapfern, dem Entschloss'nen ist sie günstig. . . .
> Nichts ist zu hoch, wornach der Starke nicht
> Befugnis hat die Leiter anzusetzen. (2014-2029)

This sentiment is not so out of character for Buttler as some later "choral" passages will be, but the exalted view and poetic diction are distinctly above his range.[2]

Buttler recognizes the similarity between his career and Wallenstein's, both being sons of fortune lifted by war from obscurity to positions of eminence: "Ich liebe einen Weg, der meinem gleicht" (*P* 2006–2012). Later—to anticipate for a moment—Buttler will come to recognize, besides this positive kinship, a negative one: besides vaulting ambition the tenacious pursuit of vengeance. As Wallenstein is motivated by rankling resentment of the disgrace put upon him by the Emperor at Regensburg, so Buttler will be motivated by revenge for the humiliation brought upon him (so he believes) by Wallenstein. Buttler (or Schiller) expressly points out this likeness between them in a later soliloquy: "Nimm dich in Acht! dich treibt der böse Geist/Der Rache—daß dich Rache nicht verderbe!" (*T* 2443 f.). It is thus, ironically, some-

---

[2] For the "choral function" of Buttler and other characters in *Wallenstein*, see my essay, "Chorus and Choral Function in Schiller," in *Schiller. 1759/1959*, ed. John R. Frey (Urbana, 1959), especially pp. 158-64.

thing of Wallenstein's own self that reacts upon him fatally in one of his own followers.[3]

These ultimate consequences, however, are not yet in sight. In the vivid banquet sequence, Buttler is still wholeheartedly with Wallenstein. He coolly rejects Octavio's advances (2168 ff.). He sees through but accepts Illo's "Revers" trickery (2192) and does his best to save it and secure the co-operation of the others (2250 ff.). The important part played by Buttler in Act IV is entirely Schiller's invention, and it is played entirely in Wallenstein's interest.

When Buttler next appears, we see a sudden and radical change take place in him, a break in his dramatic character and "value." This crucial scene of Octavio's conversion of Buttler (T II, 6) invites our special scrutiny. From entrance to exit it offers in every respect a striking contrast to the just preceding scene with Isolani. Octavio deals with each man according to his nature. He disposed of the unprincipled Isolani in short order; it requires twice as many lines and a wholly different method to cope with Buttler. He bears himself at the outset with wonted restraint and dignity. On hearing Octavio accuse Wallenstein and indicate his precarious position, Buttler gets up and declares simply "Sein Los ist meines" (1087). How different from Isolani's reaction! It is clearer than ever that Schiller meant to make Buttler a man of high moral character.

Octavio, on the other hand, is clearly the crafty manipulator. He lets Buttler get as far as the door and then plays his trump card. Buttler's first reaction shows he is proud and quick to anger, but he has himself in hand. He is candid, indeed naive, in telling Octavio all the steps in his quest of the title. Why should he, we wonder, be so confiding to Octavio at this stage? There are some implausibilities in his speech, too: it is not true, according to our previous information, "daß Geburt und Titel/ Bei der Armee mehr gelten, als Verdienst" (T 1110 f.). There has been no evidence to contradict Wallenstein's assertion that birthplace, religion, and ancestry have never weighed with him as against personal merit (P 1266 ff.). Nothing has been made of the importance of nobility among officers, and Buttler's own rise rebuts his present plaint. Nor has there been any evident ground for the word "Schmach," which he applies to his birth: it was humble, but not disgraceful, so far as we know. There

---

[3] The later Buttler too, like Wallenstein, likes to invoke Fate when he is really obeying the impulses of his heart. His lines T 2875-79 sound like a briefer echo of Wallenstein's in T I, 4.

is no apparent reason, either, why the court should have come down so hard on him: "mit schwerem Hohn zermalmend niederschlagen" (*T* 1119). This would seem to be a case of overmotivating.

Given Buttler's proud and resentful nature, it is surprising that he should have pocketed the defeat, barbed with insult, and remained so vague about his presumable enemy (*T* 1124 ff.). Given his previous relations with Octavio and estimate of him, it is strange that he should accept Octavio's story unquestioningly and the letter at a mere glance,[4] and should never challenge the "Zufall" (1136) of Octavio's possession of it or his thereby confirmed connection with a court which Buttler supposedly distrusts and hates.

Why, on the other hand, should Buttler throw overboard in an instant his long years of devotion to Wallenstein and all he knows of Wallenstein's treatment of his men? Why does he fail to see that Octavio is pursuing with him the same "deutliche Absicht" (1146 ff.) that he imputes to Wallenstein? Instead of being skeptical and suspicious, as he should be of anything that comes via Octavio from Vienna, Buttler believes every word and collapses in abject contrition: his knees give way so that he cannot stand, his voice trembles so that he can hardly speak. There has been nothing to prepare us for this labile emotionality in Buttler. He is overcome with the Emperor's "Gnade" when all he gets is confirmation in his command of his regiment—he could tell himself that it is very much in Octavio's interest to have him, reformed, in charge of it! Speechless with a sense of utter unworthiness, he surrenders his sword, and when he receives it back he vows not only to forsake Wallenstein but to kill him. Buttler's volcanic outburst here, "furchtbar losbrechend" (*T* 1168+), stands out as something unique: never before and never again do we see him display such passion. Henceforth he is quite calm, almost dispassionate, at times even philosophical, in his pursuit of Wallenstein; there is no resumption of the wild hatred that flares here for an instant. Neither, it may be added, do we hear any more of the letter; it has no before and after, but exists only in this scene.

It is clear also that Octavio must hear Buttler's bellowed "O, er soll nicht leben!" (1169), as he must Buttler's last words, "Bei Gott, ihr überlasset/Ihn seinem guten Engel nicht!" which are a direct reply to a direct question (1181 f.), so that Octavio's later protestation of innocence

---

[4] Schiller assures us "Buttler hat den Brief gelesen" (1143), but he has allowed him only an interval of six lines to do so, during which Octavio is speaking to him.

(*T* 3782 ff.) has little foundation and is one more evidence of the duplicity of his character.

Buttler asks to be left with his regiment in Wallenstein's camp "auf Ehrenwort" (*T* 1177). On the face of it, this means only that Buttler gives his word of honor to remain loyal and to bring his regiment out safely to join the imperial forces (as Max does, *T* 1272 f.).[5] Later, however, in arguing with Gordon, Buttler conveys the impression that he has pledged his word of honor to kill Wallenstein (*T* 2692 ff.). This, too, throws a light on Octavio's real intentions as Buttler understands, or is led to understand, them and detracts from Octavio's claim of innocence. When, in his final speech in the play, Buttler asks whether Octavio has any *other* orders to give him ("Habt ihr sonst einen Auftrag mir zu geben?"), he implies that the killing of Wallenstein was an "Auftrag," given here in *T* II, 6, which he executed "geschwind und pünktlich" (*T* 3810, 3814).

When Octavio departs (at the end of *T* II), Buttler takes over his function as the hidden enemy in the heart of Wallenstein's camp and confidence, the unrecognized "böser Dämon" behind the hero. Very soon after Octavio has left the stage, we hear Wallenstein speaking of Buttler in the same spirit of misguided trust that he lavished on that other viper in his bosom. Buttler, hitherto the honest, forthright soldier, develops Octavian arts of deceit.[6] Already in Act III, Scene 10, Schiller assigns to Buttler the role of dissembler as well as messenger of misfortune. To Wallenstein's warm and appealing speech he replies "Vergeßt den Falschen!" (*T* 1704), thus maligning his new friend Octavio and showing himself utterly two-faced. Earlier, Buttler had been represented as an honorable, superior person; now we must think of him as a hypocrite and a heartless scoundrel capable of killing in cold blood a man who completely trusts him.

Buttler functions repeatedly as the bringer of evil tidings. He tells of the interception of Wallenstein's courier and his fateful message. One may suspect that Buttler was "in on" this interception "vor mehrern Stunden" (*T* 1728) and kept the information from Wallenstein. Again

---

[5] One wonders, incidentally, how Buttler's men are henceforth to conceive their status in the camp. And why do not Illo and Terzky become suspicious of Buttler when he is so conspicuously excepted from the outlawry proclaimed against Wallenstein, Illo, Terzky, and Kinsky (*T* 1738 f.)? As far as they can see, Buttler has equally deserted the Emperor to stay with Wallenstein in Pilsen.

[6] The scene in which Buttler persuades the murderers (*T* V, 2) is a kind of parody of the one (*T* II, 6) in which Octavio persuaded Buttler. He too deals with each man after his nature: his procedure with Deveroux is different from that with Gordon. It is a nice touch that he gets rid of Gordon at a critical moment by reminding him of his duty as commandant (*T* 3730).

in *T* III, 16, he comes in with bad news that spoils Wallenstein's chances of winning over the cuirassiers and causes him to lament "Buttler! Buttler!/Ihr seid mein böser Dämon, warum mußtet ihr's/In ihrem Beisein melden?" Buttler, of course, did so intentionally, and the "Eifer" with which he entered was feigned. It might be argued that he could not have known what was going on in the room, so as to burst in at the critical moment; but the very fact that the conference was going on so long would have made him suspect that it was going in Wallenstein's favor. It is an Octavio-like maneuver of alienating followers from Wallenstein.

Buttler is on stage as one of the "inner circle" during *T* III, 17, 18, 19, and 20, and is witness to crucial developments. With Illo and Terzky he accompanies the general on his futile appearance before his rebellious troops. Thereupon Wallenstein orders him to write to his friend Gordon, the commandant at Eger, and thus Buttler is officially accredited to his final scene of operations. He is still on the stage, however, to be made the object of Max's special appeal for protection of the endangered leader. He refuses, ambiguously, to give Max his hand on this, and Max, the "ideal spectator," couples him with Illo as an untrustworthy character. Thus an opportunity is given for tragic irony, and Buttler again figures as a traitor and dissembler. In this aspect he is a projection of Octavio, as Gordon is of the idealist Max.

When we next see Buttler, however, as the curtain rises on Act IV, he is invested with the majestic mantle of a chorus. The sonorous soliloquy of IV, 1, is an assignment. Buttler speaks it, not in his real character, but on behalf of the meditative historian and moralist Schiller, commenting on the career of the hero whom Schiller the dramatist has brought to his last stand. Buttler here exemplifies Schiller's irrepressible "choral" tendency, that "poeti ventriloquism" that Coleridge censured particularly in *Wallenstein*.[7] A moment later, Buttler doffs the honorific costume and speaks once more with his own voice, asking Gordon, in effect: "Did you get my special-delivery letter?" (*T* 2450 f.).

In the inconclusive debate that follows (*T* IV, 2), Gordon in turn assumes the role of a chorus, in defense of Wallenstein. Buttler appears curiously casual and dispassionate as he encourages Gordon to relate

---

[7] Coleridge speaking to Henry Crabb Robinson, 1812; see Robinson's *Diary*, I, p. 396, quoted by Frank W. Stokoe, *German Influence in the English Romantic Period*, (Cambridge, 1926), p. 134. It is interesting to note that even the emissary of the opposition, Questenberg, gets a touch of the Schillerian choral character; his observation on Wallenstein: "Zu stark für dieses schlimmverwahrte Herz/War *die* Versuchung! Hätte sie doch selbst/Dem bessern Mann gefährlich werden müssen!" (*P* 306 ff.), anticipates Gordon's later apologia (cf. *T* 2482-2493).

anecdotes from Wallenstein's past. It seems in bad taste for Buttler to engage thus in gossipy small talk about the man he is supposed to hate enough to murder.

Near the end of the next scene, Wallenstein gives Buttler military orders over Gordon's head (*T* 2637 f.). Buttler, remaining on stage (*T* IV, 6), explains to Gordon the significance of the news of Max's end and uses this technical "victory" of the Swedes as an additional argument for murdering Wallenstein. He represents the securing of the general's person, living or dead, as the wish of the government which he has pledged his life to fulfill (*T* 2692 ff.); as yet he keeps his personal motives to himself. In the ensuing controversy, Gordon, as it were, passes the judgment of the "ideal spectator" on Buttler, as Max did earlier. Continuing his hypocrite role, Buttler speaks sympathetically of Wallenstein and Max (*T* 2768 f.) and converses amicably with Illo and Terzky, whom he has marked for slaughter. Only his ominous last words, "zu rechter Zeit" (*T* 2831), hint, for us, at his intention.

In the following scene (*T* IV, 8), as the debate with Gordon is prolonged, Schiller again raises Buttler out of his normal character to choral dignity. Suddenly, after some quite practical remarks, he delivers himself of an elevated, poetic speech (*T* 2847 ff.) comparable to his opening soliloquy in style, in philosophical depth, and in learned allusion. Instead of honestly admitting a personal grudge, he poses as the reluctant instrument of impersonal Fate: "nicht mein Haβ. . ./Sein böses Schicksal ist's. Das Unglück treibt mich,/Die feindliche Zusammenkunft der Dinge." He moralizes gratuitously on man's illusion of free will: "Es denkt der Mensch die freie Tat zu tun," etc. (*T* 2873 ff.). This momentary imposition of "choral" utterance on Buttler unhappily muddles his dramatic character and motivation and gives him a repulsive air of sanctimoniousness quite out of keeping with his earlier portrait.

Schiller's friend and critic Christian Gottfried Körner rightly saw this weakness in Buttler's role. In his long and detailed letter of January 16, 1800, he advised Schiller to reduce Buttler's monologues and self-justifications. He wanted Buttler kept darker in coloring and less talkative: "Ich wünschte ihn finsterer und verschlossener."[8] What Körner put mildly, Jakob Minor put sharply when he judged Buttler a splendidly conceived character killed by verbosity.[9] It was this pose as the instru-

---

[8] *Schillers Briefwechsel mit Körner*, ed. Goedeke, 2. Aufl. (Leipzig, 1878), II, pp. 341 f. A fuller reproduction of this letter, with further criticism, in *Briefwechsel zwischen Schiller und Körner*, ed. Geiger (Stuttgart, 1893), IV, pp. 124 ff.

[9] *Schillers sämtliche Werke*, Säkular-Ausgabe, V, p. 418.

ment of Fate that most puzzled Otto Ludwig about Buttler: "aus Buttler wird man nicht klug." If he is indeed "das willenlose Werkzeug des Schicksals," Ludwig reasoned, why should he get a reward at the end?[10]

Buttler comes closer to the plain truth of the matter when he says "meines Wortes Ehre muß ich lösen./Und sterben muß er, oder . . ./Ich bin entehrt" (*T* 2894 ff.). Gordon's next argument, touching Buttler's pride, at last brings out his true motive: "Den Menschen macht sein *Wille* groß und klein,/Und weil ich meinem treu bin, muß er sterben" (*T* 2909 f.).

For the rest of the play, from the beginning of Act V, where he arranges the details of the murder, until the end, when he claims his reward for it, Buttler is kept in his straight and unembellished villain-character. The protracted scene of negotiation with the murderers (V, 2) serves to lower him still further in our estimation, though Schiller did not think so. He wrote to Goethe, March 7, 1799, of the "größre Breite" and "theatralische Bedeutsamkeit" now given to the preparations for the murder, and believed "dadurch kommt auch Buttler höher zu stehen"—a strange misjudgment.

In history, Buttler was not present at the murder. Schiller makes him appear an active participant, having his hand also in the slaughter of Illo and Terzky and the stabbing of a guard (*T* 3362 f., 3698 ff.). His "blutend Schwert" (3812) is not merely figurative. He is on stage through Scenes 6, 7, 9, 10, and 11, and, by the same sort of moral relativity that makes Wallenstein appear virtuous in contrast to the baseness of his faithless friends, Schiller manages to give Buttler a comparatively elevated and virtuous station at the close, at the expense of Octavio. Though he acknowledges Octavio as in command (3780 f.), he defies him with impunity and upbraids and brands him publicly (3800 ff.). Octavio stands as the pusillanimous plotter and equivocator who "would not play false and yet would wrongly win," Buttler as the man of clear vision and action who saw what needed to be done and did it: "Ich wußte immer, was ich tat, und so/Erschreckt und überrascht mich kein Erfolg" (3808 f.—"Erfolg" in the older neutral sense of "outcome," like earlier English "success").

Thus Buttler can boast of having done "eine gute Tat," ridding the empire of a fearsome foe. He becomes almost a Wilhelm Tell, a tyrant-slayer. Like Tell, he has acted primarily from personal motives, but his action, coinciding with the public interest, makes him a patriotic hero. By the same token, what kills Wallenstein finally is not his treason

---

[10] *Gesammelte Schriften,* ed. Stern and Schmidt (Leipzig, 1891), V, p. 301.

to the Emperor but his treason to Buttler. It is personal revenge, masked as patriotic justice, that brings him to his fall. Like Maria Stuart, he suffers a vicarious punishment for a past misdeed, not the one with which he is at present charged. And if, as an unkind critic once remarked, Johanna's tragedy hinges on an insecure helmet-fastening, one could say that Wallenstein's hangs by an imprudent letter.

At any rate, Buttler towers over the debased Octavio at the end as, after a ringing speech of self-justification, he departs for Vienna to reap the praises and rewards to which his useful deed entitles him. With his exit the curtain virtually falls on the long and complicated action of *Wallenstein*. What is left to say is Gräfin Terzky's valedictory, full of pathos and tragic dignity, and Octavio's weak rejoinders. What remained of his stature after Buttler's arraignment and the countess' reproaches is finally cut down by Gordon's closing words and glance. Ironically, Octavio has this in common with Buttler: he has a coveted title, gained by dubious means, but he has no son to leave it to.

Thus Buttler has run his changeful course. Now change as such in a dramatic character is not open to question; often it makes the very essence of the play. What may be questioned is the manner and motivation of the change, the extent to which it is made credible. The crucial about-face in Buttler, as we noted, takes place in *T* II, 6. Schiller's earliest critic, Körner, apparently was not satisfied with this scene nor with the character of Buttler. In his letter of April 9, 1799, he says with tactful understatement, "vielleicht bedarf dieser noch einiger Nachhilfe." The fact that in the latter part of the play Buttler is not for one moment swayed by Wallenstein's trust and Gordon's appeals, by the memory of all that once bound him to his leader, seems to Körner something revolting (Empörendes) which calls for the strongest motivation. And "Wallensteins Beleidigung langt dazu nicht aus."[11] In other words, Körner feels that the letter-business of *T* II, 6, is insufficient motivation for the radical change in Buttler, and moreover that his character lacks ethical conflict and therefore depth. These are serious misgivings that deserve our consideration.

In his sources, Schiller found the story of a treacherous letter ascribed to Wallenstein in connection with Illo's (or Isolani's) application for a title. This motif he transferred to Buttler in an effort to make his vicious act plausible. It was an expedient altogether characteristic of Schiller. His fondness for intrigue, especially by letter, is mani-

---

[11] *Schillers Bfw. m. Körner*, ed. Goedeke, 2. Aufl. (1878), II, p. 323.

fested in his plays from *Die Räuber* to *Demetrius*.[12] Various missives circulate in *Wallenstein* too, from the "memorial" of the *Lager* to the royal letter delivered to Octavio at the last, but not all of them are convincing.[13]

Certainly Schiller would have been less likely than another playwright to cavil at a letter-trick such as that by which the transformation in Buttler is effected so instantaneously in *T* II, 6. He therewith gave his play a second villain, which seems quite unnecessary in view of Octavio's eminent qualifications. He, the "Fuchs," the "falsche Katze," the "Schleicher," the "Schlange," who surrounds his trusting friend with spies and gets reports on his slightest moves; who with cool duplicity signs the treasonable *Revers;* whose ways are crooked; who plots to rise by Wallenstein's fall[14]—Octavio would have been more than equal to the minor task of fabricating this letter.

If one accepts it as not his, but a genuine letter by Wallenstein to the court, one must assume either (a) that Octavio procured it from the court earlier, on the chance of using it to alienate Buttler from Wallenstein (but then why did he not use it sooner, since it is not conditional on the latter's overt treason with the Swedes?), or (b) that Octavio had it sent him from Vienna for this particular occasion—but how could he have foreseen the occasion in time? And how would he have learned of the existence of such a letter? Already in *P* 284–86, Octavio knows what is wrong with Buttler and how to right it at a time when Questenberg is still quite baffled. That is to say, Questenberg knows nothing of Wallenstein's letter and the "handle" it provides for dealing with Buttler—yet Questenberg comes from Vienna, where he functions, as Waldecker has pointed out, as the special *Referent* for

---

[12] Oskar Seidlin, "Schiller's 'Treacherous Signs,'" in *Schiller. 1759/1959* (Urbana, 1959), p. 136, points out "the pattern of the letter as the instrument of trickery and treachery" established in Schiller's earliest plays.
[13] The letter deposing Wallenstein and putting Octavio in command (*P* 2499 ff.) must be assumed to have been in Octavio's hands far in advance of developments; it was not brought by Questenberg, merely discussed with him (*T* 1658-60).—For Gordon to receive the imperial letter ordering him to obey Buttler's orders blindly (*T* 2454 f.), it would be necessary for Octavio to know that Wallenstein was going to Eger (which Wallenstein decided on only the day before), notify the court, and cause this letter to be sent to Gordon. This would have been impossible to accomplish in the interval, and may again be charged to Schiller's fondness for such epistolary maneuvers. That Octavio, knowing Buttler's intent, thus secures carte blanche for him, is incidentally, further proof of Octavio's guilt.—In *T* 2728 ff., it is Buttler's turn to "flash" a letter to persuade a hesitant subject; in his argument here, Buttler is again an echo of Octavio.
[14] Respectively *P* 885, 2207; *T* 1613, 2795; *P* 341 ff., 2163+; *T* 1192, 1210. For further telling judgments on Octavio by the "ideal character" Max, see *P* 2437 ff., 2604 ff.

Wallenstein and his army.[15] Had this letter been known at the court, which is hostile to and suspicious of Wallenstein, Questenberg would have come provided with it, whereas it is obviously not "in the record" as far as this important official knows.

While the assumption that Octavio forged the letter for his purpose is wholly plausible,[16] the assumption that Wallenstein wrote it raises serious difficulties. It contradicts everything we have been told about his relations with his troops. From the *Lager* to the last act of the *Tod* we get evidence not merely of Wallenstein's munificence but of his genuine benevolence for his men. Even if we should suspect a selfish motive in his repeated paying of Isolani's debts, it would be hard to see one in the gift of a warm coat to the unimportant Deveroux (*T* 3317 ff.). There is testimony to Wallenstein's "Vatersorge" for his army (*L* 1032, *P* 193, 1136 ff.). He consistently supports his men in dealings with Vienna (e.g., *P* 53 ff., 166 ff.); why should he "sell out" one now to the court he detests? And why should he, who knows men, adopt *this* means to bind one particular officer to his cause (there is nothing to show that Buttler needed special binding). How could he be sure that the "rebound" of resentment would go in this desired direction? Would not the positive reaction of gratitude for procuring the title (Wallenstein's own suggestion, *T* 1132) be a surer way of attaching Buttler to him than an unfocused indignation against a collective court? The procedure attributed to Wallenstein is altogether too round about, risky, and unpromising.

Furthermore, it would entail the writing of two letters—one of recommendation which Buttler saw (*T* 1134) and one of condemnation that Octavio produces; in other words, the double-document trick used in the banquet scenes. The virtual repetition of this device shows how it fascinated Schiller, but the repetition should also give us pause.

We are told more than once (also by his wife, *T* 1405) that Wallenstein is "argwöhnisch." Would he then not be suspicious of Buttler, knowing he had written this treacherous letter? Would he trust him as he does? Would he, who makes it a rule never to commit himself in writing (*P* 854, *T* 62), have taken such a risk with the court, where he knows he has powerful enemies who would welcome the opportunity to betray the betrayer?[17] What could he suppose the court to assume as

---

[15] See Ludwig Waldecker, *Schillerstudien* (Bonn, 1934), p. 29.

[16] An older article by Ad. Sütterlin, *Zeitschr. f. d. dt. Unterricht*, 13 (1899), 119-30, argues ably for Octavio's "Fälschung."

[17] Richard Plant, "Gessler and Tell," *MLQ* 19 (1958), 62, fn. 15, considers the intrigue too clumsy for Wallenstein, who could have foreseen that somebody in Vienna

the motive behind his interference? Would they not "smell a rat"? And would he, who takes not even his aide and brother-in-law Terzky into his confidence (*P* 863 f.), put himself with such a letter into the hands of Vienna? The danger in such a course is indicated in the play itself: Illo is sure the officers who signed the *Revers* will be incriminated even though they aver innocence: "Am Hofe glaubt man ihrer Unterschrift/Doch mehr, als ihrem heiligsten Beteuern" (*P* 1323 f.).

And there are other, deeper objections founded on considerations of psychology and character portrayal. The passage in the *Tod*, lines 1443–1455, is a weighty argument against Wallenstein's authorship of the letter—unless we suppose he is "acting" here, which would be completely groundless and farcical:

> So hab' ich diesem würdig braven Mann,
> Dem Buttler, stilles Unrecht abzubitten;
> Denn ein Gefühl, deß ich nicht Meister bin,
> Furcht möcht' ich's nicht gern nennen, überschleicht
> In seiner Nähe schaudernd mir die Sinne,
> Und hemmt der Liebe freudige Bewegung.

These words prove that his conscience is free of any sense of guilt in respect to Buttler—else he would needs betray at this point some awareness of a much greater wrong done to this man than the mere unspoken one of harboring a vague, irrational suspicion of him. Furthermore, a character capable of such low double-dealing could not successfully take the noble attitude Wallenstein takes toward the treason of Isolani and Octavio (*T* 1619 ff., 1668 ff., 2105 ff.). The fine passage on "Treue" (*T* 427-37) would be hollow pretense. Psychologically it would be quite impossible for a man who had tricked a comrade as Wallenstein is alleged to have tricked Buttler, to speak and act to him as Wallenstein does to Buttler in *T* III, 10, particularly lines 1689-1703.

We have the choice of concluding that Wallenstein is a cold-blooded hypocrite and consummate actor or a pathetic victim of amnesia. In either case the tragic effect is lost and the hero's character gravely impaired. The second alternative, moreover, conflicts with evidence of Wallenstein's excellent, indeed phenomenal, memory even for his ordinary soldiers (see the cuirassier scene, *T* III, 15). What is more, this alleged letter-fraud on an important officer was perpetrated within the last half year, as is to be inferred from Buttler's words in *P* 1972 ff. If Wallenstein has simply forgotten this egregious and recent wrongdoing,

---

would divulge the matter to Buttler. Plant regards this as an instance of Schiller's occasional "overplotting" because of his fondness for conspiracy.

then he becomes a pathological case and ceases to be a subject for high tragedy.

Despite all these difficulties and discrepancies, most people—theatergoers, readers, critics, and scholars—from Schiller's day to ours have accepted his letter-intrigue without demur or with a bit of rationalization.[18] And Schiller himself and those most closely in touch with his work seem never to have questioned Wallenstein's authorship of the letter on which the whole plot turns. In his *Geschichte des Dreissigjährigen Kriegs* (4. Buch), Schiller relates the anecdote of the "double-crossing" of Illo, introducing it with the statement that Wallenstein "auch die niedrigsten Mittel nicht verschmäht hatte, die Zahl seiner Anhänger zu vermehren."[19] The Wallenstein of the play of course is not the Wallenstein of history, but the passage throws a light on Schiller's conception of his hero. In an essay (hardly more than a résumé) which Goethe wrote for the *Allgemeine Zeitung* in 1799 on the première of *Die Piccolomini*, it is said that Octavio convinces Buttler "durch Vorzeigung authentischer Dokumente" that Wallenstein was the author of his disgrace.[20] Since this essay was a joint production of Goethe and Schiller,[21] we may be sure that this was also Schiller's understanding of the matter. Körner, too, implied his acceptance of Wallenstein's treacherous letter even while he questioned its adequacy as motivation. Even Otto Ludwig, who had so deadly an eye for the inconsistencies in Wallenstein's character, accepted the letter as his "gemeine und kleine Art" to snare Buttler.[22]

Why has Schiller's procedure been so little questioned? The answer lies, I think, in his superb stagecraft, which carries along not only his immediate audience but to a large extent his readers. We tend to forget that Schiller was not just a dramatic poet but a writer for the living stage. In the dilemma between poetic consistency and stage exigency, he was apt to decide in favor of the latter. How willing he was from the very first to alter and cut his texts in the interests of presentation! For Schiller, the play was the thing rather than the flawless portrait. His compelling interest lay in action, interplay of figures on boards, and he did not scruple unduly, here and in other plays, about the means by

---

[18] William F. Mainland, *Schiller and the Changing Past* (London, 1957), Chap. 2, reviews some of the scholarly opinions on the authorship of the letter; he himself concludes that Schiller left the matter in doubt.

[19] Säkular-Ausg., XV, p. 356.

[20] Jubiläums-Ausg., XXXVI, p. 182.

[21] See *ibid.*, pp. 342 f.

[22] *Gesamm. Schriften,* ed. Stern & Schmidt, V, p. 302.

which he produced the situations and effects he wanted. In the present case, he found the letter-business ready to his hand and used it, undeterred by any consideration of its inconsistency with the pictures he had previously drawn of Wallenstein and Buttler.

Perhaps he was influenced by the example of another practical playwright, Shakespeare, whose hand can be seen at various places in *Wallenstein.* Shakespeare similarly has Macbeth engage two men to murder Banquo, they too not professional assassins but desperate gentlemen whose fortunes, Macbeth persuades them, were ruined by Banquo. Shakespeare, to be sure, wisely leaves the evidence for this off stage and does not resort to a letter.

A personage in a play represented for Schiller not only a character but a function, and sometimes he sacrificed the former to the latter. At other times he found it convenient to transfer a needed function from one person to another. Thus, we noticed, he has Butler take over functions of the absent Octavio, and at the end, faced with a surplus villain, he depresses Octavio and elevates Buttler to relative hero rank. Schiller knew, with the instinct of the true *Theaterdichter,* that an audience, sufficiently impressed, would not question the credentials of villainy where villainy was wanted. If he but made his operations convincing up to a certain point, that was all that was required. That he did this, in his greatest play, with a mastery that carried far beyond the audiences of his time, the record proves.

Grillparzer As a Critic
of European Literature

by FRANK D. HORVAY

FRANZ GRILLPARZER is best known as a dramatist; as a literary critic, though deserving considerable credit, he has been virtually without recognition. Profiting from Fritz Strich's study *Franz Grillparzers Äs-thetik*,[1] I have examined elsewhere in depth Grillparzer's criticism of German literature.[2] In this paper I should like to investigate some of Grillparzer's observations in the field of European literature, which, in turn, force him to reflect on the German literary products of his time.

It should be stressed from the start that Grillparzer's often sharp and contradictory observations, as for example in regard to the works of Goethe,[3] must not be taken entirely at face value but rather as an expression of his over-all concern for the didactic and sentimental quality of the Austro-German literature of his age. Yet Grillparzer's criticism, which is largely buried in his letters, diaries, conversations, etc., reaches well beyond his age and can in its total effect almost be compared to Goethe's conversations and correspondence concerning aesthetics and literature. In the first half of the nineteenth century, much Austro-German literary criticism was in a pitiful state and consisted more often than not of a display in cleverness and an enjoyment of debunking. It

---

[1] (Berlin, 1905.) As valuable as Strich's analysis is, it has two limitations: He dwells too long on the aesthetical and philosophical sources of Grillparzer's drama-turgy and thereby neglects the universal aspects of Grillparzer's aesthetics; second, as Strich himself admits in his "Introduction," he was not familiar with Sauer's com-prehensive edition of Grillparzer's *Gespräche* (see footnote 13), which appeared after Strich's book was written and while it was being printed.

[2] Frank D. Horvay, "Grillparzer as a Critic of German Literature" (doctoral dissertation, Washington University, St. Louis, 1949), *passim*.

[3] For an analysis of Grillparzer's relationship to Goethe cf. Frank D. Horvay, "Goethe and Grillparzer," *The Germanic Review* (1950), 85-94.

was not supposed to indicate an appreciation or even an understanding of the work scrutinized. This was especially true in Grillparzer's native Austria, where literary critics such as Hebenstreit, Ebersberg, Jeitteles, Pietznigg, and Saphir hampered creative effort with their vitriolic pens. To a lesser extent this was also true in Germany where, for example, Adolf Müllner, the author of "fate tragedies" and a popular critic, wrote a scathing criticism in the *Stuttgarter Morgenblatt* against Grillparzer's *Das goldene Vliess* without having read or seen the trilogy on the stage. He based his judgment merely on a discussion of the plays in a Viennese periodical.[4] In contrast, Fred O. Nolte described Grillparzer as "an unsurpassed master in the delicate art of literary appreciation." Nolte went on to say, that Grillparzer

> with incomparable sensitiveness and honesty . . . observed the finest achievements of others; with unswerving insight and modesty, he examined his own productions in the light of these achievements. Of Grillparzer it may truly be said: no poet ever judged his own work more critically; no critic ever judged the work of others more poetically.[5]

I

The worth of Grillparzer's literary criticism, as displayed in his essays, diaries, and conversations, rests on two solid foundations. First, his background as a cultured citizen of the cosmopolitan capital of the Austrian Empire and, secondly, his moral sensitivity. Grillparzer read Greek, Latin, Italian, Spanish, French, English, and German literature in the original; he was familiar with Scandinavian and Slavic literature; and he was well versed in the literature of the minorities of his native Austria. He was thoroughly familiar with the contemporary aesthetic, philosophical, and historical studies. He had a fine appreciation of the visual arts; and his critical observations on Raphael's pictures, the architecture of Prague, the statues of Thorwaldsen, and Fanny Elssler's talent for ballet reflect the extent of his taste and interest. Music was his second nature which, on occasion, threatened to overwhelm the dramatist in him. Above all, he was an author of great literary works, a dramatist who was fully conscious of his deserved greatness, whereas the professional critics of his day were for the most part frustrated scribblers, whose failures as authors, according to Grillparzer, were well earned. His moral sensitivity and sense of beauty caused him to combat in his

---

[4] Franz Grillparzer, *Sämtliche Werke* (hereafter referred to as *Werke*), Ausgabe der Stadt Wien, ed. August Sauer (Vienna, 1909 ff.), I, xiv, p. 242.
[5] *Grillparzer, Lessing, and Goethe in the Perspective of European Literature* (Lancaster, Pa., 1938), p. 55.

literary criticism all authors who betrayed the purity of art. Thus he criticized Arndt, Freiligrath, Prutz, and Grün for catering to popular trends, Frankl and Mosenthal for being propagandistic, Hebbel and Zedlitz for professional authorship, and Freytag and Prokesch von Osten for employing extraneous allusions.[6] Above all, he was critical of those in whose writings he had detected even the slightest vulgarity and lack of good taste, as in Goethe's *Wahlverwandtschaften*, Halm's *Die Braut-nacht*, Hebbel's *Agnes Bernauer,* and Friedrich Schlegel's *Lucinde.* About these he wrote:

> Glaubt ihr, man könne kosten vom Gemeinen?
> Man muß es hassen, oder ihm sich einen.
>
> (*Werke,* I, x, 178)

II

Only on rare occasions did Grillparzer criticize individual foreign authors; rather he employed, in general terms, his appreciation and vast knowledge of West-European civilization as a corrective in censuring the shortcomings of German literature. In his own genre, the drama, for example, Grillparzer felt that the German accomplishments were woe-fully inadequate.

> Whereas the British with their Shakespeare possess a complete theatre repertoire which will be adequate for centuries to come; and the Spaniards need only turn the spade in order to unearth ever-lasting treasures; and whereas the French may light-heartedly dis-card two centuries of literature and still satisfy with their recent works the needs of the present, there are hardly a dozen German plays that can be saved from the past to please the connoisseur . . . of the mediocre ones a few are tolerable, but the recent plays are altogether bad.   (*Werke,* I, xiv, 72 f.)

Grillparzer loved the ancients and felt an intimate attachment to their thoughts and sentiments. Sensitively aware that Greek civilization enabled even the average citizen to appreciate that which was excellent and distinguished, he was perturbed that Gervinus and other con-temporaries, rather than encouraging art and beauty for their own sakes, persisted in subordinating them to utilitarian goals.[7] He greatly ad-mired Herodotus and Plutarch and observed what a wealth of dramatic source material their works contained in contrast to anything the Germans had to offer.[8] Also, he properly felt that as poetry the *Odyssey*

---

[6] For Grillparzer's literary criticism of these and other German authors, see Index to footnote 2.

[7] *Werke,* I, xiv, 116 ff.

[8] *Werke,* II, viii, 179.

was immeasurably superior to the *Nibelungenlied,* of which the romanticists made so much.[9] He further realized that the ancient dramatists were writing for an audience entirely different from his own, and he could not condone the efforts of Tieck and others to adapt Euripides and Aeschylus to the stage of the nineteenth century.[10] The essence in the writings of the ancients was, as he saw it, the intimate relationship between life and art. Scornful of the abstractness in the works of German authors, he wrote: "The ancients acquired . . . knowledge of human nature by active association with one another . . . we Germans expect to do the same by contemplation. Our best writings are proof enough whether we are succeeding."[11]

III

Grillparzer was a literary gourmet whose apprehension of hidden beauty enabled him to find enjoyment in all literature, regardless of repute. In this respect he differs sharply from the French critic Joseph Joubert, who was only interested in the total effect of a work of art and who said, "I love few pictures, few operas, few statues, few poems, and yet I am a great lover of the arts."[12] Certainly, many times Grillparzer found flashes of beauty where less sensitive and less broad-minded authors would have passed them by unnoticed, as in two lines of Homer's *Iliad,* a sole clause in Pindar's eighth Nemeic ode, a speech by Polyxena in Iousa Barnesi's *Vita Euripidis,* a recurring expression in Old High German poetry, a single poem, *Adventslied,* among Rückert's many mediocre ones, or the works of Hornbostel and other obscure Austrian authors. Grillparzer's recognition of even the isolatedly perfect in literature is the key to his appreciation of Lope de Vega, of whom he said that he had not written a single play which could be called perfect but that at least one scene in each play he had written could be compared to Shakespeare's best.[13] Grillparzer acknowledged that much which Lope de Vega had put on paper was in bad taste and, from the modern point of view, was even lewd; but he felt that as in *Llegur en occasion* and *Venus y Adonis,* Lope richly compensated his audience with flashes of incomparable beauty.

---

[9] *Werke,* I, xii, 39; II, ix, 299 f.; I, xiv, 142 f.
[10] Cf. *Werke,* II, xi, 66; II, x, 253, 328.
[11] *Werke,* II, vii, 66, 308.
[12] As quoted by Irving Babbitt, *The Masters of Modern French Criticism* (Boston, 1912), p. 49.
[13] *Grillparzers Gespräche und Charakteristiken seiner Persönlichkeit,* ed. August Sauer, scattered volumes in "Schriften des Literarischen Vereins in Wien" (Vienna, 1904 ff.) (hereafter referred to as *S.*), XV, 41.

As the magic of the Viennese *Volkstheater* is discernible in Grillparzer's *Die Ahnfrau, Der Traum ein Leben,* and *Libussa,* so European, Imperial Austrian, and particularly Spanish motifs are present in many of his plays. We are reminded that through the masterful translation of a few scenes from Calderon's *La vida es sueño* the young Grillparzer awakened the interest of Josef Schreyvogel, who eventually staged his first mature work, *Die Ahnfrau.* Grillparzer's lengthy juvenile play *Blanka von Kastilien* has a Spanish theme; Calderon influenced his *Der Traum ein Leben;* motives in *Die Jüdin von Toledo, Medea, Esther, König Ottokars Glück und Ende,* and even in *Treuer Diener seines Herrn* originate from Lope de Vega's treasure chest. Grillparzer's attachment to Spanish literature was inherent. It was a direct heritage through the Habsburg Catholic tradition, and that is why he distrusted A. W. Schlegel's glorification of Spanish literature which, in Grillparzer's view, was religiously as well as aesthetically questionable.[14] Grillparzer himself wrote:

> What makes the dramatic poetry of the Spaniards so different from ours is the different disposition of the two peoples. The German is soft and sentimental. He wants to draw poetry into life and then flatters himself with the lifelike quality of the composition. Hence, the conclusion of a drama is of greater interest to him than the plot. . . . To the Spaniard, on the other hand, a drama is merely a play. He abandons himself to the plot with sympathy and enthusiasm, he does not object but rather loves to see the tension whipped to its highest peak and the spectator then shocked by the disappointment of being given back to himself by an abrupt, disillusioning end. Thus Calderon's characters revert back to being actors before the curtain falls and, by addressing the spectators with a "perdonen sus muchas faltas," destroy the illusion. Poetry is like a house to the German in which he would like to dwell, but it is like a garden to the Spaniard in which he likes to stroll. Whereas the former *appears* more poetic, the latter actually *is* so.
>
> (Werke, II, x, 281 f.)

Perhaps the beauty of the Spanish language also contributed to Grillparzer's interest and love for the works of Lope de Vega, Calderon, Moreto, and Alarcon. On one occasion he called Spanish the language of love[15] and, as a whole, treasured it more than his native German. He paid the highest tribute to Spanish when he said: "The Spanish language will always be dear to me . . . for it stimulated me in the appreciation of poetry" (*S.* VI, 242).

---

[14] Cf. *Werke,* I, xv, 40, 218.
[15] *Werke* II, viii, 148.

IV

In turn Grillparzer saw little beauty in the English language and called it a ragged and ugly tongue. Nevertheless, next to reading the works of the Spaniards, the reading of Shakespeare in the original was one of Grillparzer's favorite pastimes. He detested, however, the glorification of Shakespeare by his German contemporaries, and warned aspiring authors against imitating him. Grillparzer thought that an author of Shakespeare's magnitude could properly disregard the Aristotelian laws, but that it behooved playwrights of lesser talent to devote time to study them.[16] Likewise he maintained that German history, unlike English history, was not a suitable subject for historical plays. He believed that Raupach, Grabbe, Saar, and others who attempted to deal with German emperors and the tumultuous German history in the manner Shakespeare dealt with English history, should have followed Schiller's example by choosing themes (*Maria Stuart, Jungfrau von Orleans, Wilhelm Tell,* etc.) from foreign historical sources.[17]

> Where in German history do we find such definite triumphs of a victorious party as, for example, in *Richard the Third,* where, after so many horrors, the marriage between Richmond and Elizabeth really and truly ends the War of the Roses and reminds the reader, almost against his will, of the proverb: "All's well that ends well"? Did not in Germany a new rebellion flare up as soon as one calamity was stilled or a rebellion suppressed? And does this not make it impossible to find even the tiniest spot [in history] where a tragedy can come to a conclusion and a rest?   (*S. XV,* 190 f.)

Grillparzer also believed that a play like *Henry VIII,* with a purely patriotic background, where everything seems to revolve around the birth of Elizabeth (". . . whose christening the theatre audience is still there to witness") would never have pleased German spectators. The English are interested primarily in the patriotic and the Germans in the ethical motives or, to put it differently, whereas the English prefer historical truth, the Germans prefer poetic truth in their plays.[18]

Generally speaking, Grillparzer admired the English authors for their human understanding, based on actual human relationships. He compared them, in this respect, to the Greeks and contrasted both with the Germans, who preferred "reflections about human nature."[19] He also praised English scholarship by stating that men like Gibbon could

---

[16] *Werke* II, viii, 24.
[17] *S.* XV, 191, 186 f.
[18] *S.* XV, 185 f.
[19] *Werke,* II, vii, 66.

make a single volume their life's work. Although the Germans might have patience to gather data, they had neither a sense of composition nor the ability to let their works mature. In 1845, nearly ten years after his visit to England, Grillparzer reminisced as follows:

> Geht ihr nach England, meine Zeilen,
> O nähmt ihr mich, den Schreiber mit!
> Dort wo sie schreiten statt zu eilen,
> Doch eine Spur läßt jeder Tritt.
> (*Werke,* I, xii, 169)

V

Grillparzer showed little interest in Italian literature. He ignored its drama and thought that in the sonnet alone did it deserve high praise.[20] Much as he loved Ariosto, Lope de Vega, and Calderon, and revered Dante, Shakespeare, and Goethe, Grillparzer felt that they were not representative of a universal civilization such as the Greeks had possessed. On his trip to Italy he admired the flow of beautiful melodies from the lips of average citizens: Venetian gondoliers, shopkeepers, farmers, and fishermen. But in spite of Grillparzer's many fine words for Italian music, his preference for literary accomplishment as the first mark of civilization led him to look upon the French as universally the most polished, most cultured, and most civilized people of modern Europe.[21]

Grillparzer was an admirer of Molière, Diderot, and Rousseau, and once placed Voltaire on the same pedestal with Goethe and Cicero.[22] He viewed Racine's and Corneille's accomplishments with the greatest respect and took sharp issue with those Germans who, since Lessing, had been belittling the importance of their works.[23] But Grillparzer, who believed that only the great and small authors together can give a comprehensive picture of accomplishment, also found much that was estimable in the works of such minor authors as Ponsard, Soulié, and Saintine. Interestingly enough, he showed the least sympathy for the works of his well-known French contemporaries, Dumas père and Victor Hugo, who, according to Grillparzer, had been adversely influenced by German romanticism in general and German sentimentality and conceit in particular. Referring to them he stated: "In France only the first-class authors exaggerate—the second-raters make enjoyable reading" (*S.* VI, 247). And in general terms Grillparzer observed:

---

[20] *S.* VI, 334. Cf. *Werke* II, xi, 112 f. Grillparzer had some good words for Dante's *Inferno* but disliked his *Purgatorio* and *Paradiso*.

[21] *Werke,* II, x, 257.

[22] *S.* VI, 239.

[23] *Werke,* II, xi, 220.

"German literature is enervating. For us it is the best, because we have no other—but all foreigners should keep away from it" (*Werke,* II, viii, 108). In another reference to French authors (and he had Hugo and Lamartine in mind particularly) Grillparzer lamented the influence which the German *Bildungsdichter* exercised upon their works. While reading *Littérature et Philosophie Mêlées,* he was surprised to note that the theatre, according to Hugo, had "other tasks" besides fulfilling the conditions of art; and pertinently noted: "What other tasks does it have?" (*Werke,* II, ix, 214.) He likewise objected to Hugo's sentence: "Le théâtre est une chose qui enseigne et qui civilise," and stated: "Why not? Indirectly and incidentally, but to proceed toward such goals on purpose is about the most inartistic thing one could imagine" (*ibid.*). As if to sum up his objections to those who utilized the drama for educational purposes and strove to make a reformatory of the theatre, Grillparzer declared: "The theatre must be treated with moral indifference or it will corrupt morals" (*Werke,* II, viii, 180), and continued with considerable exaggeration:

> I never liked the recent educator-poets including even Schiller and Goethe; . . . true dramatic poetry seems to me to be that which, by virtue of its mere existence, impels faith, rather than that which, by virtue of plausible evidence, demands approbation.
>
> (*Werke,* I, xvi, 214)

Grillparzer's numerous comparisons of French and German authors resulted perhaps in a more scorching censure of the latter than any other criticism he offered. Specifically, he defended French literature against the often-voiced German criticism that it was immoral. Was it really more immoral, Grillparzer asked, than German literature? Whereas French immorality, he continued, is presented with impudence and without disguise, the German is sugar-coated with euphonious philosophic ideas which are presented as a sort of moral code to the unsuspecting public. The latter is the more dangerous, because criminals can be jailed but there is no protection against lack of ethics.[24] Grillparzer also childed the Germans, these late-comers in world literature, for trying to dominate minds: "German authors always want to instruct; to do that one needs only copious reading; French authors want to entertain—for that one needs talent" (*S.* XX, 103). Likewise he berated the Germans for their lack of composition and praised the French, whose worst writers still had an appreciable command of their craft.[25] As if

---

[24] *Werke,* II, ix, 157.
[25] *Werke,* I, xiv, 77.

to summarize, he pointedly stated: Characteristics in which the French surpass the Germans in literature are logicality, warmth, disposition, practical sense, and manliness, as it contrasts with German puerility, rather than with femininity.

VI

Few, if any, of Grillparzer's contemporaries were as aware as he was of the shortcomings of German literature in the light of Western European civilization and tradition. Having been last to arrive on the modern literary scene, the Germans believed that with the brilliancy of the "Age of Weimar" they had caught up with the others. Trying to outdo their Western neighbors, Grillparzer's German contemporaries were aiming at originality, whereas he recommended adaptation of the literary tradition; they were endeavoring to become learned, whereas he expected of them a civilized taste.

Yet the totality of Grillparzer's literary criticism is not bound to his age; rather is it modern because of its strictly literary quality which, with the exception of Goethe and Schiller, was rare on the German-speaking literary scene. His main criterium, whether he is discussing literature, music, or the visual arts, is the emphasis on art for art's sake. The ageless quality which he seeks in all artistic endeavors is repeatedly evident in his comments:

> Der Geist der Zeit ist nur ein Traum
> Oft ist nur Mode das Bewunderte:
> Doch ein Geist macht sich immer Raum,
> Der Geist, der stille, der Jahrhunderte.
> (*Werke*, I, xi, 241)

Narrative and "Musical" Structure in *Mozart auf der Reise nach Prag*

by RAYMOND IMMERWAHR

Mörike's *Mozart*[1] is acknowledged to be one of the finest German prose narratives and a unique achievement in its literary evocation of creative genius in another art,[2] but it is only in recent years that scholarship has attempted a serious evaluation of the formal principles by which the story evokes its image of Mozart and his age. Franz H. Mautner has traced the delicate stylistic means by which the narrative counterbalances its tragic undertones to achieve a total impression of warmth and radiance in harmony with the human and musical personality of Mozart and the graceful style of rococo.[3] Benno von Wiese has identified the unifying theme and central climactic symbol of the story, but he and other critics[4] who have attempted to account for its structure in terms of traditional principles of the novella have reached conclusions even more diverse than their methodological premises. Indeed, the one finding on which von Wiese and another critic starting from an opposite

---

[1] A preliminary version of this paper was read in Discussion Group German IV at the meeting of the Modern Language Association in 1959. Its development has benefited from stimulating exchanges of ideas, orally and in informal correspondence, with a number of colleagues, among whom I should particularly mention Liselotte Dieckmann, Erich Hofacker, Franz H. Mautner, Helmut Rehder, William H. Rey, and René Taube.

[2] Benno von Wiese calls it "die vollendetste Künstlernovelle, die wir bis heute in Deutschland besitzen." *Die deutsche Novelle*, 2nd ed. (Düsseldorf, 1960), p. 235 f.

[3] "Mörikes *Mozart auf der Reise nach Prag*," *PMLA*, LX (1945), 199-220, reprinted separately with minor revisions, Krefeld, 1957; references below are to this separate edition.

[4] von Wiese, *Die deutsche Novelle*, 213-37, and *Eduard Mörike* (Tübingen and Stuttgart, 1950), pp. 270-95; Erich Hofacker, "Mörikes Mozartnovelle in ihrem künstlerischen Aufbau," *The German Quarterly*, VI (1933), 106-13; Karl Konrad Polheim, "Der künstlerische Aufbau von Mörikes Mozartnovelle," *Euphorion*, XLVIII (1954), 41-70.

approach, Karl Konrad Polheim, are able to concur is a rupture of symmetry which neither can justify on formal grounds.[5]

The root of this difficulty, I believe, lies less in the confusion of critical tongues than in the novella itself. To recognize this, however, is not to return to once-current views that Mörike's narrative technique must be either defective or inscrutable. *Mozart auf der Reise nach Prag* has special structural peculiarities, but if it is truly a consummate literary masterpiece, we must be able to account for these by clarifying our conception of the unusual literary task which the author set out to accomplish.

Let us first assume that our story is a successful and representative example of the novella, as this form is understood in German literary history, and briefly outline its principal features.[6] We can then examine the difficulty that this approach fails to resolve and modify accordingly our strategy for a second attack. This novella has to do with a "remarkable occurrence,"[7] the chance introduction of Mozart, on his way to the premiere of *Don Giovanni,* into the household of a German count celebrating the betrothal of his niece in his rococo castle. The occurrence is remarkable because it results from Mozart's transgression against what turns out to be a symbol of the cultural tradition that this household and its festivities represent; yet the transgression gives these festivities an unexpected fulfillment. The reader senses that the "remarkable occurrence" of the plot is on a deeper level an epochal but incongruous event of cultural history: the happy encounter of superlative, timeless genius with a graciously beautiful but frail, transplanted, artificially nurtured culture. The orange tree is the striking thematic symbol—what criticism of the German novella since Heyse has called a "falcon"[8]—around which this whole plot revolves. It symbolizes at once Mozart's creative genius and the rococo culture which this genius violates and yet brings to fruition. His plucking of one orange; his account of the associations, memories, and creative conception within him that attend upon this unconscious outward act;[9] and the manifold allegorical reference of the tree to

---

[5] von Wiese, *Eduard Mörike,* p. 287 f., *Die deutsche Novelle,* p. 231; Polheim, *op. cit.,* p. 70.

[6] Here I shall follow an approach that is perhaps best exemplified in the two studies of Benno von Wiese but shall incorporate some elements from the argument of Polheim. Cf. also R. B. Farrell, *Mörike: Mozart auf der Reise nach Prag* (Studies in German Literature, No. 3 [London, 1960]).

[7] Goethe, *Gespräche mit Eckermann,* 25 January, 1827: "Was ist eine Novelle anders als eine sich ereignete, unerhörte Begebenheit."

[8] From the falcon in Boccaccio's *Decameron,* Ninth Story of the Fifth Day.

[9] See the perceptive analysis of the creative process in the orange tree episode by Liselotte Dieckmann, "Mörike's Presentation of the Creative Process," *JEGP,* LIII (1954), 302 ff.

rococo culture developed during the ensuing afternoon of gay festivities
—all these together constitute the climactic summit of the narrative action.[10]

A story symbolizing the auspicious encounter of a creative genius
and a cultural epoch necessarily involves portraiture as well as action.
In this case, the narrative as a whole evokes the image of Mozart, but the
portrayal of his genius creating in felicitous harmony with rococo culture
is concentrated in the orange-tree section. His portrait as a human
personality is drawn in two retrospective sections immediately preceding
and following: his conversations with Constanze during their journey in
the morning and her account, presented to the ladies of the household
at sundown, of Mozart's visit and purchases at a country shop. These
two retrospective flanks about a summit provide a symmetry that is
compatible with both plot and portraiture, and criticism has demonstrated that this symmetry is reflected also in parallel details of narrative
presentation.[11]

However, this symmetry is broken by a second climactic peak, a
tragic fourth section that is shorter and less elaborate, to be sure, than the
gay, festive one we have until now been taking as the centre, but certainly no less intense: Mozart's poignant account of his conception of the
daemonic music in the cemetery scene and the finale. This second climax
presents a side of his musical creation that cannot be explained in terms
of a fruitful conjunction with rococo, that indeed shatters all rococo
forms;[12] here the exponents of rococo only play the part of mute witnesses
to a tragic intensity beyond their comprehension.

Criticism sometimes obscures the problem by identifying the tragic
second peak with "the music of *Don Giovanni*."[13] In each of the two
climactic sections, the crux of the narrative is Mozart's creation of music
for *Don Giovanni*: in the one the rustic wedding dance, in the other the
music of the statue and of infernal retribution. Both times he tells how

---

[10] Polheim, *op. cit.*, introduces quite unnecessary difficulties by arguing against
von Wiese that the precise apex of the narrative is not the transgression against the
orange tree in the garden but the Neapolitan reminiscence and inferring that the
narrative is "eine Figurennovelle, keine Handlungsnovelle" (*op. cit.*, p. 68). Essentially, the elaborate symmetrical scheme that results from Polheim's phenomeno-
logical approach (*ibid.*, p. 51) buttresses von Wiese's arguments for a symmetrical
plot. Cf. *Die deutsche Novelle*, p. 221 f. For criticism of Polheim's analysis, see also
Farrell, *op. cit.*, p. 28 f.

[11] See Hofacker, *op. cit.*, p. 110, and Polheim, p. 50 f.

[12] As Hofacker puts it: "Auf dem Gipfel des ersten Teils hat der Künstler die
anmutigen Formen der zierlichen Rokokokultur mit seinem befreiten Geist erfüllt
. . . auf dem Gipfel des zweiten Teils aber hat er diese Formen durchbrochen" (*op.
cit.*, p. 113). Cf. also Polheim and von Wiese (references above, note 5).

[13] Polheim, pp. 50 f., 60, 70.

he created the music in question after some of his other music has been played and sung: an aria from *The Marriage of Figaro* and part of a concerto in the afternoon, some of the brighter numbers of *Don Giovanni* in the evening. But each time the true climax is his account of the creation of particular music epitomizing one side of his genius. The crucial concern of the fourth section ought to be clear from the name by which the author himself introduces it, *Höllenbrand*.

The two-peaked structure was thus imposed upon Mörike by the musical subject of his novella. The festive and comic tone of most of the opera buffa *Don Giovanni* and the cheerful radiance of a great part of Mozart's work could be reflected in a fictitious plot accounting for the creation of the rustic wedding-dance theme as a common product of Mozart's genius and the style and spirit of rococo. But the tragic element in Mozart's music epitomized in the "legion of terrors" called forth by the Commandatore's statue demanded separate treatment. The symmetrical three-part symbolic plot had to be expanded into a four-part dynamic alternation: the principle of polar counterpoise that Mautner has demonstrated throughout in the style is equally characteristic of this narrative's structure.

A literary composition manifesting dynamic balance and alternation invites comparison with music, and at one point a character, Eugenie, metaphorically calls an important passage, the Neapolitan reminiscence, "a painted symphony from beginning to end" (1038). She is referring to the development in three stages of two counterbalanced themes that characterizes the sonata form, the basis of the classical symphonic movement.[14] Max Ittenbach, the critic who first recognized the four-part structure of the story, has attempted to compare it as a whole with the four-movement classical symphony. The four parts of the story he finds "keyed" to one another, balancing their paces and moods as the movements in a symphony balance tempos, keys, and themes. There is an alternation between the quiet tempo of the first and third "movements" of the literary composition and the animation of the second and fourth; while the melancholy first and tragic fourth movements symmetrically set off the festively gay second and idyllically serene third. But Ittenbach emphasizes musical structure to the point of virtually denying any

---

[14] Page references in parentheses in my text are to the one-volume edition of Mörike's *Sämtliche Werke,* ed. Herbert G. Göpfert (München: Hanser, 1954). In this edition *Mozart auf der Reise nach Prag* is on pp. 1012-1070. The analogy to the sonata is elaborated in the article of Hans Hering, "Mörikes Mozartdichtung," *Zeitschrift für deutsche Bildung,* X (1934), 365 f. Benno von Wiese suggests similar symbolic connotations in Mozart's rejoining of the two halves of the orange (*Eduard Mörike,* pp. 282, 286 f.). Cf. also Mautner, p. 37.

significance to narrative action. He views the "real action" of the story as a thematic development for which the sequence of events in the plot has only peripheral significance.[15] He takes as the "theme" of the whole work simply the polarity of the cheerful and the tragic, as the themes of its four movements respective aspects of this underlying polarity: anxious restlessness versus wholesome simplicity, historic remoteness versus festive immediacy, darkness versus light, the sublime versus the intimate.[16]

If the principle of dynamic polarity is to serve as a key to the structure of this novella, the polarities will have to be conceived in literary terms with much more specific reference to the genius and human individuality of Mozart and to the spirit and style of his age. But for meaningful literary themes to be developed, interrelated, and balanced in any fashion analogous to the themes of music, they must be manifested through sensory images. The following analysis will be concerned with the underlying thematic polarities of our narrative as they are expressed through thematic symbols in each of the four main sections.[17] This approach does not, of course, eliminate the consideration of a prologue or prelude, an epilogue or postlude, and some transitional passages. The prelude is readily identifiable through the thematic image most closely linked to the title. Mozart is journeying to Prague, to the fruition of his genius in the premiere of one of its greatest creations. The journey is made in two carriages, and the graceful ornamentation and "coquette" lines of the first carriage typify the cultural setting of his life and professional career. It is in this vehicle that Mozart converses with Constanze about the yearnings, cares, and tensions, the insecurity and agitation, of his personal, domestic, and professional life. This is the carriage that conveys Mozart to his encounter, at the manor of Count Schinzberg, with the cultural and social embodiment of the finest elements in German rococo tradition. As this first conveyance symbolizes the rococo setting of Mozart's human existence, the second carriage, presented to him by Count Schinzberg, in which he travels on to Prague, symbolizes

[15] "Mozart auf der Reise nach Prag," *Germanisch-Romanische Monatsschrift*, XXV (1937), 338-54.
[16] *Ibid.*, pp. 340 ff. Cf. also Farrell, *op. cit.*, p. 50.
[17] Nearly all the symbols to be discussed below have been identified and interpreted by other scholars; my purpose here is to clarify their bearing on the structure of the narrative. Ittenbach's treatment of symbolism is inconsistent, and he fails to realize fully the importance of imagery for his "musical" approach, but he recognizes the significance of several symbolic images, as does Benno von Wiese. The latter is especially interested in Mörike's use of symbols to fuse past and present, an aspect treated in more detail by Wolfgang Taraba in his unpublished dissertation "Vergangenheit und Gegenwart bei Eduard Mörike" (Münster, 1953). My interpretation of the carriage symbol and of the artifacts in the third section is particularly indebted to Taraba (pp. 176, 185 ff.).

the apotheosis of the rococo made possible by its encounter with the genius of Mozart. A third horse-drawn conveyance implicit in the "folk song" of the postlude is the hearse that will carry Mozart's body to the grave. Thus the image of the carriage is associated with the story as a whole, with Mozart's journey through cultural history, artistic creation, and mortal existence. The description of the first carriage and of its passengers' dress constitutes a prelude introducing both the narrative as a whole and its first main section.

The first section, which begins with the stop at the edge of a Bohemian forest, is introduced by a new thematic image: "Indem sie sich beide erhoben, kam ein kleines Unheil an den Tag. . . . Durch seine Achtlosigkeit war ein Flakon mit kostbarem Riechwasser auf-gegangen und hatte seinen Inhalt unvermerkt in die Kleider und Polster ergossen" (1013). The theme of the ensuing conversations with Con-stanze is the heedless and aimless spilling of Mozart's personal, financial, and artistic resources, wasting his own substance but enriching and refreshing the era through which his life is racing away.[18] He has repeatedly allowed social pleasures to distract him from the considera-tions of prudence, self-preservation, and duty, "weil es dann immer galt, den glücklichen Moment *bis auf die Neige auszuschöpfen* (1017).[19] Indiscriminate generosity has again and again prompted him to lend money without security, and "am liebsten *schenkte* er gleich *hin* . . . , besonders wenn er meinte, gerade *Überfluss* zu haben" (1018). Con-stanze struggles valiantly to stop such drainage at its source, but "da *stieg ihr* wohl mitunter *das Wasser an die Kehle*" (1019). The survey of the problems of their life in Vienna in her conversations with Mozart in the carriage tempts Constanze to play "mit bunten *Seifenblasen* einer erträumten Zukunft" (1024), the new existence that might await them were Mozart to be offered a reportedly vacant musical directorship in Berlin. And in this soap-bubble-pipe dream there emerges the image of an ideal new Mozart, still fluid, but with all the substantiality he has lacked in Vienna, "rund und beleibt und *vif wie Quecksilber*" (1022).

The topical content of this section, the manifold problems, friction, tension, instability, and wastage of Mozart's personal and professional substance in the artificial environment of the Viennese rococo—a condi-tion nevertheless deriving in part also from his own temperament and from the existential situation of the artist in any age—emphasizes the

_____

[18] "Allmittelst geht und rennt und saust das Leben hin" (1016).
[19] Italics in quotations from Mörike's text are mine except where otherwise indi-cated.

negative implications of this drainage for Mozart as a human individual and for his and Constanze's domestic stability. But we are reminded that this same outpouring of resources has positive implications for Mozart's art, that the vital fluid pours into the spring of essential humanity that feeds the beautifully ordered fountain of Mozart's genius:

> Doch wissen wir, auch diese Schmerzen rannen abgeklärt und rein in jenem tiefen Quell zusammen, der, aus hundert goldenen Röhren springend, im Wechsel seiner Melodien unerschöpflich, alle Qual und alle Seligkeit der Menschenbrust ausströmte (1018).

This variant image of ordered flow points ahead to the next section of the narrative. Within the first section, however, the wanton outpouring of substance is contrasted with the theme of wanton but substantial growth symbolized in the firmly-rooted natural life which Mozart sees as he steps into the Bohemian forest. In another dimension the natural growth of the forest contrasts with the artificiality of rococo Vienna, and this latter antithesis is emphasized in Mozart's playful eulogy of the forest, singling out every aspect that distinguishes its organic vitality from the artificial society and culture, even from the theater and literature, with which his career is associated:

> Mir deucht, ich . . . besinne mich jetzt erst, was es doch heißt, ein ganzes Volk von Bäumen beieinander! Keine Menschenhand hat sie gepflanzt, sind alle selbst gekommen und stehen so, nur eben weil es lustig ist beisammen wohnen und wirtschaften.

He is amazed at the discovery:

> daß solches Wesen irgend existiert, nicht etwa nur so una finzione di poeti ist, wie ihre Nymphen, Faune und dergleichen mehr, auch kein Komödienwald, nein aus dem Erdboden herausgewachsen, von Feuchtigkeit und Wärmelicht der Sonne großgezogen! Hier ist zu Haus der Hirsch mit seinem wundersamen zackigen Gestäude auf der Stirn, das possierliche Eichhorn, der Auerhahn, der Häher.
> (1014)

How different, he remarks to Constanze, is this forest from the Prater, noisy with popular music and entertainments, its ground strewn with discarded corks, crammed with carriages, uniforms, robes, and fans. As we read on beyond this section, the natural forest will also become a point of reference to which we shall compare the carefully ordered and potted plantings of the Schinzberg park, the fields, vineyards, and vegetable plots of the idyll related by Constanze, and finally the young fir and rosebush of the "Bohemian folk song." Organic life, growth, and regeneration, in forest, park, garden, or graveyard, constitute a *leitmotif* that runs through the whole narrative and links all its parts with the unifying symbol of cultural growth and artistic generation, the orange tree. The forest at the beginning of the first section is comparable to the quiet and firmly-rooted but spontaneous natural growth of an organic human society and of an indigenous folk tradition (suggested in the images of animal life)—everything from which Mozart feels cut off by the wastage and breathless haste[20] of his career and the stylized artificiality of rococo society and culture.

The stop at the village inn and the description of the bed in which Constanze rests are a transition between the first and second sections. Mozart can be refreshed by a stop in the woods or by contact with simple, rustic craftsmanship, but the curtained rococo bed with its painted canopy and green lacquered posts affords rest only to Constanze.[21] Her husband walks into the park of the Schinzbergs; it is here that the new major section begins, again with images of growth and flow, but this time a growth that is painstakingly guided and nurtured by human hands and water that pours out in the artful symmetry of the fountain. An avenue of lindens, trees that are old and indigenous but planted in geometrical order, leads him to a scene of more exotic plantings: potted orange trees alternating with laurel and oleander, a trellised arbor. As he stops to enjoy the cooling refreshment and rhythmic movement of the fountain, the color, roundness, and fragrance of the oranges, this combination of rich tropical sensations with a symmetrical pattern of arching motion awakens the reminiscence of orange-colored balls flying back and forth between two barques on the Bay of Naples to the accompaniment of lively Italian melodies in a harmoniously resolved conflict of youthful love. The images and associations fuse into a spontaneous new musical conception, the theme for the rustic wedding dance of Zerlina and Masetto.[22]

We observe that the two thematic images of the first main section are retained in this second one, but with the chief stress shifted from flow to growth and the connotation of aimless spontaneity replaced by that of artistic direction and order. The waters that give and drain away life now pour through the jets of the fountain in man-made patterns.

---

[20] The polarity here is heightened by overtones of Goethe's "Schwager Kronos" in Mörike's remark to the coachman: "Deine Tiere, Schwager, mögen ein bißchen verschnaufen" (1013), as is pointed out by Farrell, p. 27.

[21] She is resting in this bed when Mozart conceives the theme of the rustic wedding dance, and we hear later that she was asleep in bed at home during the other instance of musical creation related in the story, the composition of the cemetery scene and the finale of Act Two.

[22] See above, note 9.

The potted orange tree with its nine fruits is an organic growth nurtured, transplanted, and revived by human care, symbolic of cultural growth originally rooted in the Italian renaissance, transplanted to the French baroque of Versailles, and from there to the German rococo. The water-pageant is an expression of youthful love, vitality, and rivalry on a beautiful natural bay, but it is also a mock drama in costumes of classical mythology, a baroque masque at a site of ancient Greek culture. All these traditions are given new life by the creative genius of Mozart. The thematic images of flow and growth are now in harmony rather than in conflict with each other. Viewed from the standpoint of Mozart's personal existence and professional career in the first section, his contact with rococo had appeared largely negative, a meaningless drainage of resources, and he had seen rococo society and his own life in that society as the antithesis of natural growth. But in the second section we view Mozart's contact with rococo from the standpoint of his artistic creation; the vital energies now flow out in the beautiful patterns given them by creative genius, and this genius is stimulated by stylized forms that, for all their frailty and artificial nurture, are nevertheless a living organic tradition of rich beauty. The fruit of this union between Mozart's genius and a frail, transplanted culture is a gay dance melody epitomizing the lightness and charm of all the elements in Mozart's music that can be contained within the graceful conventions of rococo style. The harmony of the encounter is simultaneously expressed in the human action of this part of the narrative: momentary embarrassment followed by warm hospitality, the gaiety and hearty humor with which the Count and his household react to Mozart's account of the adventure in the garden, the resourceful wit that makes it possible for Max to accommodate the stylized allegory of his poem to the new situation, Eugenie's ideal appreciation of Mozart's music, and the merriment with which the Mozarts and their aristocratic hosts join in toasting and in the improvising of humorous verse and song.

The orange tree is a "lebendes Symbol der feingeistigen Reize eines beinahe vergötterten Zeitalters" (1043), but since this was an age that delighted in classical myth and allegory, the tree must also be given allegorical identity as the golden apple tree of the Hesperides revived by the touch of Phoebus Apollo. The jesting presentation of this allegory in Max's poem causes it to lighten rather than weigh down the spirit of the narrative,[23] but taken in the same light spirit the allegory may still have some significance. The tree of the Hesperides is saved from death

---

[23] von Wiese, *Die deutsche Novelle,* p. 226.

and brought to fruition by Phoebus Apollo, the god of music, who dedicates one of its nine golden apples to Amor. If, as criticism sometimes suggests, we must assign an allegorical meaning to the plucking and cutting of one of these fruits, it had best be one in harmony with Max's myth. Divine genius does not destroy[24] but revives the tree. There can be no suggestion of the impending death of the plucking deity, for the genius of musical creation, Phoebus Amadeus Apollo, is immortal. If he has violated the convention of nine fruits dedicated to the Muses, he has done so for Amor, to give supreme musical expression to the innocent gaiety of youthful love. And we may ask whether even this immortal genius could have performed the miracle of bringing the dying tree to such beautiful fruition without transforming and transcending its conventions.

Turning from allegory back to symbol, however, we are reminded by the author that the almost deified age of baroque and rococo "schon eine unheilvolle Zukunft in sich trug, deren welterschütternder Eintritt . . . bereits nicht ferne mehr lag" (1043). The cataclysmic eruption of destructive social forces is delicately suggested in imagery as well, but in association with the fountain rather than the tree. For in the background of the fountain of arching orange balls on the Bay of Naples there lurks a dormant fountain of fire, and a jesting allusion to the gardener as a threatening Nemesis compares the terror he inspires in Mozart to that from the "rain of ashes" which Vesuvius might have poured down on the spectators and actors of the pageant (1040). Here we see illustrated the stylistic principle stressed by Mautner: Mörike's use of a comic context to mute tragic undertones and thus preserve—at all events in this part of the story—the over-all impression of good-humored gaiety.

A paragraph devoted to the "peak of social pleasure"—everyone joining in gay dancing as Mozart implants kisses on the lips of both Eugenie and Franziska—leads over to the third part of the story. Just before sunset the gentlemen withdraw to the billiard room, and the ladies go out into an informal part of the Schinzberg park to enjoy the coolness of evening and the view from a vine-clad hill out over the fields toward

---

[24] This negative interpretation is suggested by Walter Heinsius, "Mörike und die Romantik," *Deutsche Vierteljahresschrift für Literaturwissenschaft und Geistesgeschichte*, III (1925), 228 f.; by Hermann Pongs, "Ein Beitrag zum Dämonischen im Biedermeier," *Dichtung und Volkstum*, XXXVI (1935), 253 ff.; to some extent also by Farrell, p. 26. An interpretation closer to the spirit of Mörike is suggested by Bernhard Seuffert, *Mörikes Nolten und Mozart* (Graz, Wien, Leipzig, 1924), p. 32: "Mozarts Leichtigkeit des Schaffens [wird] dadurch bedeutet, daß die Pomeranze, nach der er versonnen greift, sich vom Zweige löst und ihm in der Hand bleibt; so fällt ihm eine Melodie zu."

the village. This setting prepares us for the new variant in which the organic growth image of the first two sections is now to appear: the rustic increase of cultivated fields. But in this section the produce of field, garden, and vineyard will for the most part be represented indirectly through the thematic image of the simple artifact used in their cultivation and in the household of a patriarchal agrarian society. The ladies enjoying the rural view hear Constanze relate the history that makes one such implement that is "anything but an article of luxury and fashion" (1049) significant for Mozart and a fitting gift from the domain of rustic *crescentia* (Kreszenz) to Eugenie, the bride of noble birth. The second part of the story has symbolized the contribution of rococo culture to Mozart's creative genius in a beautiful living tree that had become frail and artificially stylized. In this third part, the contribution of Mozart's human spirit to aristocratic rococo is presented in the form of a homely and lifeless utensil which, like its inorganic content, "noble salt," can become a durable "symbol of domesticity and hospitality" (1060).

Mozart purchased this saltcellar along with other household and garden implements on his excursion to the village inn and shop of a master ropemaker. In their totality they embody the essential human qualities of honest simplicity and firm substantiality that Mozart missed in rococo society and in his own life as an artisan of a very different kind:

> Ist aber mir mit meiner Kunst ein anderes Tagwerk anbefohlen, das ich am Ende doch mit keinem in der Welt vertauschen würde: warum muß ich dabei in Verhältnissen leben, die das gerade Widerspiel von solch unschuldiger, einfacher Existenz ausmachen? Ein Gütchen wenn du hättest, ein kleines Haus bei einem Dorf in schöner Gegend, du solltest wahrlich neu aufleben! ((1054)

Ittenbach has shown that this third section resembles the first in its expression of Mozart's yearning for a life more natural and stable than either his temperament or the social setting of his career permitted.[25] However, the polarity no longer takes the form of direct conflict and negation. Whereas in the first part Mozart was seen yearning for something actively denied him by his cultural era, we now observe him aspiring after something which the rococo cannot give him but which he in a certain sense can attain and present to the rococo. Indeed, the very negative elements of his own human temperament that before had resulted in a draining away of his resources now indirectly lead to his acquisition of firm substance. Restlessness, the craving for sociability, even the erotic side of his temperament and the unstable physical and

---

[25] *GRM,* XXV, 348 ff.

nervous constitution that worries his physician, all result in the new
practice of walks to the country and in the quarrel with Constanze
occasioning the particular half-day excursion to the ropemaker's shop.
Mozart's observations and personal contacts at this shop bring out the
warm sympathy for fundamental human concerns expressed symbolically
in the articles he buys there and realized practically in his benefit
concert to make possible the marriage of the ropemaker's young cousin
Kreszenz.

To be sure, Mozart's yearning for a simple patriarchal existence of
his own cannot be realized. To this extent there is an ironic aspect to
the rustic idyll,[26] an irony delicately suggested by the inappropriateness
or uselessness of some of these utensils for the Mozart household: We
smile at the interest the delicate composer displays in a stick intended
for the butcher driving livestock to the slaughter. Nor will Constanze
have use for the garden tools which her husband buys her, for she has
long since abandoned the little plot on the river Wien where her
attempts to raise asparagus had been foiled by water damage (1059)—
the stream that sustains an enduring rustic society only washes away
agrarian efforts of the Mozart household![27] But if Mozart cannot make
this aspect of human experience part of his own life, the warm sympathy
displayed in his constructive activity for Kreszenz is instilled in his music,
giving it the timeless, universal humanity which he could never have
found in his immediate cultural and social environment.

This section contains some additional variants of its thematic image,
the solid artifact, with more than fortuitous symbolic connotations.
When his doctor first recommended walking, Mozart sought out a cane
inherited from his father. For some weeks he was fascinated, first by
this and then by a succession of other walking sticks acquired in the hope
that with these tokens of upper-middle-class respectability he might also
take on something of the diligence, order, composure, and self-satisfac-
tion manifest in such worthies as his neighbor the *Kommerzienrat*. The
brief duration of the walking-stick hobby shows that this stolid kind of
substantiality was alien to Mozart, a fact underscored also by his learn-
ing, just at this time, of the humiliating comparison of his face to that
of a fat little pig by Signora Malerbi, the Circe who had been "keeping
him hot on her spit" for some months (1051 f.). That the utensils of a
patriarchal rustic economy have a positive significance for Mozart quite

---

[26] Ittenbach overstresses the negative ironic significance of the episode, p. 350.
[27] In this sole instance of the flow image in the third section it carries a negative
sign, as it does everywhere in the story in its application to Mozart's personal, human
existence as distinguished from his artistic creation.

unlike the canes is suggested by the happy surprise he experiences on his way home from the ropemaker's shop: The postman hands him a heavy parcel of gold pieces from Prince Esterhazy accompanied by a letter from Haydn, through whose auspices the gift comes. The very resources that we have seen most wantonly spilled out in the first part of the story are carried back to Mozart's door in ideally substantial form after his refreshing contact with a simpler, more natural society. Moreover, this turn of fortune has been made possible by an artist whose work exemplifies the links between genius and craftsmanship and whose personality embodies the patriarchal stability for which Mozart yearns.[28]

The artifacts of the third section illustrate most strikingly a theme running through the whole story: the gift that at once honors and strengthens ties of love and friendship. The saltcellar is introduced as a wedding gift for Eugenie, and it was purchased, together with the garden tools, in a gesture of reconciliation and atonement toward Constanze. The delivery of these gifts by Kreszenz inspires Mozart with the idea of his all-important gift for her, the benefit concert, and the purchase of them is followed by the gift to Mozart from Esterhazy. The theme of the whole third section is Mozart's gift of warm, substantial humanity to a culture inclined toward empty formalism. The giving of the first section takes the form of an indiscriminate generosity which seems wantonly squandered on the individual recipients but nevertheless refreshes the whole environment and contributes indirectly to the supreme gifts of Mozart's musical genius. In the second section the orange branch presented to Eugenie's ancestress by Mme de Sévigné, the hospitality presented to Mozart and Constanze by the Schinzbergs, Eugenie's gift of ideal appreciation to Mozart, his presentation of a fresh musical creation to her, even the unwitting contribution of the tree to the apotheosis of youthful love—all are cultural gifts, symbolizing the transmission and interchange of cultural and artistic values; as such they are summed up in the gift presented to Mozart at the end of the fourth section, a carriage of ideal grace and beauty (which is therefore not described). While the fourth section itself is also concerned with gifts, they are of a different order, from superhuman sources.

The gifts of the second and third sections are nearly all, in one sense or another, wedding presents. The autograph manuscript of the rustic wedding song and the saltcellar are wedding presents from Mozart to Eugenie; they also link her aristocratic wedding with two peasant wed-

---

[28] See Ittenbach, *GRM*, XXV, 350: "das Geordnete, Gesunde, Einfache, als dessen Verkörperung Haydn hier erscheint."

dings, those of Kreszenz and the locksmith in the narrative and of Zerlina and Masetto in the opera.[29] But the most important wedding celebrated in *Mozart auf der Reise nach Prag* is that of the genius and humanity of Mozart with the elegance and grace of the rococo.

The thematic images of the second and third sections have been centered in individual tangible objects expressly termed symbolic by the author, the orange tree and the saltcellar. The flow and growth images of the first section are more general in character, at times clearly symbolical, as in the instances of the forest, the spilled perfume, and the fountain, at other times figures of speech which implicitly remind us of the guiding themes. We have observed also the continuing symbolic function of the fountain in association with the orange tree, and that of growth in fields, vineyards, and gardens associated with the artifacts. The fourth section returns to symbolic imagery of a more general character; its principal thematic image, consuming flame, appears in the opening paragraph in two forms, applying respectively to Don Juan and to Mozart:

> Es war schon fast acht Uhr; man nahm den Tee. Bald aber sah sich unser Musiker an sein schon am Mittag gegebenes Wort, die Gesellschaft näher mit dem *"Höllenbrand"* bekannt zu machen, . . . dringend erinnert. Er war ohne Zögern bereit. . . . Das Textbuch wurde aufgeschlagen, und schon *brannten die Lichter* am Fortepiano. (1060)

After a brief presentation of numbers from other parts of the opera, Mozart turns to the music directly associated with hell-fire, the cemetery scene and finale, and then through the remainder of this section the infernal flames avenging the sin and defiance of Don Juan are accompanied by the fire of superhuman inspiration, illuminating the musical creation and steadily consuming the life of the creator, that is symbolized in the candle flame. Like the principal thematic images of the two preceding sections,[30] the candle flame links present and past—the late evening at the Schinzberg castle in which Mozart plays the music of the cemetery scene and finale and the late evening at home a few weeks before when, in Mörike's fictitious account, he created it. He had returned home that evening from a dinner to find a package on his desk containing Da Ponte's manuscript libretto for these two tragic scenes.[31] When

---

[29] There are indirect associations with two other bridal couples in the opera, both aristocratic: Anna and Ottavio will wed in spite of Don Juan's "gift" of murder; his own broken vows and infidelity prevent his marriage to Elvira.

[30] See von Wiese, *Die deutsche Novelle*, p. 231, and Taraba, *op. cit.*, pp. 180 ff.

[31] There is a certain parallel between this parcel post and the one from Haydn in the third section. Haydn is the channel for a gift from a socially higher human

he came to the statue's threat to Don Juan in the cemetery, "Your laughter will end before dawn," he struck a chord and felt that he had knocked on the gate that would let loose the "legion of terrors" in the finale; at this point in his narration in the castle, he extinguishes the candles at the piano and lets sound out through the deathly silence the terrifying chords of the apocalyptic *Posaunen* in his score (1063 f.).[32] Mozart tells the company in the Schinzberg salon that he composed this music and almost the entire finale "in *einer* Hitze fort."[33] But when the task was not quite finished, he thought of the unrest he would feel in the grave were he to die at that moment, and fixed his glance "am Docht des Lichts in meiner Hand und auf den Bergen von abgetropftem Wachs." It occurred to him that a lesser composer, finding the nearly complete score, might try to finish it and take credit for the whole. "Er sollte aber wohl die Finger dran verbrennen" (1065).

We have already noted that the fire image of the fourth section was anticipated and fused with the earlier image of outpouring liquid in the second section, when Mozart thought of the potential volcanic fountain pouring out a rain of ashes from Vesuvius. In that anticipation he had also implicitly linked his own peril with the fate of Don Juan, for the gardener compared there to Vesuvius was also a "Satan," his "face like bronze," making things "hot" for Mozart (1040). There are additional associations of fire with water in and after the fourth section. The sensations with which we hear the terrifying music of Don Juan's retribution in the finale are likened to the terrified awe with which we witness the burning of a splendid ship at sea (1064 f.). Afterwards Eugenie feels the certainty "daß dieser Mann sich schnell und unaufhalt-sam in seiner eigenen Glut verzehre, . . . weil [die Erde] den Überfluß, den er verströmen würde, in Wahrheit nicht ertrüge" (1068). But the antithetical complement of the fire image in the fourth section is ice. The chords of the fateful *Posaunen* that we hear when Mozart puts out the candles fall "eiskalt, Mark und Seele durchschneidend, herunter durch die blaue Nacht"; the creative drive that carried Mozart from these chords through the composition of the finale was like a crack in the ice

---

source, Prince Esterhazy; this part of Da Ponte's libretto is the channel for inspira-tion given Mozart from a source beyond the reach of human comprehension.

[32] Mozart uses the modern trombone to express musically the connotations of the ancient instrument of the Apocalypse called *Posaune* in Luther's Bible, *trumpet* in English Bibles. Musical productions sometimes maintain the supernatural effect of these chords by placing the instruments that produce them back in the wings, out of sight of the audience. Mörike too has in mind here both the trombone and its apocalyptic prototype. Cf. Mautner, p. 37, and my article "Apocalyptic Trumpets: The Inception of *Mozart auf der Reise nach Prag*," *PMLA*, LXX (1955), 396, 401.

[33] Italics here are from the source.

at a single point spreading over the entire surface of a lake (1064). It is as though the flames that consume the lives of titanic sinner and sublime genius alike are coupled with the chilling mystery that awaits their souls beyond death.[34]

In the imagination of Mörike, transcendent artistic genius and demonically destructive energy appear as gifts from a single realm beyond human comprehension, in either case exacting a price in human life, even though we assume the source to be divine in one case and infernal in the other. The association of the opera's hero, Don Juan, with the story's hero, Mozart, in this part of the narrative is at times so close as almost to justify the words of one critic, "Mozart wird Don Juan selbst."[35] The section as a whole leaves the impression of a translation into literary terms of the music of the cemetery scene and finale. There are also parallels in the structural relation of the corresponding portions of opera and novella to the respective wholes. The tragic section of *Don Giovanni* occupies approximately the second half of Act Two, corresponding to the position of the fourth main section in Mörike's narrative. In both instances the impact of the tragic sections is offset by bright or humorous elements in the work as a whole, in the parts immediately preceding these sections, in the brief concluding passages that follow them, and in interruptions of the tragic continuity (in the opera, the brief lyric scene devoted to the love of Donna Anna and Ottavio that separates the cemetery scene from the finale; in the narrative, Mozart's presentation of other, more lyric numbers of the score between his first mention of the "hell-fire" music and his account of its composition).

But the spirit and structure of the opera are also reflected in another part of Mörike's *Novelle*. The second section, accounting for the conception of the rustic wedding theme, resembles the sequence of scenes in the opera from Don Juan's meeting with the rustic youths and maidens as they sing this melody through the finale of Act One. In either instance we have a second of four main parts which is nevertheless more than a quarter of the whole. Obvious differences in the action of the libretto and the narrative need not conceal similarities in both situation

---

[34] For the connotations of icy cold in Mörike's personal religious experience, cf. my "Apocalyptic Trumpets," *PMLA*, LXX, 398.

[35] Gertrude Lenhardt, "Mörikes Märchen und Novellen," *Zeitschrift für deutsche Bildung*, X (1934), 359. Cf. also Bernhard Seuffert (*op. cit.*, p. 34): "Viel mehr ist er der Don Juan, dessen Vollnatur alle besticht, . . . der seinen Lebenstrieb auslebt, der die Selbstvernichtung der freiwilligen Aufgabe auch des kleinsten Teiles seiner Kraft vorzieht."

and spirit. Don Juan comes upon Zerlina, Masetto, and their friends as they are preparing to celebrate their wedding in a country village; he invites them to celebrate the festivities in his own adjacent gardens and mansion. Mozart wanders from a village into the gardens of a household about to celebrate a betrothal, and he is invited to take part in the festivities in the castle. The intruder, who is host in the opera, guest in the narrative, plays the dominant part in the ensuing festivities. Although the relative social position of intruder to celebrators is reversed, in both story and opera the intruder is from a higher cultural plane, and this superiority makes a particularly deep impression on the respective brides. In the opera the continuity of the festivities is interrupted by the additional intrusion of Elvira, Anna, and Ottavio, who suspect that Don Juan is the murderer of the commandatore. Later a tragic end to the festivities is threatened by Don Juan's attempt on Zerlina and Ottavio's effort to punish him. But the act ends with everyone unscathed, so that for the most part the action in this part of the libretto is a sequence of gay feasting, song, dance, and sociability, just as in the second section of Mörike's narrative. Disturbing elements are also present in the latter, even though less conspicuous than in the libretto: the threatening figure of the gardener near the beginning of the section and the author's reminder, near the end, of the disaster impending over the rococo era. But on the whole, the spirit of Mörike's novella in this section is even closer to Mozart's music than it is to Da Ponte's libretto. The predominantly gay and festive character of the score, in which the graceful minuet of the instrumentalists on the stage is repeated even at the tensest moments of the vocal dialogue, almost completely overshadows the tragic elements in this longest continuous sequence of the opera. The bright rococo spirit of the music in this section also acts as a counterpoise to the intense tragedy of both music and action in the finale of Act Two.

The asymmetrical concentration of the greatest length, most elaborate symbolism, and most crucial action in the second of four main parts of Mörike's novella is thus partially conditioned by the example of the opera. Mozart had to present the tragic destiny of Don Juan in a work that in its totality was to exemplify the spirit of opera buffa. Mörike had to point ahead to the tragic destiny of Mozart in a narrative celebrating the happy union of his genius with the graceful forms of the rococo. The very opera with which his story was concerned helped him to accomplish his own analogous artistic mission. However, the parallels are largely confined to the two sections of the story directly concerned with the creation of the opera,[36] and they are of course limited by differences in the media and the artistic personalities of composer and author. In general, Mörike commands a narrower range than Mozart and works with less extreme contrasts. Mörike's prose beautifully characterizes the tragic impact of Mozart's music in Act Two of the opera, but he could not and would not emulate directly the tragic intensity of this music. His humor, too, is less robust than the musical humor of Mozart, and of course far removed from the buffoonery of Da Ponte; his novella could therefore not accommodate the rough comedy of a Leporello.

Taking as his principal theme Mozart's fruitful encounter with rococo elegance, Mörike constructed a symbolic plot around the fiction of the orange episode and made some effort to frame this episode symmetrically. But he could not do justice to the whole genius of Mozart or even to its manifestation in *Don Giovanni* within any such symmetrical frame. The solution was a four-part composition alternating between Mozart as a human personality and Mozart as a creative genius. The first two sections present Mozart in his encounter with the rococo, showing how it wastes his human resources but bears splendid fruit in that part of his musical creation which was adaptable to rococo style. The last two sections present the Mozart whose warm humanity transcends the limits of rococo and whose tragic genius transcends human comprehension. The balance of gaiety and tragedy, harmony and conflict pervading Mörike's narrative is symbolized within each part in a pair of thematic images: spilling liquid and spontaneous growth, the artfully nurtured tree and the symmetrically ordered fountain, solid handicraft and agrarian cultivation, consuming fire and icy cold. All four parts of the composition employ a technique of thematic balance and interaction, variation and development that is in a measure analogous to music; and the two parts concerned with the creation of *Don Giovanni* reflect the particular structural influence of this opera. Mörike could not represent the meeting of Mozart and the rococo on their journeys through history as a perfect union, but he could celebrate it as an auspicious cultural wedding, rich in gifts for Mozart, for his age, and for mankind.

---

[36] One might perhaps compare the restlessness and heedless extravagance of Mozart in the first part of the narrative to Leporello's statistical account of the erotic career of Don Juan, Mozart's contacts with peasantry in the third part to Don Juan's assumption of Leporello's role in the first half of Act Two. But I see no resemblance between the general character of Mozart's music at these points in the opera and the respective elegiac and idyllic qualities of Mörike's first and third sections.

Faust Ohne Transzendenz:
Theodor Storms *Schimmelreiter*

by ERNST LOEB

EINE Ähnlichkeit der Thematik in Goethes *Faust* und Storms
Schimmelreiter darf als Tatsache angenommen werden und läßt sich
daher als Ausgangspunkt unserer Untersuchungen rechtfertigen. Bio-
graphisch lassen sich die unverkennbaren *Faust*-Spuren mit Storms
starkem *Faust*-Interesse in der unmittelbaren Entstehungszeit des
Schimmelreiters in Verbindung bringen,[1] und im einzelnen hat schon
Silz auf weitgehende Parallelen und charakteristische Abweichungen
aufmerksam gemacht.[2] Wie der Faust des zweiten Teils, nimmt auch
Hauke Haien den Kampf mit dem Element auf und entringt dem
zurückgedrängten Meere fruchtbaren Boden—auch er im scheinbaren
Bunde mit unheimlichen und für "teuflisch" gehaltenen Mächten, auch
er mit gewaltsamen, oft tyrannischen Mitteln. Wie Faust ist auch er von
der Unvergänglichkeit seines Nachruhms überzeugt, obgleich ihm—ein
bedeutsamer Unterschied—das hohe Glück des "Vorgefühls" versagt
bleibt, das Fausts letzten Augenblick zugleich zu seinem "höchsten"
macht (11585-86).[3] Und wie bei Faust werden auch in Hauke Haiens
Lebenswerk, obgleich hier wie dort auf das Gemeinwohl gerichtet, die
Spuren einer Zwiespältigkeit offenbar, die wir in der Doppelseele beider

---

[1] Siehe Robert Pitrou, "Storm et Goethe," *Études publiées pour le centenaire
de sa mort par l'Université de Strasbourg* (Paris, 1932), S. 463. Siehe auch S. 468
über Storms besondere Vorliebe für den zweiten Teil des *Faust*: ". . . décidément,
c'est l'oeuvre préférée de Storm."
[2] Walter Silz, *Realism and Reality. Studies in the German Novelle of Poetic
Realism*, University of North Carolina Studies in Germanic Languages and Literatures, XI (1954), 121.
[3] Die auf *Faust* bezüglichen Zitate folgen Band III der Hamburger Ausgabe,
hg. von Erich Trunz, 3. Auflage (Hamburg, 1957). Die arabischen Nummern
bezeichnen jeweils die Zeilenzahl.

verankert wissen. Wie Goethe stellt uns auch Storm die Gewalttätigkeit seines Helden dar und "verhindert durch die Unterstreichung des Ehrgeizes, daß wir den Bau des Deiches nur als Ausdruck edler Gesinnung nehmen."[4] Wenn aber den Schimmelreiter nicht das Schicksal einer endlichen "Erlösung" erwartet, die Doppelnatur seiner irdischen Existenz vielmehr durch die Doppelzüngigkeit seines Nachruhms ins Unendliche verlängert wird,[5] scheint uns hier eine aufschlußreiche Abweichung vorzuliegen, die eine nähere Betrachtung der unterschiedlichen Schicksale und ihrer tieferen Gründe nahelegt.

Storms *Schimmelreiter* als eine in spätere Zeit projizierte, um ein halbes Jahrhundert hinausgeschobene *Faust*-Thematik! Dabei ist es nur natürlich, daß die äußeren Dimensionen—auch der Faustgestalt selbst—"zeitgemäße" Einbußen erleiden mußten. Aber eben nur die äußeren Dimensionen, nicht die eigentlichen Konturen dieser Gestalt, die auch dann deutlich bleiben, wenn Hauke Haiens Wissens- und Erfahrensdrang nicht auf Wesen und inneren Zusammenhang der Welt, sondern eben nur *seiner* Welt gerichtet, seine Erlebnissphäre statt der "groß und kleinen Welt" auf jene kleinste Welt eines friesischen Dorfes beschränkt bleibt. Auch wenn man dem "Unbehausten" und großen Einzelgänger Faust den offenbar so ganz anders gearteten Stormschen Familienmenschen entgegenstellen möchte, kann der tiefere Grund dieser verzweifelt gesuchten Bindung nicht übersehen werden: eine wachsende Vereinsamung, die immer deutlicher als unabwendbares Schicksal empfunden wird. So wird denn dieser Einsame, im Gegensatz zu Faust, in "unbehauster" Todesstunde vergeblich die Hände nach einer Liebe ausstrecken, die ihre Transzendenz, und damit ihre erlösende Kraft, verloren hat. Unüberbrückbar, auch für die Liebe, ist die durch den gnadenlosen Triumph der Elemente aufgerissene Kluft, die Mann und Weib ihrem einsamen Untergang überantwortet: Zerweht ihre Worte, ihre ausgestreckten Arme eine klägliche Geste der Vergeblichkeit, denn "von ihr zu ihm, von ihm zu ihr waren die Worte all verloren," und alle Fragen "blieben ohne Antwort" (374).

Auch in der Liebe, für den jungen Storm noch verpflichtendes Gottesgeschenk und ein Auftrag, durch dessen getreuliche Erfüllung sich der Mensch des Lohnes einer eigenen Unsterblichkeit würdig

---

[4] Wolfgang Kayser, *Bürgerlichkeit und Stammestum in Theodor Storms Novellendichtung* (Berlin, 1938), S. 48.

[5] "Bei den Drachen" sollen derlei Geschichten nach der Meinung des neuen Deichgrafen "am besten in Verwahrung sein," Theodor Storm, *Sämtliche Werke in acht Bänden*, hg. von Albert Köster (Leipzig, 1920), VII, 256. Alle auf den *Schimmelreiter* bezüglichen Zitate folgen dieser Ausgabe. Die arabischen Nummern beziehen sich auf die Seitenzahl von Band VII, 252–377.

erzeigen kann, klafft eine Tiefe, "die unerschöpflich ist." Dem alten
Dichter erscheint sie nur mehr ein Schleier, durch den ihm, "solange er
glücklich war, die trostlose Nacktheit des irdischen Seins verhüllt wurde."
Verloren ist der Zusammenhang mit dem Ewigen und damit ihre Unsterblichkeit. Was bleibt, ist "das hilflose Bemühen des Menschen, die
trostlose Kälte einer Wirklichkeit zu durchwärmen, in der alles Schöne
und Edle der Vernichtung preisgegeben ist."[6] Hatte an Fausts Erlösung
". . . die Liebe gar von oben teilgenommen" (11939-40), so daß ihm der
Willkommengruß der Ewigkeit winkt, der er sich, ein Liebender im
Reich der ewigen Liebe, verbindet, so wird sich des Schimmelreiters
ungeeinte Zwienatur auch in alle Ewigkeit erhalten. Ehrsucht und
Haß, die schon "in seinem jungen Herzen neben der Ehrenhaftigkeit und
der Liebe" gewachsen waren (299), das aus widerstrebender Achtung
und abergläubischer Scheu gemischte Bild seiner Zeitgenossen, wirken
fort in dem zögernden, mehr aus Angst als Dankbarkeit gewährten
Nachruhm, der sein Werk zwar preist, ihn selbst aber für alle Ewigkeit
zum "Spuk und Nachtgespenst" macht (376).

Der Entwertung der Liebe entspricht ein ähnlicher Wandel des
"strebenden Bemühens" als der zweiten Erlösungsmöglichkeit des
Schimmelreiters. War der faustische Widerstreit des aufwärtsgerichteten
Strebens und eines der Welt "mit klammernden Organen" verhafteten
Willens (1115) noch auf eine wandellose, in allen Irrungen des Weges
unveränderte Zielvorstellung gerichtet, so ist nun Zweifel an die Stelle
der Zielklarheit, Kompromißbereitschaft an die Stelle der Weggewißheit
getreten.[7] Von einem verlorenen, oder doch ins Ungreifbare gerückten,
Ewigkeitsglauben ist bei Storm nur mehr "das eigene Verlangen des
Dichters" übriggeblieben,[8] das aus verlorener Gewißheit um eine letzte
Verankerung im Unbegreiflichen ringt: kein Glaube, sondern ein
Glauben-Wollen, dessen brave Entschlossenheit sich immer aufs Neue
dem nagenden Wurm des Zweifels ausgesetzt fühlt.

Finden wir aber bei Hauke Haien auch die Perspektive verengt,
dem Weltbild Storms entsprechend auf das Irdisch-Gegenwärtige bezo-
gen, so bleiben doch die wesensbestimmenden Merkmale des "faustischen" Menschen: "Urgewalt der Verbindung von Menschentragik und

---

[6] Harry Sievers, "Storms Gedanken über Unsterblichkeit und Tod in ihrem inneren Zusammenhang," *Schriften der Theodor-Storm-Gesellschaft*, V (1956), 26, 30, 31.

[7] Siehe dazu auch Silz, *op. cit.*, 122: "Conversely to Faust, he meets disaster by ceasing to strive, by lying down for one fatal instant on the 'Faulbett' of compromise."

[8] Sievers, *op. cit.*, 22.

wildem Naturgeheimnis" erkennt Thomas Mann in dieser Gestalt,[9] ein Willensmenschentum, das sich aus eigener Kraft neue und eigene Aufgaben stellt. Im Kontrast zu Storms früheren Novellengestalten steht hier "ein Wirkender und Schaffender" vor uns, ein Fertiger, "von vornherein geprägt," von dem Stuckert sagt: "Er entwickelt sich nicht, sondern wächst nur in größere und weitere Zusammenhänge hinein."[10]

"Ehrenhaftigkeit und Liebe" sind die Beweggründe seines gemeinnützigen Strebens, in dem wir die vertrauten Züge einer faustischen Vision erkennen: "Welch treffliches Weide- und Kornland mußte es geben und von welchem Werte, wenn das alles von seinem neuen Deich umgeben war! Wie ein Rausch stieg es ihm ins Gehirn," und trotz aller Schwierigkeiten, die seinem klaren Verstande nur zu bewußt waren— "als er vom Deich hinab und den Fußsteig über die Fennen auf seine Werfte zuging, ihm war's, als brächte er einen großen Schatz mit sich nach Hause" (311). Es ist ein gutgerichtetes, ein ethisches Streben, denn vielleicht ist "der größte Lebenswert der Ethik eben der, daß sie ein Gebiet ist, wo es bestimmte Gemeinschaften gibt, ein Gebiet, wo die ewige Einsamkeit aufhört. . . . Die Ethik zwingt jedem Menschen das Gefühl der Gemeinsamkeit auf. Wenn schon anders nicht, so doch gewiß durch das Erkennen der unmittelbaren und berechenbaren Nützlichkeit, der vollbrachten Arbeit . . ."[11]

Doch ist es auch hier der Wille, der dem befreienden Zug zu menschlicher Gemeinsamkeit den dämonischen Drang der Selbstverwirklichung entgegenstellt, eine Dämonie der Selbstsucht, deren abgründiges Dunkel, selbst der Geliebten verborgen (299), auch die verderbliche Flamme des Hasses birgt. Wie bei Faust ist also auch bei ihm das gemeinnützige Anliegen des Deichbaus von einer Hybris der Selbstüberhebung durchtränkt, die sich zum Wettkampf mit den dämonischelementaren Mächten des gleichgearteten Meeres aufgerufen fühlt.

Von "kühnem Fleiß" hatte Faust gesprochen (10184), dem, sehr im Gegensatz zu Goethes Naturfrommheit, die "zwecklose Kraft unbändiger Elemente" nur "Verdrossenheit" und "Mißbehagen des Gefühls" bereitet. Kein anmutiger Anblick mehr ist ihm die Meereswoge, an der er nur den nutzlosen Aufwand verspielter Kräfte zu tadeln weiß. Groß und gut erscheint der Plan, hier nützlich wirkend Wandel zu schaffen, trüge er dem Ursprung nach nicht die unverkennbaren Züge

---

[9] Thomas Mann, "Theodor Storm," *Adel des Geistes* (Stockholm, 1948), S. 509.
[10] Franz Stuckert, *Theodor Storm. Sein Leben und seine Welt* (Bremen, 1955), S. 404, 405.
[11] Georg von Lukacs, "Bürgerlichkeit und l'art pour l'art: Theodor Storm," *Die Seele und die Formen. Essays* (Berlin, 1911), S. 125.

der faustischen Doppelseele. Und wie er dem "herrischen" Meer das "köstliche Genießen" des eigenen herrischen Willens entgegensetzen, "Herrschaft" und "Eigentum" gewinnen will (10187-10233), so auch Hauke Haien: Ein "zorniges Lachen" entrang sich ihm, wenn er als Knabe dem tobenden Treiben der Wasser zusah. "Ihr könnt nichts Rechtes," schrie er in hohnvoller Überlegenheit in Wind und Wetter hinaus, "sowie die Menschen auch nichts können!" (261). Schon der Knabe empfindet: Beiden, dem Meer und "den Menschen," wird er sein Lebenswerk abtrotzen, gegen beide es behaupten müssen.

In Wahreit wird er nicht eigentlich zwei Feinde haben, sondern nur *einen*: Ist doch der irrationale, stumpf-kreatürliche Unverstand nur die in die menschliche Sphäre übertragene Kehrseite der elementaren, widervernünftigen Dämonie der Naturgewalten.[12] Beides in seiner Zusammenwirkung aber stellt jene überdimensionale Macht des Irrationalen, des Abgründigen und Daseinsbedrohenden dar, der er den eigenen Verwirklichungswillen entgegensetzen muß, die eigene Willensdämonie, die sich an der klaren Überlegenheit seines Geistes und der visionären Kraft des Bildes entzündet, dessen Konturen ihm unverrückbar vor Augen stehen. Eine Willensdämonie mit klarer, vernunftbestimmter Ausrichtung—darin liegt kein Widerspruch: Denn das Dämonische, das in der Sphäre der äußeren Natur "nicht böse, nicht teuflisch ist, nur übermächtig und unmenschlich," ist ja, wie Goethes "Urworte" bekräftigen, "in der Sphäre des Menschlichen . . . der kosmische Ursprung des Individuellen."[13]

Der Konflikt, den beispielsweise Fritz Böttger dogmatisch auf einen "Gegensatz von rationalistischer Einstellung zur Arbeit und traditionalistischem Schlendrian" reduziert,[14] stellt sich in Wirklichkeit als ein überzeugendes Beispiel dessen dar, was für Wolfgang Kayser der vielleicht "reinste Ausdruck der Bürgerlichkeit" bei Theodor Storm ist: Immer wieder muß "der Bezirk des persönlichen Glückes" gegen ein "gefährliches, unberechenbares, unheimliches Draußen" abgeschirmt werden,[15] unberechenbar vor allem, weil in ihm ja auch die Schicksalsmächte beheimatet sind. Und eben weil diese Mächte von außen kommen, folgert Lukacs, "muß das Schicksal stehen bleiben auf der

---

[12] Siehe dazu auch Silz, *op. cit.*, 120.
[13] Paul Hankamer, *Spiel der Mächte. Ein Kapitel aus Goethes Leben und Goethes Welt* (Tübingen und Stuttgart, 1948), S. 312, 124. Siehe dazu auch Hans Joachim Schrimpf, *Das Weltbild des späten Goethe. Überlieferung und Bewahrung in Goethes Alterswerk* (Stuttgart, 1956), S. 308: "Der Dämon also ist das individuelle Müssen, der von der Natur ausgesprochene Zwang, so und nicht anders zu sein."
[14] Fritz Böttger, *Theodor Storm in seiner Zeit* (Leipzig, o. J.), S. 355.
[15] Kayser, *op. cit.*, S. 26.

Schwelle des Hauses in dem die Seele wohnt, und kann niemals dort eintreten"; es "widerfährt den Menschen," die es nicht selbst heraufbeschwören. Schuld und Unschuld aber, sowie "der Wert, der Unterschiede einsetzt zwischen den Menschen, offenbart sich in der Antwort der Menschen an das Unentrinnbare."[16] Hauke Haiens rationale Antwort an diese Mächte des Irrationalen, sein Versuch, sich und die Seinen abzuschirmen gegen die tragische Unentrinnbarkeit ihres Vordringens, sein Kampf und Unterliegen im Ringen um Lebenssinn und Selbstbehauptung: das ist der tiefste Sinn dieser Novelle.

Mit kühler Entschlossenheit aus heißem Herzen, ein "Rechner" aus Anlage und Besessenheit, nimmt er den Kampf auf. Schon sein Vater, der an langen Winterabenden zu Hause saß und "maß und berechnete" (257), war ja "der klügste Mann im Dorf" gewesen (282, 299), und Hauke selbst, der sich in einsamer und lernbegieriger Abgeschlossenheit von den Schulkameraden seinen Euklid erarbeitet, wird uns immer wieder als "Rechner" geschildert: Die Deicharbeit seiner Knabenzeit kann ihn nicht von der "Denkarbeit" ablenken (260), er sitzt, nach den anerkennenden Worten des alten Deichgrafen, "lieber vor der Rechentafel als vor einem Glas mit Branntwein" (273), in seinem Dienst soll er zeigen, daß er rechnen kann (275), und selbst in Elkes Gegenwart finden wir ihn "in seine Rechnerei vertieft" (276). Als Deichgraf wird er "vertieft in Rechenaufgaben, Zeichnungen und Rissen" seine Sonntagnachmittage, Feierabende und oft den größten Teil der Nacht verbringen (313), selbst "sein eigen Christentum" hat er sich "zurecht gerechnet" (335) und sein Gebet, das sich in Elkes schwerer Erkrankung an einen allweisen, aber eben deshalb nicht allmächtigen Gott richtet, entspringt der Vorstellung einer vernunftgegründeten Ordnung, die auch durch ein noch so heiß begehrtes Privatwunder nicht gestört werden darf.

Auch bei Elke werden die gleichen Eigenschaften hervorgehoben. Elke "kann rechnen," stellt der junge Hauke bewundernd fest (270), und auf die sarkastische Frage des Vaters, ob er glaube, dort "mitrechnen" zu können, hat er eine entwaffnend ernste, bejahende Antwort bereit (270). Elke "rechnet mich selber dreimal um und um," bemerkt ihr Vater (274), und die Tatsache, daß "beide geborene Rechner" sind (275), wird von Storm als der wahrscheinliche Grund des Zusammenfindens der beiden jungen Menschen vermerkt.

---

[16] Lukacs, *op. cit.*, S. 143.

Diese Eigenschaft wird denn auch Haukes Widersacher die erste und augenscheinlichste Angriffsfläche bieten. Von Ole Peters' frühem Haß gegen "den verfluchten Schreiberknecht" (276) bis zu seiner Warnung vor dem neuen Deichgrafen, der "zu rechnen versteht" (331), zieht sich eine Kette der Verleumdungen, die den Dorfgenossen den einsamen Mann, "der immer grübeln geht" (308), immer fremder und unheimlicher macht.

Ein eigentlich "Zugehöriger" war er nie gewesen. Selbst der Sieg, den er beim "Eisboseln" für sein Dorf gewonnen hatte, hatte ihn nur vorübergehend zum Helden des Tages machen können. Elke und Hauke "entschlüpften beide dem Gedränge" der siegesfrohen Menge (289); schweigend stand er am Türpfosten "und blickte in das unruhige Gewimmel" der Tanzenden, die längst nicht mehr daran dachten, "wer vor einer Stunde erst das Spiel gewonnen hatte" (290). Beliebt war er schon als der "Schreiberknecht" des alten Deichgrafen nicht gewesen, da es ein offenes Geheimnis war, wem man die strengere Handhabung der Deichordnung zu danken hatte, und das "ungewaschene Wort" seines Widersachers (333), daß er nur "von seines Weibes wegen" Deichgraf geworden sei (308), war später auf fruchtbaren Boden gefallen. Es hatte Hauke Haiens grimmige Entschlossenheit vertieft, und damit die Kluft, die ihn von den Dorfleuten trennte, so daß "sein Verkehr mit anderen Menschen außer in Arbeit und Geschäft" fast ganz aufhörte (314). Und als die Worte seines Gebetes die Runde machten und nur zu bereitwillig mißdeutet wurden, "entstand trotz aller lebendigen Arbeit eine Einsamkeit um ihn, und in seinem Herzen nistete sich ein Trotz und abgeschlossenes Wesen gegen andere Menschen ein" (338).

Gewiß kann, wie der alte Jewe Manners sagt, "nur die Unvernunft bestreiten," daß sein Deichbauprojekt, wenn nicht den Dank der Mitwelt, so doch den "Ehrenkranz" der Enkel verdienen müsse (328), aber in eben diesem Unverstand war Hauke Haien der große Gegenspieler erwachsen, böswillig und lauernd wie das feindliche Element vor den Deichen, dessen unbewußter Helfer er war. Immer unheimlicher wurde den Menschen der herrische, unzugängliche und verschlossene Mann, der die "Faulen und Ungeschickten ohn Erbarmen aus der Arbeit wies" (333) und dessen karges Lob man nur "düster" und "widerwillig" ertrug (334). "Seine hagere Gestalt auf dem feurigen Schimmel" erregt Furcht und Unbehagen der rastlos zur Arbeit Angetriebenen (341), in deren primitiver Welt sich das rätselhaft Überlegene und Dämonische bald unterschiedslos mit der Vorstellung des "Teuflischen" mischt.

Die absichtsvolle Eigenart des Dichters, die das Irrationale ein seltsam unverbundenes Eigenleben neben der Welt des Rationalen führen läßt, führt diesem Teufelsglauben reichliche Nahrung zu: das Nebelgebilde des gespenstischen Pferdes, das auf nächtiger Hallig im Mondschein weidet; das bleiche Pferdegerippe, das auf unerklärliche Weise verschwunden und ebenso unerklärlich in Haukes Schimmel wieder verleiblicht scheint; dieser Schimmel, ein wahres "Teufelspferd" (326), in seltsamem Handel von einem Slowaken erstanden, der unverkennbar mephistophelische Züge trägt, und schließlich die erstaunliche Verwandlung dieses Pferdes, hinter dessen kläglich verwahrloster Außenseite nur Hauke—wie Faust bei seinem Pudel—den eigentlichen Wesenskern erkennt. Der Teufelsglaube des Dorfes aber vermeint hier ganz anderes zu erkennen: den Leibhaftigen selbst, der seinem geheimnisvoll Mitverschworenen fortan nicht mehr von der Seite weichen und ihn schließlich in den Tod—und darüber hinaus in ein unerlöstes Jenseits—tragen sollte.

Obgleich im einzelnen "zwar zweifelnd, oder gar ungläubig," steht Storm diesem Komplex des Über- oder Unnatürlichen "im allgemeinen . . . anheimstellend" gegenüber.[17] Mit diesem "Anheimstellen" scheint uns des Dichters eigene Stellungnahme hinreichend geklärt. Wie es dem "aufgeklärten" Schulmeister anheimgestellt bleibt, sich nachdrücklich von diesem—obzwar unumgänglichen—Teil seines Berichtes zu distanzieren (315), muß dem Volk seine eigene Deutung anheimgestellt bleiben—jene seltsame Mischung aus "Begier, Unheimliches zu schauen" (316), mit banger Scheu und widerstrebender Bewunderung.

Wie das Antlitz des Meeres selbst erscheinen die "schwarzen Menschenmassen" (341), deren Feindschaft dem Schimmelreiter entgegenbrandet, und gegen deren Widerstand er ganz alleine "die Räder schieben" muß (330). Denn das Meer im *Schimmelreiter* ist ebenso wie "das Moor in *Renate*, die Heide in der *Chronik von Grieshuus* . . . nicht traulich und idyllisch, sondern fremd, unheimlich, ja schicksalhaft" geworden, und "von der Natur als Resonanzboden der menschlichen Stimmung" kann in Storms Spätwerk keine Rede mehr sein.[18]

Schon der Reiter des "zweiten Rahmens" dieser Erzählung sah am Meere "nichts als die gelbgrauen Wellen, die unaufhörlich wie mit Wutgebrüll an den Deich hinaufschlugen . . ." und wünscht sich "in

---

[17] *Briefwechsel zwischen Theodor Storm und Gottfried Keller*, hg. von Albert Köster, 4. Auflage (Berlin, 1924), S. 108.
[18] Kayser, *op. cit.*, 57–58, 59.

sicheres Quartier" (252-53). Das Meer, im Herbst eine "weite, wilde Wasserwüste" (259), wirkt im Winter, "als liege die ganze Welt im weißen Tod" (262); selbst an einem Maiabend herrscht "Novemberwetter" (275), wie denn überhaupt in der ganzen Novelle eine trübe spätherbstliche Stimmung vorherrscht: "Wenn im Herbst die Fluten höher stiegen," sah der Knabe stundenlang in Wind und Wetter hinaus (259); den Allerheiligentag, "um den herum die Äquinoktialstürme zu tosen pflegen," erwartete er "wie heut die Kinder das Christfest . . . am Deich mutterseelenallein" (261), und "vor Allerheiligen," im Oktober 1756 (365), wird auch sein Schicksalstag sein.

Unheimlicher aber noch als das gefahrdrohende, das offen feindliche Meer, ist die gleisnerisch trügende Maske, die es zuweilen trägt, um den Menschen in falsche Sicherheit zu wiegen. Hauke, "der nicht wußte, wie uns die Natur mit ihrem Reiz betrügen kann" (360), läßt sich, geblendet von strahlender Frühlingssonne und lachendem Himmelsblau, über das wahre Ausmaß des Schadens am Deiche täuschen—wie auch Elke sich von der Illusion des plötzlich eingekehrten "Friedens" blenden läßt (362), alle im Verborgenen schwelende Feindschaft der Menschen überwunden und ein lange entbehrtes Glück endlich gekommen wähnt.

Es war ein doppelter Ring der Abwehr und Selbstbehauptung, den Hauke um sich gezogen hatte, und wie der Mäuseschaden den Deich, so sollte das Eindringen irrationaler Mächte auch die Geborgenheit seines "sicheren" Hauses untergraben und hier wie dort die unterwühlten Fundamente dem nagenden Werk der äußeren Zerstörung öffnen. Sein Haus, die Stätte der Zuflucht und des Heiles, glaubte er gegen alle Gefahren gefeit. Eine Tiefe des gegenseitigen Verstehens, das kaum noch der Worte bedurfte, hatte die beiden Menschen in Abwehr und einer Liebe zusammengeschlossen, die Haukes einzige Verankerung in der Welt einer menschlichen Gemeinsamkeit war: ein seit Elkes todesnaher Erkrankung und nach Wienkes Geburt noch enger gezogener "Bezirk des persönlichen Glückes." Wienke, das geistesschwache Kind ihrer Ehe, Wienke mit den stumpfen und dennoch so seltsam überwachen Sinnen, die das Meer "sprechen" hören (352), und denen das Element seine ganze angst- und grauenerregende Botschaft mitzuteilen scheint— welch hinterhältiger Triumph des Dämonischen inmitten der rationalen und sorglich gegen alles Widervernünftige abgeschirmten Welt der Eltern! Charakteristisch für diese Welt des Rationalen ist ja auch das Schweigen des sechsten Sinnes, jener Hellhörigkeit, die dem Menschen nur beschieden ist, wenn er welt- und lebensabgekehrt ganz nach innen lauschen, die Stimme der wesensverwandten Elemente des eigenen Ursprungs vernehmen kann, der sich das wache Bewußtsein verschließt. Elke im Todesschatten ihrer schweren Erkrankung, Trin' Jans in ihrer Sterbestunde, beide hatten sie diese Stimme gehört, in deren Bannkreis Wienke ständig zu leben schien.

Noch aber sollte der entscheidende Schlag aus dem Dunkel erfolgen—Haukes schwere Erkrankung, die ihn selbst hart an des Rand des Grabes brachte. Und als er sich wieder vom Lager erhob, "schien er kaum derselbe Mann. Die Mattigkeit des Körpers lag auch auf seinem Geiste, und Elke sah mit Besorgnis, wie er allzeit leicht zufrieden war" (356). Aus untergrabener Entschlußkraft erwächst auch seine Kompromißbereitschaft, die zum schweren Verschulden wird—eine zwar "menschlich verzeihliche" Schuld, die aber keineswegs "zurücktreten" darf, und die der Deichgraf nach des Dichters eindeutigem Diktum selbstverantwortlich zu "tragen" hat.[19]

Den verderblichen Rat anderer einholend, wo er sonst aus eigener Entschließung gehandelt und das Nötige und Erforderliche ihm unverrückbar vor Augen gestanden hatte, versündigt er sich aus gebrochener Widerstands- und Willenskraft an Leben und Werk.[20] Notdürftige Ausbesserung, ein trügerisches Verdecken des inneren Schadens, wird angeordnet, wo bessere Einsicht und Treue zur eigenen Überzeugung die grundlegende und entschlossene Tat zur Rettung des Deiches gefordert hätte, und in überdeutlicher Symbolik hat Storm hier die Parallele des von Mäusegängen zerfressenen, notdürftig überdeckten Deiches und der "Gewissensbisse" gestaltet, die Hauke Haien unter der Außenseite seiner scheinbaren Ruhe nicht mehr zum Schweigen bringen kann (362). Äußerlich scheint dieser Gewissensbiß, der gleichsam "außer ihm Gestalt gewonnen" hatte (361), eine gewisse Ähnlichkeit mit der—allerdings keineswegs gewissensverankerten—faustischen "Sorge" aufzuweisen, die als "Entwerterin alles Errungenen" die Grundfrage nach "Sinn und Wert des Lebens überhaupt" stellt.[21] Doch während wir Faust angesichts der drohenden Gefahr einer solchen "Entwertung" zu fieberhafter—obschon kaum "geläuterter"—Tätig-

---

[19] Siehe Storms Brief an F. Tönnies, 7. April 1888, zitiert nach Heinrich Meyer, "Theodor Storm und Ferdinand Tönnies," *Monatshefte*, XXXII (1940), 377.

[20] Im Gegensatz etwa zu der von Blankenagel vertretenen Auffassung, ist es nicht der Mangel an Kompromißbereitschaft, sondern gerade der Kompromiß, der zum Untergang führt. Siehe John C. Blankenagel, "Tragic Guilt in Storm's 'Schimmelreiter,'" *The German Quarterly*, XXV (1952), 171: ". . . he feels little or no need for making concessions which some degree of diplomacy might have dictated."

[21] Heinz Moenkemeyer, *Erscheinungsformen der Sorge bei Goethe* (Gießen, 1954), S. 144–45.

keit angetrieben sehen, verfällt Hauke Haien einer ausweglosen und lähmenden Untätigkeit. Einem Faust auf der Höhe seines Selbstseins, in einer tragischen Größe, die eben darin liegt, daß er "seinen Weg" zu Ende gegangen und noch in der unveränderten Zwielichtigkeit selbst seines letzten Werkes dem "Ziel" treu geblieben ist, steht des Schimmelreiters verlorene Weggewißheit gegenüber, Ursünde der Selbstverleugnung, die ihn, den zur Unkenntlichkeit Veränderten, selbst dem geliebtesten Menschen entfremden und in letzte Einsamkeit treiben muß.

Er schweigt vor Elke, läßt ausweichende Lüge an Stelle der unbeirrbaren Wahrheit treten, die doch das Band ihrer Gemeinsamkeit war, denn "ihm unbewußt war die klare Einsicht und der kräftige Geist seines Weibes ihm in seiner augenblicklichen Schwäche ein Hindernis, dem er unwillkürlich auswich" (360), und "niemandem, selbst nicht seinem Weibe, durfte er davon reden" (361). "Er machte sich los, um weiteren Fragen des geliebten Weibes auszuweichen" (362) —eine beredte Geste, wie sie bei Storm so häufig für das Unausgesprochene steht: Loslösung, in diesem Falle, von allem Heile einer verstehenden und erlösenden Liebe.

Letztes überdeutliches Zusammenspiel der inneren und äußeren Mächte, als Ole Peters den Deich, den Hauke-Haien-Deich, Sinn und Symbol seines Lebens, einreißen, dem Element Einlaß gewähren und seinen Namen hinwegwaschen will aus dem Gedenken der Menschen; letzte Täuschung Elkes, den Herrn um Schutz für den geliebten Mann anflehend, denn "nur du und ich, wir kennen ihn allein" (368)—ihn, den sie in Wahrheit nicht mehr kannte, seitdem er sich selbst ein Fremder geworden; und "eine Stimme aus dem Haufen" (372), gesichtslos und feindlich geballt wie das in Nacht, Sturm und Flut verbündete Element, ist der letzte Menschenlaut, der in seine Todesstunde dringt: der böswillig-mißverständliche Vorwurf einer "Schuld," die doch eine ganz andere war, als im Begreifen der Menge stand. Denn nicht mangelnde Nachgiebigkeit, sondern im Gegenteil die Schuld der Selbst- und Pflichtvergessenheit ist es ja, die den Mann, der "seines Amtes schlecht gewartet" hat (373), in den einsamen Opfertod seiner ausweglosen Verzweiflung treibt.

Der Lichtschein von hoher Werfte, der ihm als "Gruß von Weib und Kind" Trost zu spenden scheint (373), erweist sich als letzte und grausamste Täuschung. Noch blinkt ihm der trügende Schein, als Weib und Kind schon in den Fluten versinken, und wie ein kalter Hohn wird er noch seelenlos über der weiten Todesfläche schimmern, die

Hauke und den Seinen zum Grab geworden war: ein entseeltes Licht, flackernd über den Wassern wie der an sich selbst irregewordene Glaube, dessen letzter Halt vernichtet war. Vernichtet im Tosen der ihn rings umgebenden Zerstörung schien sein Werk, vernichtet Weib und Kind, der Hort seines Heiles und die letzte Hoffnung seiner Unsterblichkeit. Und doch, welch' seltsames Spiel der doppelsinnigen Dämonen: War er es doch selbst, der dem Deich durch den eigenen Opfertod "etwas Lebiges" einverleibt (312, 343) und vielleicht damit—wer möchte es bestreiten?—den Fortbestand des Werkes, das ja sein ganzes Leben war, gesichert hatte.

Aber nicht auf Gelingen oder Versagen, sondern darauf kommt es an, inwieweit das Errungene—wie alles Vergängliche—als Gleichnis des Ewigen bestehen kann. Das Leben ist kein Additionsspiel des rechnenden Verstandes: Es wird auf seinen wahren Wert geprüft, auf die Unermüdlichkeit des Strebens, die es dem Ziel der Vollendung, und damit der Gottheit, verbindet. Nicht das Höchsterrungene, sondern das Höchsterstrebte, wovon auch die Liebe nicht ausgeschlossen ist, scheint uns den Schlüssel zu Fausts Erlösung sowie Antwort auf die Frage zu geben, warum Storms Schimmelreiter eines ähnlichen Schicksals nicht teilhaftig werden kann.

Zwar hat das Element, doppelsinnig auch in diesem Akt der Gnade, ihn und die Seinen unwiederbringlich aufgenommen, und nur in Verbindung mit dem Element, dem er zugehört, wird die Nachwelt von ihm zu sagen wissen: mit einem Schauder der Ehrerbietung, der zwischen beiden nicht zu unterscheiden weiß.

Symbols of Isolation in Some
Late Nineteenth-Century Poets

I‌T IS customary to connect certain late nineteenth-century poets
in almost all European countries with the idea of a withdrawal into the
ivory tower of poetry. In a strong reaction against the effects of the
industrial revolution and the urbanization of life on the literature of
their epoch, these poets consciously guarded themselves in their writings
against any concern with social or political problems, precisely those
problems explored by the so-called realistic and naturalistic writers.
Instead, the ivory tower poets felt that they were the guardians of a
poetry untinged by the prevalent realism of the day, a *poésie pure* which,
as so many of them realized, must be written and can be understood only
in solitude and contemplation.

The metaphor of the ivory tower, which is so blithely used in connection with this poetry, is almost entirely foreign to the poets themselves. Except for Henry James's unfinished novel *The Ivory Tower*
(1914), I have not been able to find anywhere a description of an ivory
tower, and only rarely the metaphorical expression of a withdrawal into
the ivory tower, among the poets under consideration. The *image* is
foreign to them. The *idea* of withdrawal, however, is common. It is
expressed in entirely different imagery, and some examples of this
imagery of isolation will be discussed in this paper.

But first a word on the metaphor of the ivory tower. The most
often-quoted passage, which probably made it fashionable among his-
torians of literature, is by Sainte-Beuve. He contrasts Victor Hugo's political and social way of writing with the "more reserved" Alfred de Vigny
who, in the words of Sainte-Beuve, "withdraws before noon as though

into his ivory tower."[1] It is generally assumed[2] that the expression is derived from the Song of Songs: "Thy neck is as a tower of ivory." However this may be, an ivory tower is certainly not a Hebrew invention and it does not carry, in the Biblical passage, any connotation of withdrawal. Henry James, in the novel mentioned, went to great length to describe an ivory tower. In his words, it is "the remarkable product of some Eastern, probably some Indian, patience"[3] (p. 148). It is round, of very fine work, and perfectly circular, "an effect arrived at by the fitting together, apparently by tiny golden rivets, of numerous small curved plates of the rare substance." It has two curved doors that can be opened with a golden key, and inside it are drawers, the topmost of which contains a sealed document. We will never discover its importance, partly because of James's style and partly because the novel was never finished. However, at the outset of the long description of this little ivory tower, the hero says, using the well-known metaphorical phrase: "Doesn't living in an ivory tower just mean the most distinguished retirement?" (p. 147). Obviously, James is conscious both of the actual elegant little ivory towers existing in Chinese as well as in Indian art and of the metaphorical usage that had become so common.

During the period under discussion, this is one of the few examples of the description of an actual ivory tower or its metaphorical usage. The attitude, however, that we have come to connect with it exists in many writers of the period. It expresses itself in two essentially different ways. The first is perhaps best exemplified by Proust, who, over-sensitive to noise and subject to very disturbing allergies, had a sound- and dust-proof room built for himself and, while writing his great novel, rarely emerged from it. Proust may be an extreme case, but to a certain degree every writer will at times need the kind of solitude so beautifully described by Lawrence Durrell in his *Alexandria Quartet* which the "I" of the novel found in his retreat to an isolated Greek island.

What is more important is the fact that for the writers under consideration isolation becomes a main theme of poetry. To be sure, very

---

[1] From the poem "A. M. Villemain" in *Pensées d'Août*, 1837. *Poésies Complètes* (édition revue, Paris, 1890), p. 378.
　　　　　　　　　　. . . et Vigny, plus secret,
　　　　Comme en sa tour d'ivoire, avant midi, rentrait.
[2] See, e.g., Erwin Panofsky, "In Defense of the Ivory Tower," *The Association of Princeton Graduate Alumni*, 3 (1953), 77-84; and Harry Levin, "The Ivory Gate," *Yale French Studies*, 13 (1954), 17-29. The chapter "Symbolist Poetry and the Ivory Tower" in Cleanth Brooks's *Modern Poetry and the Tradition* (Chapel Hill, 1939), pp. 54-68, is not concerned with the history of the image.
[3] Although *The Ivory Tower* was written in 1914, the publication date is 1917 (New York).

often, though not always, the hero of this poetry is the poet himself; however, it is the theme of isolation, regardless of the hero's calling, which, repeated in ever-recurring identical or similar symbols, gives the poetry of this period its distinguishing character. This artistically created isolation finds a rich expression in the imagery of the time. The images of isolation are like variations on one main theme, but they have received, thanks to the genius of the authors, a fullness and depth which make each variation seem worthy of our special attention. I will by necessity be selective, both in regard to authors and to imagery.

First a few general observations. The withdrawal into solitude evokes, in the different works, a great variety of emotions; it can be a blissful as well as an extremely sad experience. In almost all the cases discussed, however happy or unhappy the protagonist, it is a voluntary withdrawal, it is not forced upon the hero; rather, he seeks it out, creates it, watches it lovingly and with great solicitude. Rarely are these protagonists presented as outcasts, as the scum of society. On the contrary, they proudly carry a torch which they feel would be extinguished without their isolation. Theirs is an aristocratic attitude, their minds contemplate in solitude their own power and spiritual obligation. Far from feeling exiled by society, they have rejected it or exiled themselves from it.

Among the writers under consideration there are great personal differences. Baudelaire, in so many ways the father of the symbolist movement in France, felt strongly that he was an isolated outcast. In none of his poetry is there an ivory-tower attitude. In his poems he walks through Paris or dreams of voyages to foreign lands. With all his dandyism, his fastidiousness, his esthetic sensitivity, he did not possess that aristocratic sense of withdrawal which was Mallarmé's outstanding characteristic. One might also think of Verlaine's friend Rimbaud. Whereas the former created poems of a sadly blissful loneliness, Rimbaud wrote about the drunken boat of his life which goes out into the wild ocean and is tossed about by storms. Or we may remember Proust's hero, one of the most sociable human beings ever presented in a novel, whose desire for solitude emerges only at the end of fourteen volumes through the finally-awakened urge to write. In other words, the ivory-tower attitude is not equally present in what in so many other ways is a unified literary movement.

Thus cautioned against an oversimplification of the problem, I will analyze four poetic images, all closely related to one another: the lonely castle, the underground treasure, the deserted park, and the palace with its adjacent terrace. These images are clearly interrelated, but to each of them is given its very special form and mood of isolation. Undoubtedly one of the most completely isolated literary figures of that time is Axel, the hero of the novel by the same name by Villiers de l'Isle-Adam. It is not without reason that Edmund Wilson has entitled his collection of essays on the symbolist movement *Axel's Castle*. In the play, Axel is brought up in a medieval castle surrounded by an impenetrable imaginary Black Forest, without any contact with, but great contempt for, the outside world. When visited by a cousin, he breaks out into violent disdain for the state, its laws, the behavior of courtiers, etc.—in short, for all the conventions which human beings generally consider to be right and correct. Carefully educated by Mr. Janus, a Rosicrucian, Axel has been taught to value the mind over the body, purity of spirit over the desires of the flesh, and to yearn burningly for a reunification of his soul with the World-Soul from which man took his origin. Although carefully educated in the ways of the world, he has the most sovereign disdain for anything worldly. Temptation comes to him in two closely connected forms: a beautiful young woman reveals to him the existence of a rich underground treasure of which Axel had been unaware. With wealth and love within his grasp, Axel renounces both, and shares with the beloved woman a poison that kills them before they are sullied by either greed or sensuality.

This is simultaneously a mystic and a singularly sterile contempt for the world. Although in some essential ways a symbol of the poet and a somewhat exaggerated portrait of Villier's master, Mallarmé, Axel is not able to write poetry. His desire to reach the absolute does not allow that detour through the senses without which poetry cannot exist. Even Mallarmé, so well practiced in the experience of the absolute nothingness of the mind which contemplates only itself, could not quite renounce fragments of the sensory world if he wished to write at all. But Axel, superb, pure, proud, and in a decisive way sterile, renounces even those sensuous remnants and prefers to die a death of beauty in the presence of his beloved, who is bedecked with the jewels they have uncovered. There is no trace of creativity in him—only a very clear, uncompromising, and pure road to death in beauty.

A similar dark forest surrounds the equally dark castle to which Golo leads his strange blonde bride Mélisande in Maeterlinck's *Pelléas et Mélisande*. Like Axel, Mélisande is not an artist. If one must interpret her strange and lovely existence in the forest of symbols surrounding her, she rather represents the human soul longing for light, but which, for the period of its earthly existence, is enclosed in the darkness of this life and this body. Mélisande does not wish to be in the dark castle; she has no pride in her isolation, only the nostalgia of the lonely heart that sees an unattainable light in the far distance. Her love for Pelléas is a death-love—her surest, although unconscious, way of freeing herself from isolation through death. Compared with Axel's impenetrable forest, hers is still darker, more endless, producing in her sadness and longing rather than resistance and pride.

Axel's isolation is twofold: that of his castle in the forest and that of the accidentally discovered underground treasure which he is too proud to return to the world to which it once belonged. The treasure becomes a symbol of the purity and preciousness of his own magnificent death-in-life. Another poet adopted this underground treasure world to make it the true symbol of the poet's world: the German poet Stefan George. In the group of poems called *Das Unterreich*,[4] he made Heliogabalus, one of the late Roman-Byzantine emperors, the figure who created the individual rooms of an under-ground palace, which represent to him in various ways the artificial world of poetry. George had as a living example the underground rooms which the half-insane Bavarian King Louis II had built in one of his fantastic castles (Linderhof). In George's *Algabal*, however, these rooms are not only what they must have been for the Bavarian king—a strange refuge from the baseness of this world. George's emperor is the only true emperor that can ever exist, namely, the absolute and utterly free ruler of the creative imagination, the poet who uses his rich material to create poems of lasting loveliness. His realm is beneath and beyond the reach of human footsteps; it is filled with the choicest gems and valuables—gold, silver, ivory—but, to be sure, there is no tower. The boat on its lake[5] can be propelled without oars; the imagination alone, commanded by the poet, makes it move.

> Der schöpfung wo er nur geweckt und verwaltet
> Erhabene neuheit ihn manchmal erfreut,
> Wo ausser dem seinen kein wille schaltet
> Und wo er dem licht und dem wetter gebeut.
>
> (P. 91)

That everything in this realm is artificial, removed from nature as well as man, is the greatness and the tragedy of the poet. His realm is,

---

[4] In *Hymnen Pilgerfahrten Algabal*, 1892.
[5] Cf. Villiers de l'Isle-Adam, "L'agrément inattendu" (*Oeuvres* VI, 207-13) which, although not speaking of an underground realm, describes an unexpected underground lake. See on this subject Kurt Wais, *Mallarmé* (2nd ed., München, 1952), p. 219, and note 5, p. 666.

by its very nature, an artificial one, i.e., his task is to transform natural objects into art. At the heart of the ideas on poetry of that period— resulting in the ivory tower attitude—lies the strong conviction that unless poetry transforms nature into something no longer "natural," it does not fulfill its task. This is most poignantly expressed in the last of the *Algabal* poems, in which the dark underground garden, reminiscent of lava and made of coal, is described as the "sanctuary" through which the poet walks in search of the rarest of all flowers: the black flower. In this weird context, coal is the most appropriate symbol: it suggests the intermediary stage in the long process of development from the living plant to its final transformation into the diamond. Ultimately—and all poems in *Das Unterreich* speak of gems—nature has to be transformed into the most precious of all gems, the diamond. This process of transformation is the arduous task of the solitary emperor-poet in his lonely realm of artifice.

The reader may not feel comfortable in this cold and stern world of art, and George himself resorted, not much later, to less absolute and harsh symbols of isolation. But judging from the point of view of a development of the symbol of the underground treasure, it seems that there is an inner progression from Axel's beautiful but sterile "realm below" to George's more creative one. The hard artificiality of the latter's poetic world is matched, and perhaps surpassed, only by Yeats in his poems on Byzantium, representing an equally stern and uncompromising symbol of isolation within an artificial and precious world of gems and metals. Yeats's Byzantium is populated by equally artificial objects— real birds are transformed into golden birds, human beings into the "lords and ladies of Byzantium" who, ghost-like, move in the entirely cold, moonlit, and unnatural city. Written over thirty years after George's *Das Unterreich*, but still describing the same state of mind with almost the same words, the stanza from "Sailing to Byzantium" (1927), quoted below, shows a poetic conception amazingly similar to George's *Algabal* poems, although there is in all probability no trace of "influence":

> Once out of nature I shall never take
> My bodily form from any natural thing,
> But such a form as Grecian goldsmiths make
> Of hammered gold and gold enamelling
> To keep a drowsy Emperor awake;
> Or set upon a golden bough to sing
> To lords and ladies of Byzantium
> Of what is past, or passing, or to come.

The last treasure-world to be mentioned is again an underground treasure. It occurs in Hugo von Hofmannsthal's play *Das Bergwerk von Falun,* based on a tale by E. T. A. Hoffman. It is the story of a young sailor irresistibly drawn into the mysterious embrace of the Queen of the Mines, the goddess of the underground treasures, from whom neither the vast sea on which he used to travel nor the love of an earthly woman can detract him. In contrast to Algabal or the Emperor of Byzantium, there is neither pride nor a sense of control in the young man, but rather an uncanny, subconscious desire, repressed by him, fought by his environment, but irresistible, which leads him to death. This is not Axel's self-imposed death in beauty, yet it is a death fully as beauty-conscious, pure and cold and equally lonely. In both the story by Hoffmann and the play by Hofmannsthal, the psychological urge or drive which draws the youth into the realm of the underground queen is dominated by the artificial, gem-like world of beauty which he does not create. But both the forbidding coldness of beauty and the attraction it had for Axel are clearly present in *Das Bergwerk von Falun.*

As was said earlier, George himself felt uneasy in this world and, within a short time, found other symbols which express the same loneliness of the creative artist in less forbidding imagery. In his loveliest volume of poetry, *Das Jahr der Seele,* we find the poet enclosed in a park. But first an older poet must be mentioned to whom the image of the park was one of the most appropriate symbols of the poet's lonely life devoted to beauty in the peculiar sense of that period. The first great park-poet was Verlaine.[6] In discussing the symbol of the park, we must realize that there is hardly a poem of the period in which the image of the park evokes pleasant emotions. Life in these parks is neither easy nor pleasant; just as in the previously mentioned symbols, it rather imposes a severe obligation. It may turn out to be a failure or an error; the poet may leave the park to return to "the world." Wherever the image occurs, it evokes a stern or at least a sad mood and, despite the voluntary act which puts the poet into that setting, it is neither welcome nor gay. The parks in which these poets enclose themselves in their imagination offer no relief from the essentially demanding solitude which their concept of poetic creation imposes upon them, even when they are in the company of a beloved woman, as is often the case. In no

---

[6] Some parks are, of course, found in earlier, mainly Romantic, literature. They do not carry, however, the connotation of decay or decadence which appears strongly in the late nineteenth-century park-poems. One should also mention Baudelaire's poem "L'Ennemi," in which the park is completely ravaged by the storms and floods of time. *Oeuvres* Gd. de la Pléiade, I, 28.

way does her presence relieve the sense of severe, demanding, and sad solitude.

Although Verlaine did not write many park poems, his landscape-poems which do not seem specifically to describe an enclosed park lead to the sensation of the cultivated, secluded mood of a park environment. The famous poem "Clair de Lune" is an example.

> Votre âme est un paysage choisi
> Que vont charmant masques et bergamasques
> Jouant du luth et dansant et quasi
> Tristes sous leurs déguisements fantasques.
>
> Tout en chantant sur le mode mineur
> L'amour vainqueur et la vie opportune,
> Ils n'ont pas l'air de croire à leur bonheur
> Et leur chanson se mêle au clair de lune,
>
> Au calme clair de lune triste et beau,
> Qui fait rêver les oiseaux dans les arbres
> Et sangloter d'extase les jets d'eau,
> Les grands jets d'eau sveltes parmi les marbres.

Until we reach the last stanza we cannot be sure that the disguised figures of the woman's inner landscape move in a park. Only when Verlaine speaks of a fountain surrounded by statues do we feel that a park is established. To be sure, this is not the description of a real landscape—the exquisite landscape of the first line is only a metaphor for the woman's soul. But we quickly forget the first words, "your soul is," and feel transported into the park with its sad moonlight in which disguised rather than real people dance and sing. This is the first poem of the collection *Fêtes galantes*, the last poem of which is also a park-poem.

Colloque Sentimental

> Dans le vieux parc solitaire et glacé.
> Deux formes ont tout à l'heure passé.
>
> Leurs yeux sont morts et leurs lèvres sont molles,
> Et l'on entend à peine leurs paroles.
>
> Dans le vieux parc solitaire et glacé,
> Deux spectres ont évoqué le passé.
>
> —Te souvient-il de notre extase ancienne?
> —Pourquoi voulez-vous donc qu'il m'en souvienne?
>
> —Ton coeur bat-il toujours à mon seul nom?
> Toujours vois-tu mon âme en rêve? —Non.

—Ah! les beaux jours de bonheur indicible
Où nous joignions nos bouches! —C'est possible.

—Qu'il était bleu, le ciel, et grand, l'espoir!
L'espoir a fui, vaincu, vers le ciel noir.

Tels ils marchaient dans les avoines folles,
Et la nuit seule entendit leurs paroles.

Love ends where it began, in the park, which is now icy and deserted. Love is past. The loneliness of the participants is made evident by the dialogue between the two persons so ironically called sentimental. It is not a true exchange; each soul remains isolated and forlorn.

Stefan George's *Das Jahr der Seele* describes a similar love story. That it is a sad story is clear from the first line of the first poem: "Komm in den totgesagten park und schau . . ." To be sure, the lovers still find living things in this park—late roses not quite withered, the last asters, and so on. But the general mood is one of subdued farewell symbolized by the late autumn days which these poems evoke. Only outside of the gate do the lovers see the second blooming of an almond tree; inside they experience the last radiance of these dying weeks (glanzerfüllte Sterbewochen). Thus the first group of poems finds a late and passing autumn beauty filled with the sense of a final farewell. There follows a short group of winter poems, then a group called *Sieg des Sommers*. However, this is not the victory of love over sadness. It is the victory of the poet who has renounced the pleasures of this world in favor of undying service to art. This is a stern summer and a stern victory indeed, the ultimate demand of which is that the enjoyment of the rich summer days in the garden be only a spiritual one. A kiss received in a dream should never be exchanged for a true kiss, George says. Only the dream kiss, with which one has kissed far-away images in one's mind, is valid, and under its impact the poet will have to live after renouncing real kisses, real love, actual life.[7]

In these poems a case can be made for the idea that from the beginning there was no beloved, that they really present an inner dialogue, and that throughout the volume the poet takes farewell of his own personal life in order to achieve the victory over summer, namely, the sacrifice of his personal feelings to his poetic vocation. The poems may

---

[7] *Das Jahr der Seele* (Berlin, 1902), p. 43:
Und törig nennt als übel zu befahren
Daß ihr in euch schon ferne bilder küsstet
Und daß ihr niemals zu versöhnen wüsstet
Den kuß im traum empfangen and den wahren.

also be interpreted as the farewell to an existing beloved woman whose love he sacrifices for his future true love, the Muse. However they are interpreted, the result is the same: the summer is not the summer of sensual pleasure but the victory of the mind over the body, of the "true" use of nature over the "false" one, the victory of the spiritualized world of poetry over the merely sensuous experience of the natural summer day. A little later in the volume we find one of George's most famous poems, which ends with the stanza:

> Verschweigen wir was uns verwehrt ist,
> Geloben wir glücklich zu sein
> Wenn auch nicht mehr uns beschert ist
> Als noch ein rundgang zu zwein.
>
> (P. 93)

No matter how one interprets the "we," there is no doubt that here we witness a mood of ultimate renunciation, the withdrawal from common pleasure and a common life, in favor of the lonely, stern, and painful solitude of the creative poet.

The symbol of the park has received an exultantly rich treatment by the poets of the period, far too rich to be discussed here at any but its most superficial level. The only justification for mentioning it at all is the perspective from which it is seen in the wider context of this paper.

The German poet Rainer Maria Rilke wrote a series of seven park-poems as part of his volume *Neue Gedichte*. He describes the parks less as a symbol of the poet's solitude than as the half-forgotten remnants of former, richer times when the kings gave shape to nature and nature was happy to receive its laws from them.[8] And yet the sadness of the parks prevails, and in the last of the poems the poet feels almost fenced in. The avenues of the park are seen in the distance almost closed off by balustrades, every nightingale sounds as if it were poisoned, the shrubs do not believe in spring, and a sense of decay closes in on the lonely wanderer. For the first time there is a suggestion of what will happen to the symbols of isolation in the years to come: they will be felt as a burden, a sign of decay—we might say of decadence—and quite gradually the poets move out of their gardens or their towers or their underground treasurehouses back into the open fields of life. That this way back into so-called life will not necessarily remove the solitude of the poet will be seen later. In Rilke's park-poems there is only a first timid indication of what later appears as a strong literary movement—the

---

[8] Even here the kings might well symbolize the poet in his garden of poetry.

movement away from the ivory tower. Rilke continued to love the park, as can be seen in his French poems, one group of which is called *Verger*, i.e., the orchard. Altogether, his French poems, almost the last poems he wrote, are in a happier mood than any earlier ones, and the particular group of *Verger* poems is happy and delightful. The orchard replaces the earlier traditional and deserted parks; it is fruitful and rich and knows "how to bow its secular instinct to the youthfulness of one moment."[9] The poet admires the beauty and the order of the orchard's purpose, and ends with the stanza:

> Tes dangers et les miens, ne sont-ils point
> tout fraternels, ô verger, ô mon frère?
> Un même vent, nous venant de loin
> nous force d'être tendres et austères.
>
> (P. 29)

The identification of the park and the poet remains the same in these late poems; only the mood has changed remarkably. The orchard, unlike the park, is not decaying or sad, but rich and fertile, symbolizing a creative poet rather than one enclosed in the artificial park world, suffering from isolation. As we know from Rilke's life, he was more isolated than ever at the time of the orchard poems. But in his solitude he had been granted the poetic fulfillment of his late great poetry, and although the imagery of the enclosed garden remains the same, its meaning has completely, and for once happily, changed and reversed itself.

The last image under discussion is that of the terrace which lies outside the isolated castle and within the isolated park. It has, as a terrace, received a poetic life of its own which seems worth exploring.

One of Stefan George's early poems is called *Auf der Terrasse*,[10] a very difficult and rather controversial poem. It is assumed that the terrace described in the poem is the wonderful terrace of St. Germain near Paris. From the general context it is clear that the poet meets on this terrace whatever muse or woman or goddess endows him with the gift of poetry. For a moment he sees before his eye a train of runes (ein Zug von Wunderstaben)—the mysterious symbols of his future poetry. But the moment is short and, as always in George's early poetry, a sense of resignation is felt, a demand to overcome the life he may not "live" but rather must transform into poetry. The terrace thus is the place where he receives an inspiration, but where simultaneously he has

---

[9] *Poésies françaises* de Rainer Maria Rilke, (Paris, 1946), p. 29.
    et qui sait bien son instinct séculaire
    plier à la jeunesse d'un instant.
[10] In *Hymnen Pilgerfahrten Algabal*, pp. 40-41.

to renounce real love and real life in favor of the severe life of the poet devoted exclusively and entirely to his muse, i.e., his poetic mission.

We are on similar ground in the work of George's young friend Hugo von Hofmannsthal. His fragmentary play, *Der Tod des Tizian*, was written in 1892, the year of the publication of George's *Hymnen* and shortly after the two poets met for the first time. The scene takes place on "the terrace of Titian's villa, near Venice." Gianino, the handsome sixteen-year-old boy who is the center of the fragment, describes in those unforgettable poetic words which the young Hofmannsthal had at his command the night he became aware of the sweet sounds in the park around the terrace, the fragrant odor of the garden, the faun who holds a flute and whose marble glistens in the moonlight, the soft gleam of the moon on the quiet pond, the bees and the love dance of the gnats. But then Gianino walks on through the park to a place from which he can see the city. And he realizes in the overawareness of the night the violent difference between the protected garden and terrace and the open city at his feet outside the gate. In the city he feels the ecstasy of passion, torment, hatred, blood—life is awake, as he says. One of the friends answers Gianino's long description of his nightly adventures, which may well be called the experience of the sensitive artist: You see, the friend says, from our distance the lovely colors of the city, which is veiled by the exhalations of the evening.

> Allein in diesem Duft, dem ahnungsvollen,
> Da wohnt die Häßlichkeit und die Gemeinheit,
> Und bei den Tieren wohnen dort die Tollen;
> Und was die Ferne weise dir verhüllt,
> Ist ekelhaft und trüb und schal erfüllt
> Von Wesen, die die Schönheit nicht erkennen
> Und ihre Welt mit unsren Worten nennen . . .
> Denn unsre Wonne oder unsre Pein
> Hat mit der ihren nur das Wort gemein . . .
> Und liegen wir in tiefem Schlaf befangen,
> So gleicht der unsre ihrem Schlafe nicht:
> Da schlafen Purpurblüten, goldne Schlangen,
> Da schläft ein Berg, in dem Titanen hämmern—
> Sie aber schlafen, wie die Austern dämmern.[11]

And another friend adds:

> Darum umgeben Gitter, hohe, schlanke,
> Den Garten, den der Meister ließ erbauen,
> Darum durch üppig blumendes Geranke
> Soll man das Außen ahnen mehr als schauen.
> (Pp. 49-50)

---

[11] In *Die Gedichte und kleinen Dramen* (Leipzig, 1919), p. 49.

The description goes on and the meaning is clear: in order to create beauty, the poet has to withdraw into the enclosed garden; he must watch the city only from the distance, sitting on his terrace in quiet contemplation, allowing the evening light to throw a merciful veil over the reality of the city, which would appear ugly and even horrifying on closer inspection. Nowhere is the esthetic attitude of the period more radically expressed than in this little fragment in which, as we are told, Titian madly works in the background on his last great painting, and the mourning friends, knowing that he is to die, can calmly speak of the triumph of beauty over the ugliness of experienced life. There is in the young Hofmannsthal a luscious quality which overshadows the sterner attitude of the earlier poets discussed, an estheticism often criticized and condemned. But it must be admitted that in this contrasting description of the terrace and the distant city he has gone to the core of the esthetic problem as it was seen by the poets of that period.

It took Hofmannsthal twenty years to overcome the esthetic attitude of the *Titian* fragment. In the play *Die Frau ohne Schatten* (1911), later transformed into a beautiful prose tale, life in the enclosed garden, in the secluded palace, and on the protected terrace is condemned once and for all. A fairy, caught in the Emperor's garden, has become his wife. But in spite of her love for him she cannot bear children: she is a woman without a physical body—she casts no shadow. And in order to acquire that shadow which will make her human and give her the happiness and pain of childbirth, she must enter precisely that city which, in the *Titian* fragment, is described as ugly and distasteful. It would be just as ugly and distasteful in the later work were it not for the decency, simplicity, and honesty of a man, the dyer, who does not suffer from this ugliness but bears it with that kind of humane love and trust which cannot be found anywhere in the ivory tower environment. The young empress, fully aware of the ugliness that surrounds her, is willing to accept it because she sees simultaneously that certain human qualities are brought out, fostered, and developed only and exclusively in such an all-too-human environment, and she realizes that unless she becomes human herself, in great humility and a complete willingness to sacrifice her sheltered life, she will not bear the children she longs for— she will remain without a shadow in the only sense that matters, namely, the refusal to be human within the world of other human beings. She is willing to do the menial tasks which the wife of the dyer refuses to do, and acquires through her intimate intercourse with human beings the human lot. Thus, having gone in solitude into the world, she saves her husband, the emperor, who had not understood what she has learned, namely, that love is greater than beauty and that human understanding is more valuable than esthetic appreciation. To be sure, the empress is not a poet, and she does not need the retreat into the lonely park for the sake of poetic creation. But the amazing repetition of the same symbols— the palace and terrace on the one hand and the ugly city on the other— suggest very strongly that Hofmannsthal himself had found a way out of the ivory tower into the world of human life. The renunciation in *Die Frau ohne Schatten* is the very opposite of that in the works discussed earlier: what is given up here is not the world, or life in this world, or real life, or whatever the term may be, but rather the isolated world of the mind which, without a shadow, i.e., without the physical world of the body, is inhuman and hence sterile. The wheel has gone full circle.

It seems relevant to add some observations on another poetic character who, although going out into the world, as Hofmannsthal's empress does, remains nevertheless completely and radically isolated: Rilke's Malte Laurids Brigge, who, in his own peculiar way, leaves his sheltered home and garden in order to go into the city of Paris—ugly to a man like Malte, who, beneath the surface of splendor and beauty Paris shows to the stranger, discovers the real Paris, the ugly Paris which Bauderlaire had already seen and described, the Paris of sickness, death, and unbelievable suffering. What is so remarkable about the book and what brings it into the orbit of this investigation is the fact that Malte, while watching the terror of the city and suffering brutally from it, lives a life even more isolated and lonely than almost any of the characters discussed earlier. He does not visit any friends, he has no girlfriend, he barely speaks to the characters he so poignantly describes; rather, he carries around him an aura of complete and utter isolation. He would be untrue to himself if he were to break through this aura. It is, to be sure, self-imposed; nobody has forced it upon him except his own inner will which grows stronger the more difficult his experiences become. He is—and this brings him close to our theme—on the way to being a writer. Isolation is the only way in which he can achieve this goal. He has to be alone in a city in which other people are drawn close together. His isolation is as great a treasure as that of any of the earlier characters. But it is achieved not in beauty but in ugliness. The contact with the horror of life, which the empress had to undergo when she went to the dyer's house, has to be experienced so that the creative power of Malte can be released. He is not sheltered, but is vulnerable and wide open to life's terrors. No forest surrounds him, no fence protects the park of his soul from the ugliness of life; he is exposed, must be exposed, and yet he is alone and must be alone. Perhaps we feel his isolation as an even sterner demand than that imposed upon the underworld emperor, precisely because he is not surrounded by self-created artificial things but rather by life itself in all its nakedness and shamelessness. The demand is the same: it is the stern service expected of the writer who submits to his genius and is willing to take the consequences. But the means of isolation are utterly different.

The last two examples show the way the poets gradually found out of the ivory tower attitude. In *Die Frau ohne Schatten* this is still done in the form of great beauty. The whole work is exultantly rich in symbolic imagery and the ugliness of the "real world" is merely a facet in the realm of the emperor—a realm of splendor to which the empress will return, enriched but not sullied by her human experience. In a somewhat more complex way, this can be said of Rilke's work also. Malte, too, although describing ugliness in all its immediate poignancy, is not pulled down by it, but rather grows through the experience. Above all, the book itself is not essentially a description of the ugliness of life in the modern city; it is rather the development of the writer in this environment. In other words, even in this book, which of all the works discussed comes closest to a "realistic" work, "realism" is by no means its purpose. Rather, the isolation of the sensitive human being, the self-imposed, rigorous loneliness of the prospective writer who almost succumbs to the pressures of his environment—this is the painful but beautiful subject of a book written with too much artistry ever to be considered a realistic description of an objective reality.

In conclusion one basic question must be asked concerning this symbolic world. Whereas we will readily grant all poets their necessary solitude and isolation in order to fulfill their difficult task of compressing into verse, rhythm, rhyme, and sound their essential inner visions, why are the poets discussed here so preoccupied with this isolation that they can present little else? Why is even the description of an underground treasure or a secluded park fundamentally a narcissistic attitude, the symbolic reflection of loneliness? Even if a beloved woman shares this solitude, her presence does not detract from the self-awareness the poets express so poignantly in their rich images. To be sure, poets have always put themselves and their task on a high level. Homer gave to the bard an exalted place in his poetry, but his bard is only one, although a much honored, figure among innumerable others. In the *Divine Comedy*, too, the poet himself is the central figure, but he is concerned not merely with himself but with the characters he sees, meets, and talks to. The exalted position of the poet I have tried to describe is of a different nature. It is, as it were, more absolute and uncompromising—as if it were a sacred shrine. Most of the poets around 1900 felt with painful acuteness that it was their supreme obligation to preserve a beauty which was on the verge of being lost. Some of them, like Baudelaire, Proust, and Rilke, succeeded in transforming the essential ugliness of life into the beauty of their powerful writings. But at other times even they withdrew into the poetic symbols of the enclosed realms discussed here. Twentieth-century writers have, to a large extent, given up any ideal of "beauty." Expressionists, Marxist writers, existentialists, and modern American realists bluntly express ugliness as ugliness and consider it beneath their dignity as poets to withdraw from it. Have we then, in the ivory tower poets, a last attempt to preserve the attitudes of a dying aristocratic world whose ideal was that of a life and death in beauty? To a certain extent this is the case. The sadness so intimately connected with the imagery discussed here is in part the expression not merely of a personal isolation, but of a sense of what Spengler, shortly after the first world war, called the decline of the West.[12]

What makes these poems unforgettable and great, however, is not only their melancholy beauty, but a sense of rigorous self-discipline. In this way they differ significantly from their Romantic predecessors. Sad these poems may be, but self-pity is foreign to them. They remind the reader of a realm of the heart, an inner concentration on values too easily forgotten or overlooked, a treasure and a garden of the mind to be cultivated with admirable courage and severity.[13] These poets found one expression, utterly their own, of the esthetic sensitivity, the moral stamina, and the near-religious awe which was and will always be the mark of human individuality. They transcend their limitation in time and space, as all great writers do, by addressing themselves to what in every attentive reader is most preciously human and humane. In the middle of the twentieth century we have little patience with an ivory tower attitude. But in reading these poets, we are poignantly reminded of the quiet recesses and mainsprings of our own minds; it was their special task to explore them—fully, completely, and honestly.

---

[12] It may be significant in this connection that James stopped his work on *The Ivory Tower* at the outbreak of World War I.

[13] To be sure, they were not, as the medieval monks in their enclosed gardens, happily meditating on the soul and its relationship to God. Although most of them were genuinely religious, they conspicuously lack happiness, and what marks them as a group is not their religious, but rather their poetic search.

Das Motiv des "Stirb und Werde" bei Christian Morgenstern

by ERICH HOFACKER

Von unwiderstehlicher Macht getrieben umflattert der Nacht-falter den Lichtkegel der leuchtenden Kerze in immer engeren Kreisen, bis er von der Flamme ergriffen in ihr versengt wird. In diesem Flammentod spürt Goethe "die selige Sehnsucht," mit der der geistige Mensch dem Licht zustrebt und sein bisheriges Dasein immer wieder hingibt, um eine höhere Stufe zu erklimmen. Mit dem "Stirb und Werde" spricht der Dichter das Grundgesetz alles geistigen Wachstums aus.

Auch Christian Morgenstern beobachtet eines Abends den Flammentod eines Nachtfalters und erlebt ihn symbolisch. Aber für ihn bedeutet dies etwas ganz anderes. In acht Zeilen, impressionistisch in einfachster Sprache geprägt, hält er dieses Erlebnis aus dem Jahre 1909 fest:

> Wie still! Der Bach nur fällt und fällt . . .
> Und manchmal rollt ein hohler Ton
> von ferner Wetter schwülem Drohn—
> davor die Nacht den Atem hält . . .
> Ein Falter tupft in krauser Flucht
> der Zimmerdecke fahlen Plan . . .
> und endigt seine dunkle Bahn
> in meines Lichts verbotener Frucht.

Es ist Gebirgswelt. Das deutet schon der fallende Gießbach in der ersten Zeile an. Der lungenkranke Dichter hat ja den größeren Teil seiner späten Jahre dort verbracht und die Schweizer Alpenwelt ist ihm zur geliebten zweiten Heimat geworden. Auch sein Geist braucht die

Einsamkeit der Höhenluft über dem menschlichen Alltagstreiben.[1] Das ferne Tosen des Bergbachs als Erlebnis des lauschenden Ohrs kommt bei Morgenstern öfters zum dichterischen Ausdruck. In seiner Frühzeit spricht er von dem Frieden im stillen Alpental, wo die Bäche aus geheimen Schluchten brausen und dann wieder im "Hochlandschweigen," wo wir in der tiefen Stille "des Baches fernes Rauschen in der Kluft" vernehmen (MW, 228).[2] Das akustische Erlebnis vertieft sich schon 1902 zum Wiegenlied, wenn das Wässerlein so vom hohen Fels zum tiefen Grund hinabfällt, unser lautes Selbst zur Ruhe bringt und uns vom Eintag zur Ewigkeit wiegt (K, 67). Aber erst nach Morgensterns Begegnung mit Meister Eckhart kann er von dem göttlichen Urgrund sprechen, in den letzten Endes alles versinkt und von dem es aufgenommen wird (MW, 247). Aus seinem letzten Lebensjahr stammt das Gedicht "Wasserfall bei Nacht" (P, 70). Hier hat Morgenstern im Gießbach, der aus den Regionen des ewigen Schnees kommend zu Tal stürzt, das Einströmen himmlischer Kräfte in den träumenden Menschen erlebt.[3]

So weist wohl das doppelte "fällt" in der ersten Zeile des Faltergedichts auf ein metaphysisches Erlebnis hin, und wir werden damit auf die richtige Ebene der geistigen Deutung geführt. In diese metaphysischgeistige Höhenluft mischt sich das ferne Grollen des Donners eines nahenden Gewitters, bei dem der Atem stockt.[4] Die Angst der Kreatur treibt den Nachtfalter dem Licht der menschlichen Behausung zu. In pan-ischem Schrecken umflattert er die Flamme, stößt an die Zimmerdecke, stürzt in das Kerzenlicht und wird verbrannt. Für den Falter aber ist das Licht nicht wie bei Goethe Ziel seliger Sehnsucht, es ist für ihn

---

[1] Michael Bauer, *Christian Morgensterns Leben und Werk* (München, 1933) S. 254.

[2] Die folgenden Abkürzungen für die Werke Morgensterns werden benutzt: MW: *Mensch Wanderer;* K: *Ein Kranz;* P: *Wir fanden einen Pfad;* M: *Melancholie;* S: *Stufen;* W: *Auf vielen Wegen;* B: *Ein Leben in Briefen;* Sp: *Epigramme und Sprüche;* E: *Einkehr.*

[3] Dazu mein Aufsatz "Zur Naturlyrik Christian Morgensterns" in *Monatshefte* (November 1947), S. 430.

[4] Der Donner wird von Morgenstern nicht metaphysisch empfunden, wie etwa bei Klopstock als Ausdruck der göttlichen Majestät oder mythisch als Ausdruck des Kampfes übermenschlicher Gewalten wie bei Stefan George in dem Gedicht: "Auf stiller stadt lag fern ein blutiger streif." In den Versen "An meine Seele" vom Jahre 1897 fühlt sich der überschwengliche Pantheismus des jungen Dichters eins mit dem Weltwind, der als "der Schoß von Gewittern" erlebt wird. Das Gewitter ist für den starken Menschen also nicht Ausdruck eines metaphysisch Drohenden. Bei dem Gedicht "Der vergessene Donner" aus dem Jahr 1908, das im Stil der Galgenlieder gehalten ist, kann man von einer Verharmlosung dieses Naturschauspiels sprechen. Es beginnt mit den Worten: "Ein Gewitter im Vergehn, ließ einst einen Donner stehn."

verbotene Frucht. Dadurch wird der Erkenntnisgehalt des Gedichts ein ganz anderer. Im Gegensatz zu Goethe deutet Morgenstern sein Wahrbild nicht aus. Aber das Wort von der verbotenen Frucht weist auf das *sicut eris Deus* der Bibel hin. Und dieser Hinweis auf das menschliche Erkenntnisstreben bringt uns dem Goetheschen Gedicht wieder näher. Während Goethe das Grundgesetz der geistigen Entwicklung enthüllt, weist Morgenstern seine Schranken auf.

Als das Faltergedicht entstand, war Morgenstern bereits durch Rudolf Steiner mit der Möglichkeit der Erlangung übersinnlicher Erkenntnisse durch strenge geistige Schulung bekannt geworden. Er hörte wohl auch von der großen Gefahr, in die der unvorbereitete Geistesschüler durch verfrühte Enthüllungen aus der Geisteswelt gerät. Wie überwältigend ein solches Erlebnis selbst auf einen geschulten Geist wirkt, deutet Morgenstern in einem Gedicht seiner letzten Jahre an. Hier irrt der Suchende lange in dumpfem Streben vor jener Wand, die ihn von der Geisteswelt trennt. Endlich ertastet er die Klinke des Portals. Wenn er sie öffnet, wird der Geistesschüler überwältigt hinfallen "wie ein Leichnam" in den Sand (P, 39). In den vorchristlichen Mysterien bewahrten die Priester den Neophyten in strenger Schulung vor solchen Gefahren. Die Einzelheiten der Einweihung wurden als strenges Tempelgeheimnis gehütet. Vielleicht dachte Goethe an diese vorchristlichen Einweihungen, die den Geistesschüler durch Tod und Auferstehung führen sollten, als er sein Gedicht vom "Stirb und Werde" mit den Worten beginnen ließ: "Sagt es niemand, nur den Weisen . . ."

Im Goetheschen Gedicht ist die stille Kerze das Mittel, wodurch der Flammentod des Falters sich vollzieht; bei Morgenstern wird in anderem Zusammenhang diese selbst zum Symbol des "Stirb und Werde." Wir denken an ein Gedicht, das den Vorgang der Vergeistigung zum Ausdruck bringt und das mit den Worten beginnt: "In deine Flamme schau ich, Kerzenlicht." Hier stellt der Dichter dar, wie die Flamme ihm zum Bild der Seele wird, die ihren erdenschweren Leib wie eine Fackel hochhebend in den Raum verbrennt (M, 70). Dieses Erlebnis wird beim Besuch einer Kirche in Rom am Neujahrstag 1903 wieder lebendig. "In meiner Nähe ließ sich eine Gruppe von Nonnen nieder," schreibt Morgenstern in seinem Tagebuch." Eine davon war eine wahre junge Schönheit mit strengen, charaktervollen Zügen. Ich dachte ihrer Geschichte nach. Regte sie das mysteriöse Schauspiel des Kerzenansteckens, der soviel dunklen toten Kerzen gnadenreich nahenden, erlösenden, Bestimmung gebenden Flamme auf wie mich? Fühlte sie den Sinn des Lebens, den dieses Feuer der Kerze gab, daß sie sich leuchtend

verzehre?"[5] Denselben Gedanken hat Morgenstern noch einmal in einem
Spruch aus den letzten Lebensjahren ausgesprochen, als ein Stück
rückschauender Geisteserkenntnis, dem "Stirb und Werde" Goethes
vergleichbar:

> Wirf dich weg! Sonst bist du nicht
> meiner Art und meines Blutes.
> Wehe, wachst du zarten Mutes
> über deinem Lebenslicht,
> dessen Flamme gar nichts wert,
> wenn sie nicht ihr Wachs — verzehrt.
>
> Brenne durstig himmelan!
> Brenne stumm hinab! Doch — brenne!
> Daß dein Los von dem sich trenne,
> der sich nicht verschwenden — kann.
> Laß ihm seine Angst und Not!
> Du verstehe nur den — Tod.

Hier ist Verwandlung von Stoff in Licht, das als lebendige Flamme zum
Himmel lodert und in der Verwandlung sein stoffliches Selbst verzehrt.
Ein unübertreffbares Wahrbild für die Entwicklung des geistigen Men-
schen. Daß diese nicht zum eigenen Heil, sondern im Dienst des Näch-
sten, im Dienst der Menschheit geschehen soll, ist Morgensterns tiefste
Überzeugung, die er nicht müde wird, immer wieder auszusprechen.
"Nur wer sich selbst verbrennt, wird den Menschen ewig wandernde
Flamme," heißt es in den *Stufen* und gleich dahinter stehen die Worte:
"O helfen, helfen können—es gibt nichts Größeres für Menschenart
(148). Das wahre Verständnis des Todes aber, zu dem die letzte Zeile
des Spruches auffordert, wird Morgensterns ernstestes Bemühen, und
dazu verhilft ihm auch sein persönliches Schicksal.

Wie eine Grundmelodie begleitet das Erlebnis des "Stirb und
Werde" Morgensterns ganzes Leben und Werk. Dies sei im Folgenden
kurz dargestellt. Zuerst tritt es ihm im Gedanken der Wiederverkörperung entgegen, also gar nicht nur in Bezug auf sein persönliches
Leben, sondern im allerweitesten Sinn als ein kosmisches Gesetz der
Entwicklung des Menschengeschlechts. Durch das Studium Schopen-
hauers angeregt, wird dieses zunächst rein gedankliche Erlebnis von
dem Sechzehnjährigen in dichterische Form gebracht. Der Tod erscheint als ein Mittel, das den Menschen durch die wiederholten Erdenleben zur Freiheit reifen lassen könnte (MW, 7). Zwei Jahre
später scheint dieser Gedanke schon mehr geistiger Besitz geworden zu

---

[5] Bauer, *op. cit.*, S. 165.

sein. Es klingt persönlicher, wenn er sich fragt, wie oft er schon aus dieser Welt durch diese Welt gegangen sei, um ewig wieder anzufangen (MW, 9). Mit noch größerer künstlerischer Kraft drückt ein späteres Gedicht, "Künstlerideal," die Sehnsucht aus, nach diesem Leben in einem neuen Künstlerwerden als genialer Tonkünstler oder Bildhauer am Gewand des Scheins weiterzuweben und in immer neuen Welten als Meister der Schönheit aufzuerstehen (W, 9). Hiebel erkennt darin die Weiterwirkung Schopenhauerscher Gedanken.[6] Inzwischen hat sich das Gedankenerlebnis in jenem Lebensgefühl verdichter, daß sein Werk nicht an *eines* Lebens Spanne gebunden ist und daß sein Ich niemals sterben wird, auch wenn sein Leib zerfällt (MW, 16). So hat Morgenstern trotz seines jahrelangen vergeblichen Bemühens, das Rätsel des Daseins gedanklich zu bewältigen, gefühlsmäßig den Glauben an ein geistiges Fortbestehen nie ganz aufgegeben. Als der Dreißig-jährige während seiner metaphysischen Krisenjahre in der Dämmer-stunde sein Antlitz aus dem Grund des Spiegels betrachtete, begrüßte er "den großen Schatten" als Freund und nicht als Feind (Mw, 77).

Nach der ersten schweren Krankheit 1893 kommt die Vorahnung eines frühen Todes über ihn. In einem Brief schreibt er: "Ich habe noch nie in meinem Leben mich zu dem Glauben aufschwingen können, daß ich sonderlich alt werden würde, und ohne, daß mich diese Meinung sonderlich beunruhigt, übt sie doch indirekt Einfluß auf mein Denken und Trachten, indem mir beständig die Mahnung vorschwebt: Bringe, was du der Welt etwa zu sagen hast, möglichst schnell unter Dach und Fach, ehe es zu spät ist" (B, 40). Demgegenüber klingt der Anfang des drei Jahre später entstandenen Spruchs noch recht zuversichtlich: "Fünfzig Jahre hoff ich heiter mich durch diese Welt zu dichten . . ." (Sp, 92). Aber nach einem schonungslos ausgesprochenen ärztlichen Befund schreibt er wohl in Anlehnung an die Passionsgeschichte die ergreifenden Zeilen vom Tropfen Tod, der ihm in den Becher des Lebens fiel (M, 74). Und wenn er auch in den folgenden sieben Jahren glaubt "alt genug geworden zu sein, um sterben zu können," so muß er sich doch im Gedanken an sein unvollendetes Werk gestehen: "Es ist bitter, sich sagen zu müssen, daß man zwischen 35 und 45 zu erledigen hat, was man zwischen 45 und 60 hätte erledigen können" (S, 26). In seiner Lyrik kommt das Bewußtsein des frühen Todes nicht oft zum Ausdruck. In einigen seiner Sprüche hingegen schwingt ein tiefernster Ton mit: wenn er sich wegen seiner Schroffheit entschuldigt, weil seine Zeit kurz bemessen ist, oder wenn er von den Soldatenmanieren dessen

---

[6] Friedrich Hiebel, *Christian Morgenstern* (Bern, 1957), S. 31.

spricht, der in den Tod marschiert (Sp, 111), dann wieder, wenn er in dem Tod den Lehrer sieht, der des Menschen Trotz zur Einsicht kehrt, oder den Richter, der weise und gerecht ist (Sp, 147).

Dem vom Schicksal aufgezwungenen Stirb als biologischer Tatsache setzt Morgenstern das Werde seines Wesens und seiner künstlerischen Leistung entgegen. In einem früheren Aufsatz wurde an Hand von Briefstellen und Tagebuchnotizen gezeigt, wie dieses Werde, dieses Aufwärtsstreben, in Morgensterns Natur lag, wie er sich als Entwicklungsmenschen fühlte. Es wurde fener dargelegt, wie die treibende Kraft der seelischen Entwicklung beim jungen Morgenstern die unbarmherzige Selbstkritik war, zu der er sich von Nietzsche aufgefordert fühlte,[7] also ein bewußtes "Stirb und Werde." Aber selten kann so etwas Negatives im gestalteten lyrischen Werk künstlerischen Ausdruck finden. Das lange Gedicht "Entwicklungsschmerzen," in dem der Dichter uns einen Blick in seine inneren Nöte werfen läßt, in den Kampf zwischen dem, was er ist und was er sein möchte, klingt ungeschickt und frostig (W, 16). In einer selbstquälerischen Zergliederungskunst fürchtet der Dichter manchmal, das Firmament zu vergessen, von dem der Mensch umgeben ist, und er fragt sich, ob sein Antlitz noch um Ewigkeit weiß (W, 31). In schlaflosen Nächten fühlt er zuweilen, daß er vergeblich stritt und er bittet den Geist der Nacht, daß er ihn in einem traumlosen Schlaf bis zum Ende versenke, weil die metaphysische Ungewißheit sein Herz in Angst und Zweifel stürzt (M, 67). Es ist ein geistiger Tod, gegen den sich der grübelnde Dichter wehrt. Er träumt von dem gläsernen Sarg, der zur Zeit der Ebbe an den Rand des Meeres gestellt wird und den die steigende Flut auf den totenstillen Meeresgrund verschleppt, wo er mit schwarzem Seetang überzogen wird (W, 29). In seiner wachsenden Unsicherheit glaubt er wie auf dem dunklen Meer zu gehen, wo jeder Schritt sich wie schwankend auf den Tod zu bewegt, doch immer hält in höchster Not "den zagen Fuß ein unsichtbares Floß" (M, 80). In diesen Jahren vor der Jahrhundertwende drängt sich auch die Allmacht des physischen Todes seinem Bewußtsein auf, und er stellt sie in dem "Totentanz" dar. Hier erscheint der Tod als Säemann, als Bauer Tod, der Keime ohne Zahl um sich wirft, als Gast, der zum einsamen Trinker tritt, als fremder Sensenmann, der zum Schmied kommt, als gespenstischer Steuermann, der im Nebel das Schiff in den Abgrund lenkt, als trunkener Weichenwärter zur letzten Fahrt, als die Gestalt, die den Bergsteiger auf dem schwindelnden Pfad in

---

[7] "Ruhe und Aufstieg im Werk Christian Morgensterns" in *Monatshefte* (Februar 1960), S. 51.

den Abgrund stößt und endlich als Besucher des Schwerkranken in seinem Fiebertraum (W, 48-58).

Man kann gut verstehen, daß Morgenstern sich demgegenüber die Schönheit der Erde zu eigen machen möchte. Er nennt sich einen Naturschwärmer und berichtet: "Die Natur wird immer mehr meine Religion, mein Alles und Höchstes."[8] Dann heißt es wieder: "Ich ertrinke manchmal fast in den zahllosen Wirkungen der Natur auf mich."[9] Wenn er vom Glück des reinen Schauens spricht, erinnern wir uns an die Anschaulichkeit seiner frühen Naturlyrik und daran, daß er das Malerauge von seinem Vater und Großvater geerbt hat. In seinen frühen vorwiegend noch diesseitig eingestellten zarten und melodischen Naturgedichten, die den Ruhm des jungen Morgenstern begründeten, stellt dieser das "Werde" der künstlerischen Leistung hin als Antwort auf den düsteren Schicksalsruf. Dann kommen die Galgenlieder als positive dichterische Ernte der negativen Lebensepoche 1901-1905. Während die Galgenlieder als Auflockerungs- und Abwehrmittel, als Ventil, wirken, geht Morgensterns metaphysisches Forschen weiter. Dies wird von ihm selbst als ein "Stirb und Werde" empfunden: "Alles Große macht sterben und auferstehen. Wer an Nietzsche und Lagarde nicht immer wieder stirbt, um an ihnen auch immer wieder aufzuerstehen, dem sind sie nie geboren" (S, 78).

Im Winter 1905–1906 vertiefte er sich in die Schriften Meister Eckharts. Als er dann eines Abends das Evangelium nach Johannes aufschlug, glaubte er zum ersten Mal zu verstehen, was es heißt: "Ich und der Vater sind eins." Aus einer Briefstelle, die Michael Bauer zitiert, wird klar, was dieses Erlebnis für Morgenstern bedeutete: "Mir ist im letzten Januar oder Februar in Birkenwerder ein ungeheurer Gedanke aufgetaucht, nicht als etwas Plötzliches, sondern als Krone gewissermaßen meiner ganzen bisherigen Entwicklung, und diesen Gedanken tiefer zu denken wird meine ganze fernere Lebenszeit und künstlerische Arbeit dienen müssen. Er ist vielleicht nichts Geringeres als die Grundlage einer neuen Weltanschauung und Religion."[10] In seinem "Tagebuch eines Mystikers" hat der Dichter die neue Erkenntnis von immer neuen Perspektiven aus dargestellt. "In Christus ist zum ersten Mal auf der Erde Gott selbst sich zum Bewußtsein gekommen. In Christus erkannte Gott als Mensch zum ersten Mal sich selbst." (S, 251). Diese persönliche Erkenntnis umkehrend kommt Morgenstern

---

[8] Bauer, *op. cit.*, S. 72.
[9] Bauer, *op. cit.*, S. 120.
[10] Bauer, *op. cit.*, S. 238.

von der menschlichen Seite her zur allgemeinen Schlußfolgerung: "Religion ist Selbsterkenntnis des menschlichen, als ebendamit göttlichen Geistes. Religion ist die Erkenntnis, daß alles Denken göttliches Denken ist, wie alle Natur göttliche Natur, daß jede Handlung eine Handlung Gottes, jeder Gedanke ein Gedanke Gottes ist, daß Gott nur soweit Gott ist, als er Welt ist, daß die Welt nichts anderes ist als Gott selbst—daß in demselben Augenblick, da ein Mensch sich seines Gottseins bewußt wird, Gott in ihm sich seiner selbst als Mensch bewußt wird" (S, 222). Die Geschichte der Menschheit ist also die Geschichte des Bewußtseins Gottes, denn "Gott entwickelt sich dadurch, daß er sich selbst beständig Stationen schafft" (S, 247). Da diese Stationen aber im Vergänglichen verhaftet sind, kann Morgenstern sagen: "Gott kann allein leben durch seinen immerwährenden Tod. Gott muß fortwährend sterben, um fortwährend leben zu können" (S, 245).

In dieser Auffassung hat also das "Stirb und Werde" für Morgenstern eine ungeheure Vertiefung erfahren. Indem er an sein eigenes Leben denkt, sagt er sich: "Ich werde erst sterben, wenn ich erfüllt haben werde, was ich erfüllt haben konnte. Gott stirbt nicht vor der Zeit. Er wacht hier auf und schläft dort ein, wie es gut ist. Was sträubst du dich gegen das, was du dein Schicksal nennst? Siehe dir selbst ins Antlitz: Dein Schicksal ist, daß du Gott bist. Ich sage Gott! Aber wo uns die Wirklichkeit dieses Wortes faßte, da wäre unser Herz und Hirn auch schon dahin, wie ein Bologneser Glas, das, getroffen, zu Staub zerspringt. Gott schauen ist Tod, das wußten alle Völker. Gott erraten ist Leben" (S. 225).

In jener Zeit lernte Morgenstern die Gefahr kennen, sich durch mystische Schau im Göttlichen zu verlieren. Er war sich dieser Gefahr bewußt: "Wenn ich das Gegenwärtige nicht so liebte, wenn ich diese Liebe nicht hätte wie einen großen sicheren Fallschirm, ich wäre längst ins Bodenlose gefallen" (S, 31). Jetzt, da sein eigenes Ich mit dem Leben Gottes für ihn zusammenfiel, bestand die Versuchung, die physische Grenze zu überschreiten. Schon lange war dieser geheime Wunsch in ihm rege. Als Primaner hatte er versucht, sich eine Vorstellung von der Unendlichkeit des Weltalls zu machen, indem er sich in einen horizontal gestellten Klappstuhl legte und über das Bildhafte des Sternenhimmels hinausdringen wollte. "Es gelang mir so wohl, daß ich empfand: jetzt noch eine Sekunde solcher Erdabwesenheit, ein einziger kleiner Schritt weiter und mein Gehirn ist auf immer verloren. Und ich brach das schauerliche Experiment ab" (S, 30). Fünfzehn Jahre später ergriff ihn die gleiche Versuchung. In den Gedichten "Raumschwindelgefühl" und "Notschrei" beschreibt er die Angst, aus dem Bannkreis der Erde gerissen zu werden. Andererseits fühlt er den Drang des Mystikers, über die Sinnesgrenzen hinauszustreben. In dem Gedicht "Am Quell" ist sein Blick auf den Himmel gerichtet, die Unendlichkeit bedrängt ihn, fast hätte er sich in ihr verloren. Da hört er die Quelle rauschen. Ihre Stimme soll ihn mahnen, der Erde treu zu bleiben (E, 16). Wirklicher und dramatischer erscheint die Gefahr in dem Gedicht "Versuchung." Hier sieht sich der Dichter in der Hochgebirgswelt am Rand des Abgrunds stehen. Im Gefühl seiner Unsterblichkeit tritt die Versuchung an ihn heran, sich hinabzustürzen:

> Gott schläft hier ein, Gott wacht dort auf,—
> so sprachst du selbst. Wohlan! schlaf ein!
> Nicht einen Nu erlischt dein Sein,
> denn Form nur gibst du in den Kauf . . .
> Mein Tagwerk ist noch nicht vollbracht.
> Wer an der Schale sich vergreift,
> Bevor sie ihren Kern gereift,—
> er schläft zu früh ein—und erwacht—
> zu spät.

Der Gedanke, daß der Mensch seine Reifezeit abwarten, dem Tod ganz entgegenreifen solle, erinnert an Rilke. Was ist aber mit der letzten Zeile gemeint? Deutet sie nicht auf die Anschauung von den wiederholten Erdenleben hin, die dem Dichter ja schon lange vertraut war, damals aber durch das Studium der buddhistischen Lehre in ihren karmischen Wirkungen näher gebracht wurde? Das gewaltsame Abreißen des Reifeprozeßes wäre dann eine Tat, die sich für ein späteres Erdenleben als Hemmnis fühlbar machen würde.

Ein weiterer Grund, sich mit der Erde wieder fester zu verbinden, war der Umstand, daß der Dichter im Sommer 1908 die geistige Gefährtin fand, nach der er sich all die Jahre gesehnt hatte. Morgenstern nennt diese Lebensbegegnung das entscheidende Erlebnis seiner Gipfeljahre. Hatte sich der kranke Dichter vorher in seiner geistigen Welt eingesponnen und geglaubt, er könne "die bunte Welt" entbehren, so wurde er durch Margareta Gosebruch von Liechtenstein wieder enger mit ihr verflochten. Infolge dieser Liebe fühlte er sich nicht mehr nur Gast auf dieser Erde (MW, 203). Jetzt würde ihm das Scheiden vom Diesseits nicht mehr so leicht fallen. Im Bewußtsein seiner schwindenden Lebenskräfte bittet er die Geliebte: "Laß mich nicht allein, denn es will Abend werden" (MW, 197). Auf Margaretas Anregung hin ist Morgenstern dann mit der Anthroposophie Rudolf Steiners bekannt geworden. Es zeigte sich nun, daß für ihn das Eindringen in diese Geisteswissenschaft eine natürliche Fortsetzung seines bisherigen philosophischen Denkens war. Die Einsichten, die er sich allein erobert hatte, durften weiterhin zu Recht bestehen, und darüber hinaus erhob sich eine gewaltige Geistesschau, die seine früheren Ahnungen weit hinter sich zurückließ. In den Zeilen an Rudolf Steiner beschreibt er es so: "Ich war sozusagen bis vier Uhr morgens gegangen und glaubte kaum noch, daß es nun noch wesentlich heller für mich werden könnte. Ich sah überall das Licht Gottes hervordringen, aber . . . Da zeigen Sie mir mit einem Male und gerade im rechten letzten Augenblick ein 5 Uhr, 6 Uhr, 7 Uhr—einen neuen Tag" (S, 40). Der Lebensabendstimmung gegenüber bricht also jetzt ein neuer Morgen an. In dem Gedicht: "Knospe des Lebens, brichst du noch einmal auf?" schildert Morgenstern den Lenz seines neuen Glücks (MW, 236).

Zunächst sich zurückhaltend und vorsichtig prüfend hatte Morgenstern die Schriften und Vorträge Rudolf Steiners auf sich wirken lassen, dann aber bewegte er sich im Bewußtsein einer neuen Verantwortung entschlossen dem Ziel seiner letzten Lebensepoche zu, das er als "ein tiefdemütig lebenslanges Lernen" bezeichnete (P, 37). Wenn er in Christiania, Berlin, Kassel, Basel, München und Budapest anstrengende Vorträge anhörte und sie innerlich verarbeitete, so ging das eigentlich weit über seine physische Kraft und war nur der zähen Energie zuzuschreiben, mit der sich der willensstarke Geist die notwendige körperliche Grundlage erzwang. Erst nachdem er von dem neuen geistigen Gehalt so viel in sich aufgenommen hatte, daß er auch ohne den persönlichen Umgang mit Rudolf Steiner innerlich weiterkommen konnte, machte der Körper wieder seine Rechte geltend und trieb, zunächst noch langsam, später immer schneller dem unvermeidlichen Zusammenbruch entgegen.

Morgensterns späte Lyrik, vor allem das Bändchen *Wir fanden einen Pfad*, sowie der letzte Teil der *Stufen* geben von dem "Werde" Zeugnis, dem steilen Aufstieg, den der Dichter dem Verfall seiner physischen Kräfte, dem unentrinnbaren "Stirb" entgegensetzte. Nur weniges kann hier beispielhaft angedeutet werden. Zum alten Bestand gehörte die Erkenntnis von der Wiederverkörperung. Jetzt erst wird sie aber im Rahmen der Bewußtseinswandlung der Menschheit in ihrer ganzen Tragweite erlebt. Darüber lesen wir in den *Stufen*: "Die Lehre der Reincarnation ist längst da. Aber sie mußte eine Weile beiseite gelassen werden—die ganze europäische Zivilisation geht auf dies

Beiseitelassen zurück. Jetzt hat dieser Zyklus das Seine erfüllt, jetzt darf sie, als eine unermeßliche Wohltat, in den Gang der westlichen Entwicklung wieder eintreten. In einem Sinne, der erst jetzt möglich ist, zweitausend Jahre nach der Erscheinung des Christus, in einem ganz anderen Sinne als je vorher wird sie jetzt von neuem die Menschheit befruchten, erleuchten, erlösen" (277). Wie in dieser Stelle schon angedeutet, wird das Erscheinen Christi als das Zentralereignis, als der ausschlaggebende Wendepunkt, nicht nur in der Geschichte des Menschengeschlechts, sondern der ganzen Erde selbst erkannt. Morgenstern hatte in Christus die höchste menschliche Bewußtseinsstufe Gottes begriffen. Jetzt erfuhr er, wie der Mensch vielmehr die niederste Stufe der geistigen Wesen darstellt, die sich nach oben in die verschiedenen Engelreiche abstufen. Zu ihnen kann der Mensch der Zukunft im Wandel des Bewußtseins sich wieder einen innerlichen Zugang schaffen. Die höheren Wesen aber sind helfend am geistigen Aufstieg der Menschheit beteiligt (P, 55). Der Geist der sich opfernden Liebe durchdringt diese höheren Reiche bis zum höchsten Geisteswesen, Christus selbst (P, 59). Dem Menschen am nächsten steht sein Schutzengel, den der Dichter als "Weisheit seines höheren Ich" anspricht, "die ihn von Anfang an geleitet hat." An diesen Schutzengel wendet sich das Dankgebet für die Lebensgefährtin, die er ihm zugeführt hat, damit sie aneinander schaffen zu immer geistigerer Tätigkeit (MW, 224).

In seiner Selbstbeschreibung für den Verleger Reinhard Piper spricht Morgenstern von dem neuen siegreichen Kampf, nachdem er schon am Ende seines Wissens angekommen zu sein schien. Nun blickt er in "eine Welt unerhörter Aufwärtswende" hinein (MW, 255). Am Tor dieser neuen Welt klingt die Grundmelodie seines Lebens, das "Stirb und Werde" noch einmal kräftig an, und wenn wir dieses Motiv bisher bald im biologischen und bald im geistigen Sinn ausdeuten mußten, so können wir das folgende Zitat, das wenige Jahre vor seinem Hinscheiden niedergeschrieben wurde, im doppelten Sinne gelten lassen: "Zukunft! — un-er-schöpfliches Wort! O Lust zu leben! O Lust zu — sterben! Wohin können wir denn sterben, wenn nicht in immer höheres, größeres — Leben hinein!" (S, 273).

WASHINGTON UNIVERSITY PRESS

Papers on Classical Subjects, in Memory of John Max Wulfing. December, 1930. $1.00.
Contents:
John Max Wulfing, The Man and Scholar, by George R. Throop; Canidia and Other Witches, by Eugene Tavenner; Restoration Coins, by Thomas S. Duncan; The Lex Data as a Source of Imperial Authority, by Donald McFayden; C. Sosius: His Coins, His Triumph, and His Temple of Apollo, by Frederick W. Shipley; Concerning the Rostra of Julius Caesar, by Frederick W. Shipley.

Three Philosophical Studies. April, 1931. $1.00.
Contents:
Spinoza and Modern Thought, by Lawson P. Chambers; Existence and Value, by George R. Dodson; The Realm of Necessity, by Charles E. Cory.

Sociology and the Study of International Relations, by Luther L. Bernard and Jessie Bernard. February, 1934. $1.25.

The Facetiae of the Mensa Philosophica, by Thomas F. Dunn. June, 1934. 75c.

Forms of Address in German (1500-1800), by George J. Metcalf. December, 1938. $2.00.

Charles Sealsfield—Bibliography and Catalogue of Literature, by Otto Heller and Theodore H. Leon. September, 1939. $1.00.

Edmund Burke and His Literary Friends, by Donald Cross Bryant. December, 1939. $2.75.

Émile Zola's Letters to J. Van Santen Kolff. Edited by Robert J. Niess. May, 1940. $1.00.

The Language of Charles Sealsfield: A Study in Atypical Usage, by Otto Heller assisted by Theodore H. Leon. July, 1941. $1.50.

A Glossary of Mississippi Valley French, 1673-1850, by John Francis McDermott. December, 1941. $1.50.

The Hymn to Demeter and Her Sanctuary at Eleusis, by George Emmanuel Mylonas. March, 1942. $1.00.

Types of Utility Rate Bases under Depreciation Reserve Accounting, by William S. Krebs. 1946. $1.50.

German Literature as Reflected in the German-Language Press of St. Louis Prior to 1898, by Erich P. Hofacker. 1946. $1.50.

The Life and Works of Marie-Catherine Desjardins (1632-1683), by Bruce A. Morrissette. 1947. $3.00.

Le Philosophe: Texts and Interpretation, by Herbert Dieckmann. 1948. $3.00.

On the Edge of the Black Waxy: A Cultural Survey of Bell County, Texas, by Oscar Lewis. 1948. $3.00.

The Political History of Leigh Hunt's Examiner, Together with an Account of "The Book," by George D. Stout. 1949. $2.50.

The Wulfing Plates: Products of Prehistoric Americans, by Virginia Drew Watson. 1950. $2.50.

Studies in Memory of Frank Martindale Webster. 1951. $3.50.
Contents:
In Deference to David Hume, by Robert M. Schmitz; Leigh Hunt's Shakespeare: A "Romantic" Concept, by George Dumas Stout; Jeffrey, Marmion, and Scott, by Alexander M. Buchan; The Frustrated Opposition: Burke, Barré, and Their Audiences, by Donald C. Bryant; The First Public Address of George W. Cable, Southern Liberal, by Guy A. Cardwell; Linguistic Equations for the Study of Indo-European Culture, by Vladimir Jelinek.

The Soviet Theory of Internationalism, by Merle Kling. 1952. $2.00.

Pope's Windsor Forest 1712, by Robert M. Schmitz. 1952. $4.50.

The Esthetic Intent of Tieck's Fantastic Comedy, by Raymond M. Immerwahr. March, 1953. $3.50.

The Novels of Pérez Galdós: The Concept of Life as Dynamic Process, by Sherman H. Eoff. November, 1954. Paper, $2.25.

The Great Rimbaud Forgery: The Affair of *La Chasse spirituelle* (1949), by Bruce Morrissette. 1956. $6.00.

Theory and Treatment of the Psychoses: Some Newer Aspects. August, 1956. $2.00.
Contents:
  Psychiatry in the General Hospital, by Alan Gregg; Contemporary Problems in Psychiatry, by Stanley Cobb; Theoretical Contribution to the Concept of Milieu Therapy, by Alfred H. Stanton; Strategy and Tactics in Psychiatric Therapy, by John C. Whitehorn; Some Sociological Aspects of the Psychoses, by F. C. Redlich; What is Psychotic Behavior? by B. F. Skinner; Major Themes, by George Saslow; Conclusion, by Edwin F. Gildea; Historical Note, by Edwin F. and Margaret C.-L. Gildea.

Joseph Glanvill, Anglican Apologist, by Jackson I. Cope. 1956. Paper, $2.50.

Concurring Opinion: The Privileges or Immunities Clause of the Fourteenth Amendment, by Arnold J. Lien. 1957. Paper, $2.50.

Sprat's *History of the Royal Society*, edited by Jackson I. Cope and Harold Whitmore Jones. 1958. $7.50.

The Test of Factual Causation in Negligence and Strict Liability Cases, by Arno C. Becht and Frank W. Miller. 1961. $4.50.

Ancients and Moderns. A Study of the Rise of the Scientific Movement in Seventeenth-Century England, by Richard Foster Jones. 1961. $7.50.

Ronsard and the Hellenic Renaissance in France. Volume I. Ronsard and the Greek Epic, by Isidore Silver. 1961. $10.00.

Pope's Essay on Criticism, by Robert M. Schmitz. 1962. $5.00.

Ronsard and the Hellenic Renaissance in France. Volume I. Ronsard and the Greek Epic, by Isidore Silver, 1961. $10.00.

Pope's Essay on Criticism, by Robert M. Schmitz. 1962. $5.00.

Studies in Germanic Languages and Literatures. 1963. $4.50.
Contents:
  The Gothic Character X, by Ernst Ebbinghaus; The Composition of Eddic Verse, by Winfred P. Lehmann; The Views of Konrad Gesner on Language, by George J. Metcalf; The Languages of the World—A Classification by G. W. Leibniz, by John T. Waterman; Another Look at Lessing's *Philotas*, by Bernhard Ulmer; A Gottschedian Reply to Lessing's Seventeenth *Literaturbrief*, by Robert R. Heitner; José Ortega y Gassets Verhältnis zu Goethe, by Egon Schwarz; The Character and Function of Buttler in Schiller's *Wallenstein*, by Walter Silz; Grillparzer as a Critic of European Literature, by Frank D. Horvay; Narrative and "Musical" Structure in *Mozart auf der Reise nach Prag*, by Raymond Immerwahr; Faust ohne Transzendenz: Theodor Storms *Schimmelreiter*, by Ernst Loeb; Symbols of Isolation in Some Late Nineteenth-Century Poets, by Liselotte Dieckmann; Das Motiv des "Stirb und Werde" bei Christian Morgenstern, by Erich Hofacker.

Orders for any of these publications should be addressed to the Office of Publications, Washington University, St. Louis, Missouri 63130